Upliftment of OBCs

Upliftment of OBCs

Human Rights Perspective

Najibul Hasan Khan

RAWAT PUBLICATIONS
Jaipur • New Delhi • Bangalore • Hyderabad • Guwahati

ISBN 978-81-316-0475-5

Published by
Prem Rawat for **Rawat Publications**
Satyam Apts, Sector 3, Jawahar Nagar, Jaipur 302 004 (India)
Phone: 0141 265 1748 / 7006 Fax: 0141 265 1748
E-mail: info@rawatbooks.com
Website: www.rawatbooks.com

New Delhi Office
4858/24, Ansari Road, Daryaganj, New Delhi 110 002
Phone: 011 2326 3290

Also at *Bangalore, Hyderabad* and *Guwahati*

Typeset by Rawat Computers, Jaipur
Printed at Nice Printing Press, New Delhi

Contents

Acknowledgements

I wish to put on record the teaching and research activities of Dr Ambedkar Chair of Legal Studies and Research, Department of Law, Aligarh Muslim University, Aligarh sponsored by Dr Ambedkar Foundation, Ministry of Social Justice and Empowerment, Government of India, New Delhi. The Chair confines its thrust areas to social justice and upliftment of the oppressed segments of Indian society, based on the principles, thoughts, and convictions of Dr Ambedkar.

I express my gratitude to Dr Ambedkar Chair for selecting my research project, on which I was awarded Ph.D. in Human Rights by the Aligarh Muslim University, for publication under its publication scheme.

I also thank Professor Mohammad Shabbir (Ambedkar Chair Professor of Law), Dean, Faculty of Law, AMU, Aligarh and Dr Zafar Ahmad Khan (Research Officer, Dr Ambedkar Chair of Legal Studies and Research), who devoted their valuable time in editing, vetting and standardising the final draft of this research project giving it proper shape for publication.

Mr Zaheer Ahmad (Computer Operator) and Mr Shakeel Ahmad (Office Attendant), under Dr Ambedkar Chair of Legal Studies and Research, also deserve my thanks for adding the finishing touches to the final draft of my research project.

Introduction

The present study is an attempt to examine the status of scheduled castes and scheduled tribes and also to find out the efficacy of reservation policy and other constitutional provisions in improving the condition of this lot. India has a long history of caste-ridden society. The social relations are based on caste differentiation. In this social phenomenon, an integrated society cannot be formed. Moreover, due to unequal distribution of educational and economic opportunities, a large segment of population suffered socially and educationally and remained backward. The backwardness, developed either due to economic reasons or was embodied in socio-religious conditions, has proved to be a great stumbling block in the way of nation's progress and unity.

The evil of caste system has persisted for several thousand years in Hindu society. It is still prevalent in various forms throughout the country in the villages and more particularly in south India. The scheduled caste bridegrooms are not permitted to ride on mares in villages, *dalits* cannot even sit on their own *charpoys*, when persons of others castes pass by. These people are not permitted to draw water from the common wells and in some cases even from handpumps. In many teashops and *dhabas*, separate crockery is used for serving these people. Barbers refuse to cut the hair of these people. Often there are also reports of gang rape, public auction of women, urinating in the mouth of women, compelling boys to eat night soil, parading women naked in the villages, mass killing and destroying the houses and properties of scheduled castes and scheduled tribes by the high-caste persons. Such instances are numerous and reflect the deep-seated prejudices of caste system still dwelling in the hearts of vested persons. Not only this hatred has alienated *dalits* but has the potential of turning into militancy and fissiparous tendencies as well. No nation can progress if it is divided into countless groups and deny equality to its citizens.

Roots of reservation policy for scheduled castes in India lay deep in past. To be true, as an accepted constitutional policy, it has its origins in ancient Hindu civilisation. The hierarchical social order was created over centuries by the so-called higher-caste Hindus with a view to preserve the monopoly of their social status, property and education. As a result, property, education, freedom, justice, progress and prosperity were denied to the people of lower castes. The downtrodden in the Hindu society were stripped off even the equitable opportunities for political, social, economic and educational development. The caste system, on the one hand, bestowed hierarchically graded privileges on some sections of society and inflicted a series of disabilities, on the other. Opportunities of growth and development were contained and usurped by the higher castes with the result that the downtrodden were deprived and discriminated, symbolising a powerful institutional pattern of exploitation and suppression of the weak by the strong.

All this compelled our wise founding fathers to adopt the policy of social justice with an emphasis on compensatory discrimination as an equaliser to those who were weak—socially and economically—in the caste-ridden Indian society. They took special notice of these people and obligated the state to promote with special care their educational and economic interests, and to protect them from social injustice and exploitation. The Constitution of India also provided that the state should strive to promote the welfare of the people and in particular to minimise the inequalities in income, status, facilities and opportunities amongst individuals and groups of people, residing in different areas and engaged in different vocations. On these broad principles was based the concept of equality of opportunity in matters of public employment, which implies that no citizen should on grounds of only religion, race, caste, sex, be discriminated against in respect of any employment or office under the state.

It was apprehended that any special provision for the educational, economic or social advancement of any backward class of citizens in order to implement the mandate of the Constitution might be challenged on the ground of discrimination. Therefore, Article 15(4) was added, so as to offset the effects of fundamental rights of citizens, which directed the state not to deny admissions to anyone to any educational institution maintained by the state or receiving aid out of the state funds, on grounds only of religion, race, caste, language or any of them. The law now empowered the government to make special provision for the advancement of socially and educationally backward classes or for scheduled castes and scheduled tribes. The bedrock of the 'egalitarian social order', conceived in the Constitution, later on became the basis of reservations.

The present study is an attempt to see as to what extent the beneficiaries of reservation policy have really been benefited. It also assesses the impact of various measures adopted for the welfare of the scheduled castes and scheduled tribes. An endeavour is also made in this study to examine empirically the political, social, economic and educational impacts of reservations. It also finds out the extent to which these people have progressed by virtue of constitutional safeguards in due course of time. The transformation of the traditional caste system and practice of untouchability, which has undergone a qualitative change, have also been discussed.

A thorough study of the reservation policy in India has revealed that it has successfully built up a strong political environment and has helped the weaker sections to gain confidence. Second, the government has developed adequate and satisfactory administrative apparatus for the implementation of the constitutional safeguards in favour of scheduled castes and has achieved a great deal of success in the removal of untouchability and moving towards the goal of a casteless society. Third, the reservation policy has helped the scheduled castes economically and has raised their standard of living and social status. Fourth, the reservation policy has helped these sections in enabling them educationally to come at par with other sections of society. Fifth, this representation in public services has increased considerably and the promise in Article 16(4) to a large extent has been realised. Sixth, the benefits of reservation have reached evenly to all scheduled castes in the light of constitutional ethos and philosophy. Seventh, the beneficiaries have sufficient awareness about the welfare programmes and constitutional safeguards designed for them. Lastly, the execution of constitutional safeguards in favour of scheduled castes has enabled them to come at par with other sections of society and hence the time has come to discontinue the reservation policy in the larger interest of the other sections of the society.

The present study is divided into six chapters. Chapter 1 provides a broad historical overview of scheduled castes and scheduled tribes in India. A number of theories have been advanced to explain the origin of caste in India and it is difficult to recognise any particular factor responsible for its origin. A variety of factors have contributed to its emergence. Hindu society was classified into four *varnas,* i.e., Brahmin, Kshatriya, Vaishya and Shudra. These four *varnas* are said to have been born respectively from the mouth, the arms, the thighs and the feet of Lord Brahma, which determine their status. The Brahmins got the place at the top of the system while the Shudras were placed at the bottom. They were subjected to many disabilities, humiliations, condemnation and reduced to living a life of degradation. They were convinced that untouchability has been ordained by God and human beings have nothing to do with it. This practice continued till now in

Indian society and the habitual obedience developed with the passage of time among the *Shudras*.

Chapter 2 is an attempt to analyse the debates of the Constituent Assembly on the issue of reservation for backward classes in general and scheduled castes in particular. Actually, most of support to reservation came from such members as the Chairman of Drafting Committee, B.R. Ambedkar, who themselves were from backward classes. On the other hand, the members of the Constituent Assembly, who opposed it, mostly belonged to upper classes. As such, the entire Constituent Assembly stood sharply divided on this issue. And, it appears that it caused sufficient rift amongst the members of the Constituent Assembly. Besides Ambedkar, the prominent supporters of reservation policy included T.V. Muniswami, Pillai P. Kakkan and T. Channaiah. Ambedkar heavily relied on the concept of social democracy, equality and fraternity in support of his demand for reservation in favour of socially and educationally backward classes in general and scheduled castes in particular. Muniswami and Kakkan forcefully argued that there was discrimination against Harijans in case of jobs which could be removed only through reservation of seats. He also accepted the fact that if merit alone is taken into consideration, Harijans cannot come forward. Channaiah also spoke forcefully in support of reservation, taking social and educational disabilities as the basis for backwardness of scheduled castes and scheduled tribes. Then, there were also discussions in relation to reservation for minorities in services but the same was opposed vehemently by members like K.M. Munshi and Sardar Patel stating that such an attempt will distort the secular character of the country. However, the debates and discussions in the Constituent Assembly finally tilted the balance in favour of scheduled castes and scheduled tribes as well as other backward classes.

Chapter 3 examines the various provisions of the Constitution of India related to protective discrimination. By way of the provisions of Constitution, the first major blow fell upon this age-old barbarity. The Constitution makes it impossible to enforce any affirmative legal disabilities on the basis of caste. The Constitution of India has also dealt with the problem of untouchability in two ways: firstly, through its legal abolition and secondly, through promoting the interests of untouchables. The framers of the Constitution desired to have an equalitarian society. They enacted several special provisions of protective discrimination in favour of scheduled castes and scheduled tribes so as to provide them distributive justice. These include reserving seats in Lok Sabha, state legislatures, panchayats, municipalities, educational institutions and in employment. Unfortunately, these provisions, which were intended to bridge the gap among various sections of people, have, in fact, created a wide gap among them.

Chapter 4 deals with the politics of reservation by analysing the findings of various commissions and committees constituted on the issue of reservation. Indian politics is caste-ridden. The caste factor is dominant in every sphere of life. During the freedom struggle, untouchables were neglected by the British, the Congress and the Muslim League and none of the political and social movements have touched the problems of untouchability. Political representation, as a means to emancipate the backward sections of Indian society from the age-old disabilities, was not given due recognition during the 19th century. Thus, the Government of India Act of 1858 and the Indian Council Acts of 1861 and 1862 did not recognise the special claims of the depressed classes. Caste in India has been employed as a factor in achieving political power. One consequence of this has been the growth of competition and confrontation among the various castes. Since politics protects caste interests, the caste factor in politics has been solidified irrespective of its growing confrontational and competitive role.

Chapter 5 is a judicial response towards weaker sections. The landmark judicial pronouncements on the issues like who are the backward classes, what are the criteria of backwardness, what is the limitation of reservation, etc., constitute the focus of study in this chapter. Judiciary has also done commendable work through its judicial pronouncements for their upliftment. Last chapter is devoted to concluding remarks and suggestions.

The present study thus reveals that the objectives of social justice through reservation which could not be achieved even after decades of independence. The Constitution-makers, visualising social justice and equality, provided reservations for the downtrodden and the depressed for a period of ten years but it kept extending. The political parties saw in reservations an opportunity to garner votes on the basis of caste. The competition among political parties to woo these sections became so acute that the apex court had to pronounce that reservations, in any case, should not exceed 50 per cent. But, the study reveals that government has given scant regard to the court's ruling. Restructuring of reservation policy seems to be an urgent need. What is required is to make the policy judicious and reasonable to spread the benefits of reservation to wider sections of the society. It is, therefore, suggested that only one generation should be permitted reservation and its gains should not at all be covered by a few who are already better off. Besides, the benefit of reservation should be given only once, i.e., at the stage of admission or recruitment or promotion and not at every stage in one's career and in this process merit should not be ignored.

A change in the attitudes of the upper-caste Hindus vis-à-vis backward sections is equally necessary to generate an atmosphere congenial to social equality and social justice. Social justice is the sheet anchor of the Constitution and the reservation is the means to move in this direction.

1

Suppressed Humanity in India

Historical Perspective

It is perhaps true that the most frequently mentioned peculiarity of the Hindu society is the institution of caste or the caste system. Social institutions that resemble caste in one respect or the other are also found elsewhere, but it is only in India that it has a religious sanction. It is for this reason that the caste system has survived in a far perfect form in India than anywhere else. Hocart[1], however, considers that the Indian caste system is not an isolated phenomenon but a species of a very widespread genus. Comparable forms still exist in Polynesia and Melanesia, and its traces can also be seen in ancient Greece, Rome, and modern Egypt. Hutton[2] finds analogous institutions which resemble caste in one form or the other in various parts of the world like Ceylon. Fiji, Egypt, Somali, Ruanda and Urundi in modern Africa and Burma. Ghurye traces elements of caste outside India like Egypt, Western Asia, China, Japan, America, Rome and Tribal Europe. It is true that social and racial differences in some form or the other do prevail in other parts of the world, but the kind of system found in India is characterised more by its specific unique features like the complexity, elaboration and rigidity than by such features which it shares with caste structures elsewhere. The caste system that has developed in India is the natural result of the interaction of a number of geographical, social, religious and economic factors not found elsewhere in conjunction. It is the peculiarity of India that it recognised the social differences inherent in human nature and gave them an institutional and mystic form with a religious and spiritual background.

It is difficult to define what a caste precisely connotes. The word 'caste' comes from the Portuguese word '*casta*', signifying breed, race or kind. The Portuguese of the sixteenth century applied the term indiscriminately to the various social and occupational groups found in the subcontinent, and this confusion has continued to the present times. On the one hand, the term is used to describe, in the broadest sense, the total system of social stratification peculiar to India, on the other hand, it is used to denote three more or less distinct aspects of this system, i.e., *varna, jati* and *gotra*. *Varna* is not the same thing as *jati*, the former representing the four-fold division of society which the authors of the *Dharamsastras* sought to derive from one or other of the four *varnas*. By contrast, the *gotra*, or clan, described by Hutton[3] as "an exogamous unit of individuals descending from a single ancestor", cuts freely across *jati* lines and possibly across *varna* lines. To this confusion of interlocking hierarchies may be added a fourth division when dealing with South India, where by the time of the Chola period (AD 850–1267) there had occurred a great and still unexplained bisection of the Shudra *varna* into the "*jatis* of the left hand" and the "*jatis* of the right hand", a division that still exists today and is reflected in the continuing rivalry between *jatis* of opposing hands. Careless use of the English word 'caste' has been the source of considerable confusion. Manu distinctly says that there are only four *varnas*: Brahmin, Kshatriya, Vaishya and Shudra and there is no fifth *varna*, while he admits of over fifty *jatis*.[4]

The Hindu religious belief that "all human beings are not born equal" is deeply entrenched in the psyche of the upper-caste Hindus, leading them to see themselves as a superior race destined to rule and the untouchables or *dalits* are an inferior race born only to serve. This belief stems from the fact that the creator created these *varnas* from different parts of his body, i.e., the Brahmin was born from his mouth, the

Kshatriya from his arms, the Vaishya from his thighs and the Shudra from his feet. He created Brahmins with *Gayatri* (metre); the Kshatriyas with *Trishtubb*, the Vaishyas with *Jagti* and the Shudras without any metre. It is believed that in the beginning there were only three *varnas* and the fourth *varna* (Shudra) is an outcome of the fight between Brahmins and Kshatriyas for the supremacy in the *varna* (caste) hierarchy.[5] The caste of a person is determined by his birth. It also determines one's occupation. Salvation can be achieved by doing one's own work. It is the duty of a Brahmin to impart knowledge. The son of a barber should be a barber. It is his *karma*.

Dalit refers to the downtrodden, broken, or oppressed. Increasingly, those whom others have called untouchables, depressed classes, Harijans (Children of God), or scheduled castes are adopting *'dalit'* as a name for themselves. *Dalit* is a caste rather than a class label, it applies to members of those menial castes which have carried the stigma of untouchability because of the extreme impurity and pollution connected with their traditional occupations.[6] An attempt is made in this chapter to trace the origin of the *dalits* and the circumstances responsible for their plight. There are some archaeological and literary sources which throw light on the origin of the *dalits*. But the information available is scattered. The concern of this study is how today's *dalits,* over a period of time, have been reduced to such a plight. Most of the scholars agree that the present condition of the *dalits* is the result of the long process of our country's history through which they have been reduced to their present state of "sub-human" or "no people" (*dalit* state) existence of misery and poverty.

The moot point in this regard is to identify the time or period when the *dalits* of today started losing their identity. The *Rigveda* is the earliest written literary source of the ancient history of India. A large part of the text has been addressed to Lord Indra, which narrates a fierce war encounter having taken place among different groups. Two opposing forces may be seen in the *Rigveda:* first on whose behalf the hymns of the *Rigveda* are addressed to different gods and, second, against whom the same are addressed. Ramprasad Chanda[7] observes, "the hymns reveal two hostile peoples in the land of the seven rivers now called the Punjab – the *dinar* worshipping *Arya* and *deva-less* and the riteless *Dasyu* or *Dasa*". The archaeological sources also help in reaching the historical roots of the *dalits*. Archaeological literature, certainly, has not been written keeping the *dalit* in mind but it throws much light on the ancient people of India. The *Ancient Cities of the Indus,* edited by Geogory L. Possehl[8], is a superb work of reference. It includes the main research paper written between 1924 and 1997 and contains, among others, the works of the famous pioneer archaeologists like John Marshall, Ernest Mackay, Mortimer Wheeler and the well-known Indian archaeologists S.R. Rao, Gurdip Singh and B.M. Pandey. Four aspects are covered, namely, (a) that it was a well-established civilisation, (b) the nature of the people, (c) the date of the civilisation, and (d) how it met with its end.[9]

The *Rigveda* and the Archaeologists

A number of attempts have been made to correlate the information based upon the *Rigveda* and the archaeological works. These attempts have been made by historians like N.N. Bhattacharyya. N.N. Bhattacharyya[10], in his work on *Ancient Indian History and Civilisation,* has rejected Wheeler's view that the Aryans first destroyed the Harappans and then erected their own settlement on the same site. On that basis, later scholars have fixed the date of Harappa civilisation as 1750 B.C. not 1500 B.C.[11]

Regarding the Shudras appearing as a social class engaged in the service of the three higher *varnas*, the *Rigvedic* society did comprise men and women slaves who acted as domestic servants, but they were not so considerable as to constitute the service *varna* of the Shudras. The first and the only reference to the Shudras as a social class in the *Rigveda* is to be found in the *Purusasukta* which recurs in the nineteenth book of the *Atharvaveda*.[12] Here, it is pertinent to know why the fourth *varna* came to be referred as Shudras. It appears that just as the common European word "slave" and the Sanskrit "*dasa*" were derived from the names of conquered peoples, so also the word Shudra was derived from a conquered tribe of that name.[13]

According to Manu, the ancient Indian law-giver, untouchability is the punishment for miscegenation between a member of a high caste and that of a low caste or an outcaste. The children of such an unequal pain become untouchables, and the greater the social gap between the two parents, the lower the status of their children. The consequences are also more severe if the mother is of the superior caste. Thus, the offspring of a Brahmin father and a Shudra mother is called *Nishada*; the child becomes a fisherman. The offspring of a Shudra father and a Brahmin mother is called *Chandala*, he is the most degraded of all mortals.[14]

J.H. Hutton, eminent anthropologist and author of one of the best books on caste, *Caste in India* (1963), locates the origins of caste in the taboos and divisions of labour in the pre-Aryan tribes of India as well as in their efforts at self-preservation in the face of invasion. In his opinion, untouchability is the consequence of ritual impurity.[15] Von Fuerer-Haimendorf,[16] another eminent anthropologist, believes that untouchability is an urban development and is the result of an unclean and ritually impure occupation. Once untouchability had developed in urban or semi-urban settlements, its gradual movement to the villages was inevitable for it is everywhere the towns which set the standard.

According to some scholars, the origin of untouchables starts from the Vedic period, i.e., the coming of Aryans to India during 2500 B.C. to 2000 B.C., and from the writings of *Rigveda,* which was written during 1200 B.C. to 1000 B.C. So in the early Vedic time it is said that all men were equals and there was no trace of untouchability as we see it today. According to *Rigveda*, in those days, perfect brotherhood was prevalent. In course of time, when the Aryans having grown in overwhelming number scattered and colonised throughout the whole of Aryavartra they divided themselves into four divisions according to their different qualities (*guna*) and actions (*karmas*) in order to organise their society and set it up on sound basis. This four-fold division has been a predominant feature of Hindu social fabric. Historically, untouchability was the social fruit of the Aryan conquest of India. In the process of social interaction, a portion of the indigenous conquered population was incorporated into the Aryan fold. The most backward and despised section of this incorporated population it appears constituted the hereditary caste of untouchables. But many read a kind of caste structure with four *varnas* in the *Rigveda*, in its *Purusha Sukta*. Though doubts exist about the status of the *Purusha Sukta* as an integral part of the *Rigveda*, it is certain that functional division of society was known at the time of the *Rigveda*. The existence of the four-fold division of society in Iran, viz., *Athravans, Rathaestars, Vastria Fshouyants* and *Hinti* corresponding to the four *varnas* in India, must have been known to the early Aryan colonisers, and a functional division of society on similar lines could have been practised. So, untouchability as we now understand, was non-existent during the Vedic period. The reference about four *varnas* which we find in *Purusha Sukta* of *Rigveda* does not necessarily suggest the Brahminical supremacy over the three other *varnas*. It rather suggests that all the four groups are equally important for the preservation of total human race or *Purusjati*. Head, hand, thigh, leg, etc., are all vital aspects of human physiology and a balanced composition of all these is obviously necessary for the continuance of man. Therefore, the so-called religio-philosophical outlook of *Vedas* seems to have been more directed towards human welfare in socio-ethical plane. Any reading of transcendental, mystical and supernatural theological concept of divinity regarding caste can be said as an unwarranted interpolation from without, the distinction concerning four *varnas* is from the standpoint of certain qualitative standards (*guna, karma* and *veda*) and it need not be interpreted in terms of birth. This point has been very much supported in the Upanishadic period when one finds not only non-Brahmins like Kshatriyas, even Vaishyas and Shudras were duly accepted as Brahmins in the social plane on account of their qualitative mark and excellence.[17]

In the later Vedic period, this caste system was not absolutely rigid; rather, it was a mid-way between the laxity of the Rigvedic Age and the strong rigidity of the age of the *Sutras*. The term *varna* was now used in the sense of caste not in the sense of colour in this age. In the *Sutra* period, caste system was rigid. Untouchability had begun to creep in. The probability seems to be that in Vedic times the *varnas* were classes rather than castes, and that post-Vedic scholars, looking for authority for the caste system in the earliest *Vedas*, have interpreted the nature of the *varna* in terms of the caste system as they knew. In the Puranic period, i.e., 3rd century A.D. to 1000 A.D., due to certain economic forces the people belonging to higher castes indulged in lower occupations and naturally they were declared as outcastes and once they lost their position, it was not possible for them to regain it. Stuart Piggot, a British archaeologist and author of prehistoric India has put forward a thesis that even before the Aryan arrival in India from the North-West, the Harappan civilisation might have developed a caste system. He is, however, quite certain that the concept of caste as known in the later literature is quite unknown in Rigveda.[18]

So in the later Vedic period, specifically in the period of *Smiritis* and *Sutras,* we find little restrictions in interactions. There is the possibility that in this phase of development of human civilisation, the healthy spirit of equality, gave place, in course of time, to the tradition-bound caste system and then again to the institution of untouchability which divided the Hindu, wrapped their thinking and eroded the structure of the community. The Hindu scriptures interpolated the concept of *varna* and legitimised the concept of *chaturvarna* and gave it a divine origin. Those who did not recognise this system – mostly indigenous people who had their own gods, religions and social systems as well as those who opposed or violated this system were outcaste and were put aside the pale of Hinduism. They were forced to live outside the towns and villages and were treated as untouchables.[19]

Gradually, as the Hindu *varna* system grew fashionable, strong strict measures were adopted to enforce it. Social intercourse and intermarriage were prohibited. Society became strictly endogamous and was divided into water-tight compartments. Those who violated the law of endogamy were ex-communicated and were forced to live outside the community. In consequence they had no option other than the low and degrading occupations. The four-*varna* system was over time ideologically refined by orthodox Brahmins. The *Dharmasutras*, which were compiled between 600 and 300 B.C., represent the crystallisation of these efforts by the orthodox Brahmins whose homeland was the upper Ganga basin. However, from the very beginning, the four-*varna* system was filled with contradictions. Therefore, the Brahmins had to revise the basic principles to conform to the realities of daily relaxation of the rules.[20]

Ambedkar's thesis on the origin of untouchability, as expounded in his book *The Untouchables* (1948), is an altogether novel one.[21] There are two roots from which untouchability has sprung: (a) contempt and hatred for the broken men, as for Buddhism by the Brahmins, and (b) continuation of beef-eating by the broken men after it had been given up by the others. Ambedkar[22] tries to explain what he means by broken men. He proposes an ingenious hypothesis: when primitive society began to settle down and to cultivate, certain tribes remained nomadic and war-like. They began to attack the settled tribes as the latter were wealthier. In addition, they had grain, which the nomads wanted but did not possess. The settled men needed defenders as they had lost their war-like spirit. They employed "broken men" – defeated nomads and stray individuals – who needed protection and shelter. These became mercenaries of the settlers, but were not allowed to stay within the settlement. They were kept at a distance, as they belonged to a different tribe. They were treated with disrespect. Ambedkar provided supporting evidence for such a process from Ireland and Wales. This difference was that in those countries the outsiders were absorbed into the settled community after nine generations. This did not happen in India, for the Hindus had contempt for the broken men who were Buddhists and beef-eaters. There was, thus, a deep social cleavage between the masters and their servants. Ambedkar believes that the root cause of untouchability lies in a pronounced cultural or racial difference of contempt and hatred coupled with a close economic dependence of the inferior society on the superior one.

Stephen Fuchs[23] proposes a new theory regarding the origin of untouchability. According to him, the above proposed theories as well as various others presented by a number of Indologists seem to suffer from one great defect: they do not penetrate deeply enough into the past of the dominant Indian peoples. They restrict themselves unduly to happenings in India. It is true that the caste system and untouchability developed after the arrival of the Aryans and, most probably of the Dravidians in India, is unique and not found elsewhere in the world, and that nowhere in the world are untouchables found in such vast numbers, about 138 millions. Yet, the roots must be sought in an age when both population groups lived on the steppes of Inner Asia, where the animal-breeding societies developed a pronounced hierarchical structure. These animal breeders gave up cultivation completely and regarded manual work of any kind as unworthy of a shepherd and warrior. They also developed a social structure of their own, an extended joint family system with a patriarch at its head in whom all power was vested.

The Aryans who invaded India and disrupted the native civilisation were not necessarily superior warriors but they were aggressive and had sophisticated military technologies and military virtues. After hundreds of years of intense martial conflict, the Aryans succeeded in subjugating most of the northern India. Throughout the vanquished territories, a rigid caste-segmented social order was established and the Blacks (called Shudras) were reduced to slaves, to cater to the requirements of their conquerors. This new order was thoroughly racist, with the whites on top, the mixed race in the middle, and the overwhelming majority of black people at the bottom. In fact, the Aryan term, *varna,* denoting one's societal status and used interchargeably with caste, literally means colour or complexion and reflects a prevalent racial hierarchy. Servitude to Whites became the basis of the lives of the black people of India for generations. With the passage of time, this brutally harsh, colour-oriented, racially biased caste system became the foundation of the religion that is now practiced throughout India. The greatest victims of Hinduism have been the untouchables. Indeed, probably the most substantial percentage of all the black people of Asia can be identified among India's 160 untouchables. These untouchables number more than the combined populations of England, France, Belgium and Spain. The existence of untouchability has been justified within the context of Hindu religious thought as the ultimate and logical extension of *karma* and rebirth. Hindus believe that persons are born untouchables because of the accumulation of sins in previous lives. Hindu texts describe these people as foul and loathsome, and any physical contact with them was regarded as polluting.[24]

The caste system is known for its denouncement of the *Ati* Shudra castes. Although discrimination towards classes like the *candala* was widespread in ancient India, it does not seem likely that the members of these classes were grouped together to form a distinct social stratum (*varna*). Furthermore, the percentage of discriminated classes is considered to have been rather small in ancient India. Conversely, in the medieval Deccan, discriminated castes were grouped together as *Ati* Shudra and treated as a distinct social stratum. Moreover, the percentage of discriminated castes was also much higher than in ancient India. This mean that the medieval discrimination which was quite different from its ancient predecessor was formed during this period. Nonetheless, pinpointing the exact period of formation of this medieval discrimination is very difficult; the period between the 8th and 12th centuries might reasonably well be presumed as being the formative era. We know, in fact, that Indian society in general began to change from the bottom in the 7th or 8th century, and this social transformation gave rise to the predominant features of medieval India such as the village community and the 'district' (*pargana*) community by the 12th century. The shaping of medieval discrimination in the Deccan was also an unmistakable part of the general social transformation depicting this period, and, in particular, discrimination against *Ati*-Shudra castes in the later medieval Deccan was a direct development of this medieval system of discrimination.

The term *dalit* really denotes the abysmally low status to which a certain section of the people are reduced. They are forced to live like that. A *dalit* is not considered part of the society. The *dalits* are required to perform menial and degrading jobs and even if they perform other jobs, it is not socially recognised. They are considered as the source of pollution to the extent that if a higher caste Hindu was touched by an untouchable or even had a *dalit*'s shadow across him, he would consider himself to be polluted and have to go through a rigorous exercise of rituals to get himself clean. The plight of *dalits* is so miserable that every hour two *dalits* are assaulted, every day three *dalit* women are raped and two *dalits* are murdered and two *dalit* houses are burnt".[25] They are the most exploited segment of society.

Untouchability is used and practised to perpetuate atrocities, violence, exploitation, discrimination, violation of rights of the distressed and downtrodden. Segregation is writ large on the social life, places of worship, education, housing, land ownership, use of public wells, roads, buses, etc.

- In most of the upper caste (rich) families the servants are *dalits*. After the servant has cleaned the room, pots and pans, one of the family members will sprinkle 'holy' water to purify all that has been touched by the servant.

- *Dalits* are not allowed to wear shoes; if they do wear them, they have to take off their shoes the moment they meet a higher caste person.
- In rural areas, *dalits* are not allowed to ride cycles in the localities of higher caste people.
- The *dalits* mainly live in the peripheries of the village.
- In general, *dalits* are not allowed to sit at the bus stop. They have to stand and wait till the upper caste people have entered the bus and they are not allowed to sit in the bus even if there are vacant seats.
- Even after half a century of independence, even the educated among the *dalits* are not allowed to get for rent a house of their choice to live in.
- People can touch a cat, they may touch a dog, they may touch any other animal, but the touch of these human beings will cause pollution.[26]

The very survival of 250 million untouchables and tribals is at stake because of complete lack of respect for human dignity and equality on the part of high caste Hindus. Indeed, violation of the *dalits'* fundamental rights is a daily phenomenon despite the protection guaranteed by the Constitution of India and the human rights instruments. Although social stratification exists in almost all societies, the caste system is quite unique to the Indian society. Sanctioned by religio-philosophical system, the *dalits* are socially placed outside the four-fold caste system and they are referred to as the fifth caste (*Panchanas*), even when they live as outcastes. Perhaps nowhere else in the world has inequality been so elaborately constructed as in the Indian institution of caste.[27]

The rot lies at the root, the caste system, and thus the upper castes enjoy the privileges. Its presence is felt in every sphere. Since the system has a religious sanction the state regulations have become meaningless. In the medieval period, the shudras and the untouchables were denied the human rights of education, equality and liberty. The Islamic message of brotherhood was replaced by political expediency and the

Muslim rulers created a new class of Shudras and noblemen from the caste-Hindus, they did not confer these privileges on the untouchables. The rulers, perhaps, thought that they would have to face opposition of the caste-Hindus it they conferred privileges on the untouchables and even in the Maratha empire, though the untouchables, especially Mahars, fought heroically against the Mohammedans, they were not rewarded. Even Shivaji could not abolish the system of untouchability.

During the 11th and 12th centuries, the number of castes, sub-castes and mixed castes increased greatly with the influence of Jainism on the Vaishyas, which made them confine themselves mainly to trade, commerce and lending. The position of the shudras had improved a great deal. As the Vaishyas believed in the doctrine of *ahimsa*, the position of the Shudras gradually improved, both economically and socially. Their lot further improved when the reformist movement like Jainism and Saivism welcomed them in their fold. But, intellectually they remained rather backward, because higher education was largely restricted to the elite, the Brahmins and the Kshatriyas.[28]

The advent of the Afghans and Moghuls in the 16th century had a considerable impact on the Hindu social system. The immediate reaction, however, of the Afghan and Moghul conquest was the exodus of some people to the South. Those who remained behind became more exclusive and tried to protect themselves by early marriage and further strengthening the caste system. The Portuguese occupation of some parts of India in the early 16th century gave rise to fresh conversions of Hindus into Roman catholics. When Hindu kings conquered the areas occupied by Muslims or Portuguese rulers, Muslim and Christian converts freely got themselves reconverted to Hinduism. All these further increased the number of castes.[29]

The Muslim invaders continued to come and go with their leaders like Sultan Mahmud of Ghazni and Mohammad Ghori. After the slave dynasty, India was ruled by different Muslim rulers and dynasties, Khiljis, Sayyids, Suris, and the Moghuls.

During the long period of Muslim domination in India, one would have expected some changes in the lot of the *dalits* as Islam upholds the principle of equality of all human beings. But that was not to be.

A number of well known research works have confirmed that Muslim society itself was divided into a number of different grades/classes, through not exactly like the Hindu caste system. The highest grade, which is comparable to the Hindu 'twice-born' upper castes were Ashrafs, Shaikhs (chiefs), Mughals and Pathans (corresponding to Hindu Kshatriya). The middle group was made up of those who have clean occupations. The last group included the converts from the untouchables, who did scavenging, sweeping and other menial tasks. This division among the Muslims was confirmed by later historians and scholars. J.S. Grewal[30] observes that the "differences on the basis of religion or race or occupation were reflected in the morphology of cities and towns. Urban centres were divided into separate quarters for the various social groups. On the outskirts of towns generally lived the scavengers, the leather dressers and the poor beggars … . The respectable social groups among Muslims lived apart from the common populace …". Why did the caste distinctions continued during the Muslim period in India? There was no change in the position of even those *dalits* who embraced Islam. Acculturative influence of Hinduism can be one reason. The other possible reasons "are those elements in Islam itself which support such distinctions". Imtiaz Ahmad[31], in the introduction to his edited work *Caste and Social Stratification Among the Muslims*, has summarised these elements (based upon traditions) in these words:

(a) an Arab was superior to a non-Arab;
(b) among Arabs, all *Quraishities* were of equal social standing in a class by themselves, and all other Arabs were equal irrespective of their tribes;
(c) among non-Arabs, a man was by birth the equal of Arabs, if both his father and grandfather were Muslims, but only

if he were sufficiently wealthy to provide an adequate *mahr* (endowment);

(d) a learned non-Arab was not equal to an ignorant Arab, even if he was a descendant of Ali, "for the worth of learning is greater than the worth of family"; and

(e) a Muslim Kazi or theologian ranked higher than a merchant and a merchant higher than a tradesman.

Besides Islam, during the Muslim period, there were other religions as well. The religions which came from outside India included Christianity, Judaism and Zoroastrianism. Christianity was first to arrive and Judaism and Zoroastrianism came around the same time when Islam entered India. The indigenous religions which came into existence during the Muslim period were Lingayatism and Sikhism. Baha's religion, which originated in Iran with its founder Baha'u'llah (1819–92), is to be found in the Malwa region of Central India. As far as Judaism is concerned, there were two ancient settlements of Jews, one in Cochin and the other in and around Bombay in Western India. Historically, their presence in India is confirmed from A.D. 1020 onwards. Jewish scholar, Shalva Weil, observes that "in terms of the larger order or ranking, both these groups individually have had to internalise caste perceptions in order to provide legitimisation to their ascribed status. As intermediaries in a ranked order of things between the local king and inferior castes, they have both individually shared what Fullar (1976) has termed a common 'orthopraxy' with Hindu, while at the same time retaining theoretical adherence to the egalitarianism of the Judeo-Christian tradition". Jews, both of Cochin and Bombay, are divided into two main castes or *jatis* known as *gora* Jews and *kala* Jews. According to Mandelbaum, these two groups of Jews, "did not interdine or intermarry, though they did worship in the same synagogues. Those of the higher *jati* claimed poorer jewish ancestry. The lower, they alleged, was of mixed origins".[32]

The forefathers of the Parsees were allowed by the local king Sanjan Jadi Rana to settle in a place named Sanjan in

Gujarat subject to certain conditions, which they accepted. Since the Parsees did not believe in conversions there was no chance for them to influence the social order based on caste system. So Parsees or Zoroastrianism may be considered to be more or less unconcerned with the problem of the *dalits*.

The other religion which came into prominence during the Muslim period was Sikhism, which also upholds the concept of egalitarianism. The founder of the Sikh religion, Nanak, "did away altogether with caste distinctions and ceremonials". But there are a number of testimonies available to establish that by the time of the first half of the nineteenth century, the caste hierarchy among the Sikhs became the order of the day. While summing up the discussion on caste hierarchy among Sikhs, Ethne K. Marenco says: "the many sources show that the Sikhs maintained caste practices, despite the fact that their religious dogma was against caste … . The original converts to Sikhism were striving for upward mobility. This type of corporate caste mobility, where whole groups converted to a religion that promised them an escape from their low caste position, has occurred more than once in India, and it was the phenomenon which was involved in the original conversion of *Jat* Hindu or *Chuhra* and *Chamar* Hindus or *Chuhra* Muslims (Mazhabis) to Sikhism".[33]

An egalitarian religion which came from outside is Baha'i. Its members are limited to Malwa villages in Central India and also it has got indigenised fully under the influence of Hindus. Therefore, the Baha'i religion made very little positive contribution. A quotation from the work of W. Garlington will be helpful to clarify this point further: "by presenting Baha'u'llah as an *avatar* who has come to revitalise Hinduism rather than denounce it, Baha'i teachers do not make declarants forsake their Hindu heritage, and in effect they can psychologically remain Hindus: they are Hindus who believe in the *Yugavatar*, Baha'u'llah. On the normative level the Baha'i faith is an egalitarian religion, all believers are considered equal in the eyes of God, and therefore they all assume a similar status

– that of God's servant. This ideal is in direct contrast to the traditional Hindu view as practised in Malva villages, whereby an individual is ranked according to his status group (caste) ..."

The next important period of Indian history is the British. Technically, this period began with the inauguration of the East India Company (London) in 1599. But for the first 150 years, the East India Company showed interest only in business and trade. It was only from 1744 onwards that Lord Robert Clive turned it into a military power. In 1857, for the first time, a major revolt took place in the Indian (British) Army dominated mainly by upper castes which some of the historians see as the outcome of the threats to the religious practices. After crushing the revolt, the British with a proclamation by Queen Victoria in 1858 transferred political authority from the Company to the English Crown.[34] The British, however, maintained *status quo* as far as social and religious aspects of life were concerned. It was acknowledged that "due regard may be had to the civil and religious usages of the native ...". They recognised the integrity of caste organisation and held that social privileges of the membership of a caste were to be wholly within the jurisdiction of the caste. This was more or less their avowed policy till the first war of independence in 1857. The Rising opened the eyes of the administrators of the country as well as of the students of British Indian history to the potentialities of caste. It was almost the unanimous opinion of persons connected with the Government of India that the root causes of the rising were to be found in the fact that the Bengal Army was composed largely of the higher castes, and that the safety of the British domination in India was closely connected with keeping the Indians divided on lines of caste. Some officials like Sir Lepel Griffin thought that caste was useful in preventing rebellion, while James Kerr[35], the Principal of the Hindu College at Calcutta, commented in 1865 as follows: "It may be doubted if the existence of caste is on the whole unfavourable to the permanence of our rule. It may even be considered favourable to it, provided we act with prudence and forbearance. Its spirit is opposed to national union". The maxim of 'divide and rule' began to be preached by historians and journalists alike. Major General H.T. Tucker, while giving evidence before the Special Commission presided over by Lord Peel, appointed to suggest reorganisation of the Indian Army after the Rising of 1857, insisted on the necessity of keeping the country under British domination through the policy of dividing and separating into distinct bodies the nationalities and castes recruited to the Army. Because the Rising was largely the work of soldiers of the high caste, Brahmins and Rajputs, there was a clamour in England that the high-caste sepoys should be removed. It is perhaps no coincidence that in the post-Rising period, a large number of the British intellectuals, most of them being members of the Indian Civil Service, conducted studies of the various caste groups in different parts of the country. But for these studies, which provided a wealth of data on the life, customs, manners and religious beliefs of different castes, our knowledge about them would not have been complete. It is, however, a matter of debate whether these intellectuals were solely inspired by their intellectual curiosity or were guided by their administrative zeal to tighten the grip of British rule in India, in particular to find out about "the impact of Hinduism on the perpetuation of the ritual imbalances in the Indian caste system, the relation between clean castes and scheduled castes and scheduled caste occupation, scheduled castes and Hindu religion, etc.[36]

Initially, the British did not intervene in matters relating to caste. However, there was a change in its policy in the second half of the 19th century, specially after the rising, to a policy of active interference in caste matters so that the traditional hierarchical organisation of caste became almost irrelevant. This policy was given a new orientation in the 20th century, when the demand for independence gained momentum, to widening the existing cleavages and fostering separation and new alignments in the hierarchy so that they could perpetuate their rule by dividing and sub-dividing the Hindus on the basis of caste as well.

The impact of British rule on the traditional Indian caste system was broadly as follows:

1. The rigidity and orthodoxy of the caste hierarchy started breaking down, and at the same time, an all-round hardening of the system ensued.
2. The process of upward social mobility not only suffered a severe jolt but actually a downward mobility ensued.
3. Separatism and conflict became a permanent feature of the Hindu society.
4. Caste became a tool in the political, religious and cultural battles that the Hindus fought amongst themselves.

Thus, whatever measures they initiated in their 200-year rule, especially after 1857, in administrative, legislative, economic, educational and above all, in political fields, were aimed at achieving those objectives. The British Government assiduously nursed, rather than ignored, the spirit of caste in their actions and policies enunciated during this period.[37] Though the British Government recognised the integrity of caste for internal affairs, they did not protect the institution in all matters. At first, the British authorities wanted to sustain traditional Hindu and Muslim Laws. After 1864 a new policy was adapted and the British courts, administering a uniform criminal law, removed from the purview of caste many matters that used to be erstwhile adjudicated by it. Questions of assault, adultery, rape, and like were taken before the British courts for decision, and the caste councils in proportion lost their former importance. Even in matters of civil law, such as marriage, divorce, etc., though the avowed intention of the British was to be guided by the caste customs slowly but surely various decisions of the High Courts practically set aside the authority of caste. A number of decisions of the High Courts did embolden the non-Brahminic castes to dislodge the Brahmins from their monopoly of priesthood. In Bengal and in North India, generally it is now settled that there is no office of priest recognised as such in law, and a householder may employ anyone he likes for the performance of any priestly service and pay the fees to him. A similar view has been to taken in the Madras presidency. When the non-Brahmin reformists started the practice of performing their religious rites without the aid of the Brahmin priests, the latter lodged a complaint asking for an injunction against the persons so violating their rights. The High Court of Bombay decreed that people could engage any priest they liked, and were not at all bound to call for the services of the hereditary priest; but unlike the High Court of Madras, they decreed that the hereditary priest must be paid some fees by way of compensation. G.S. Ghurye,[38] therefore, comments that this opened the way to the dissolution of the only bond holding together the diverse castes, viz., the employment of common priesthood.

The Caste Disabilities Removal Act of 1850 struck at the roots of the caste system. The Act did not remove civil disabilities existing among castes that facilitate conversion to another religion or admission into another caste. Notwithstanding any custom of caste disinheriting a person for change of caste or religion, the Act provided that a person does not forfeit his ordinary rights of property by loss of caste or change of religion.

Under the British colonial rule, various lawsuits were brought by native Indians into the law courts established by the British. The most difficult law suits for the British judges to decide were those pertaining to Hindu family law which included marriage, divorce, succession, adoption, guardianship and maintenance. The problems were not only intermingled with Hindu religion but were deeply related with the various customs of each caste, which were quite unfamiliar to the British judges.[39] Anticipating these difficulties, Warren Hastings, the then Governor of Bengal, initiated reforms in the judicial system providing that in all suits regarding inheritance, marriage, caste and other religious usages shall be decided as per the personal laws of the parties.[40]

Although Hastings made it a rule to apply *Shastra* as such to law suits among Hindus and this rule was followed in British

India at large, the rule was not easy to practise in a specific law suit because *Shastra* as such included various law books, classical as well as medieval, and there existed among them no concrete jurisprudence. Therefore, 'Brahmins', 'Pandits' well-versed in *Shastra* were posted in the judiciary (king's courts set up in the presidency towns of Calcutta, Madras and Bombay with jurisdiction over lawsuits among British citizens and among native Indians residing in the Presidency Towns) as well; in the *Sadr Divani Adalats*. The Pandits were required to submit the 'report' pertaining to the specific case known as *vyavastha* to the courts. This gradually led to the emergence of Hindu law. The Hindu law was, consequently, not the pure classical Brahminical law itself but adjusted with the British judicial administration. In this sense, the Hindu law was the law produced under British colonial rule for administrating jurisdiction over. Hindu subjects. This Hindu law contained a kind of legal fiction. In it, Hindu society of the 19th century was presumed to be composed of four *varnas*, namely, Brahmin, Kshatriya, Vaishya and Shudra in consequence of its being based on classical Brahminical laws like *Manusmriti*. In addition, the four *varnas* were equated with castes so that Hindu society in the 19th century was assumed to be a 'caste society' to comprise four 'castes' according to Hindu law.[41]

In case of *Bhola Nath Mitter v. Emperor*, the Calcutta High Court awarded penalty in an adultery case. The accused was a man who had intercourse with a Dom woman (Dom was thought to be a depressed caste). This Dom woman was married to a Kayastha man following the Hindu marriage ritual (Kayastha in Bengal was considered to belong to the Shudra *varna*). In the trial, the accused claimed to be not guilty on the ground that marriage between a Shudra man and a woman of a depressed caste was not legal hence the charge of adultery could not be applied to the accused. The Calcutta High Court rejected his plea by declaring that both Kayastha and Dom belonged to the Shudra 'caste' and the marriage between a Kayastha man and a Dom woman was legitimate.[42]

Similar marriages between a Shudra man and a woman of a depressed caste were decided as being legal by other High Courts like the Madras High Court also.[43]

An example of social discrimination against the depressed castes, covered and kept intact by the legal fiction of the Hindu Law, was the problem of 'temple entry' of the depressed castes. In 1908, the legal committee of the Privy Council decided in an appeal from the Madras High Court that the custom of excluding a depressed caste from entry to a Hindu temple was legal. This was a suit brought against Shanars (Shanans) who forcibly entered the famous Meenatchi (Minakshi) temple of Madura (Madurai) in a procession bearing torches and music. Shanans, traditionally palm distillers, were supposed to be a depressed caste but in the latter part of the nineteenth century they began to try to improve their social status by abandoning palm distilling and taking to other professions like trading. For the first time in 1874, they asked for the right to enter Minakshi temple but were denied. After their sporadic attempts to enter Minakshi temple had failed, they decided to force their way into the temple on 14 May, 1897. The hereditary trustee of the temple, the zamindar of Ramnadu, sued Madura District Court for a declaration that Shanans were not entitled to enter the temple, and an injunction to restrain them from so doing as well as compensation of Rs 2,500 for the purification ceremony needed for the temple as it was defiled by their entry. The subordinate judge of Madura, who decided in favour of the plaintiff on the ground that entry of Shanans into the temple had been rejected by custom, observed that the "Courts of Law have recognised and enforced customs of this character although they may be repugnant to generally conceived notions of what is just and proper. It is not for this court to examine whether the doctrines or usages obtaining in a particular temple are defensible from a logical or equitable standpoint in the light of modern enlightenment and civilisation." Shanans appealed to the Madras High Court but their appeal was dismissed. They then appealed to the Privy Council which affirmed the judgment of the Madras High Court.[44]

During the British period a number of movements were launched for the uplift of the *dalits*. Before the British, during the Muslim period the *Bhakti* movement helped the cause of the *dalits*, particularly in the spiritual sphere. This happened mostly through the *Bhakti* saints, who either were non-Brahmins or themselves were *dalits*. The efforts of most of these movements during the British period were limited to reform rather than aimed at total change. But there were some personalities, who were involved directly in the struggle either for change or reform among *dalits*. They include Jotiba Phule, Ambedkar and Gandhi. Among these, the first two were for the total uplift of the *dalits*, Gandhi's work was limited to reform, more within the Hindu Society. Ambedkar dedicated his work *Who were the Sudras* to Phule and writes, "the Greatest *Sudra* of Modern India who made the lower classes among Hindus conscious of their slavery to the higher classes, who preached the gospel that for Indian social democracy was more vital than independence from foreign rule". Phule belonged to the Mali caste. In 1873, he formed an association named *Satyashodhak Samaj* with the definite purpose of "asserting the worth of man irrespective of caste". He encouraged through his writings a revolt against the tyranny of the caste system. His revolt was "against caste in so far as caste denied ordinary human rights to all". In 1851, he started a primary school for the so-called untouchables in Poona. He criticised the *Manusmriti* because he realised that it was the most weighty stumbling block in the way of social change. Phule "made efforts to unite all the non-Brahmin *dalits*". Ambedkar and Gandhi, however, approached the problem from different angles which had an impact on the history of the *dalits* for years to come.

The British Government, which was at that time also trying to help all other communities such as Muslims, Christians, Anglo-Indians, and so on, excluded them from the definition of depressed classes, while bestowing on them special benefits, such as giving them separate communal electorates. In 1931, a special committee was set up to draw a 'schedule' of the castes and classes covered under the depressed classes. Also at the same time, the Round Table Conference was called in London. At the Conference, Ambedkar demanded separate electorate for the depressed classes, whom he always referred to as 'untouchables'. At this conference, he also proposed that the untouchables be called "Protestant Hindus" or "non-conformist Hindus". But Gandhi objected to Ambedkar's demand for separate electorates. By that time, of course, Gandhi had also introduced his favourite term 'Harijan' to be used in place of untouchables. As Gandhi and Ambedkar did not agree with each other at the Round Table Conference, no final decision was taken. Finally, the whole matter of a separate communal electorate was left to the chairman of the conference, Prime Minister Ramsay MacDonald, who in 1932 issued the Communal Award. In this he also replaced the expression "Depressed Classes" with "Scheduled Castes". From then on the untouchables of India were known as "Scheduled Castes". Later, the same expression was included in the Government of India (Scheduled Castes) Order, 1936. Gandhi opposed the Communal Award because of the fear of their getting separated from Hindu fold. He went on fast unto death which prompted Ambedkar to agree to make certain modifications in the Communal Award in a manner satisfactory to Gandhi. According to this agreement, in place of the separate electorate, joint electorate for the scheduled castes with the caste-Hindu majority was accepted.[45] This, according to Upendra Baxi, was a defeat for a political liberal Ambedkar by his shrewd opponent Gandhi. "Gandhi gambled on Ambedkar's self-restraint and won", says Baxi, "the costs of the victory would have to be recorded by untouchable historians of future India." In this way one more chance of effective liberation and freedom was lost by the *dalits*.[46]

Gandhi dominated the Indian political scene for well over a quarter of a century (1920–1948) and by and large influenced most of is contemporaries. There were very few who differed with him, and fewer still who challenged his supremacy. Ambedkar was one of those few prominent Indian leaders who clashed with Gandhiji. He clashed with the Gandhi not for any personal reasons but on account of the ideological differences and his approach to the problem of the untouchables. For Ambedkar, the cause of the untouchables was the first and the foremost. From the very beginning, Ambedkar was of the view that the problem of the depressed classes was a political problem. Emphasising this he said in the Round Table Conference on 20 November 1930:

> "We are often reminded that the problem of the depressed classes is a social problem and that its solution lies elsewhere than in politics. We take strong exception to this view. We hold that the problem of the depressed classes will never be solved unless they get political power in their hands. If this is true, and I do not think that the contrary can be maintained then the problem of the depressed classes is, I submit, eminently a political problem and must be treated as such."[47]

Impressed by the weighty arguments of Ambedkar, the Round Table Conference decided in principle to treat the untouchables as a separate unit, and to give them special representation in the future set-up of India. But, the matter could not be finalised as the Congress had not participated in the first session of the Round Table Conference. Gandhi participated in the second session of the Round Table Conference as the sole representative of the Congress. In his very first speech on September 15, 1931, Gandhi opposed the special treatment for the untouchables, and said, "the Congress has reconciled itself to special treatment of Hindu-Muslim Sikh tangle. There are historical reasons for it, but the Congress will not extend that doctrine in any shape or form. I listened to the list of special interests, so far as the untouchables are concerned I have not yet quite grasped what Ambedkar has to say. But, of course, the Congress will share the onus with Ambedkar of representing the interests of the untouchables are as dear to the Congress as the interests of any other body or any other individual throughout the length and breadth of India. Therefore, I would most strongly resist any further special representation."[48]

In 1944, when India was on the threshold of freedom and negotiations were going on between the Congress and the Muslim League to arrive at a settlement, Ambedkar wrote a letter to Gandhi saying that in addition to the settlement of the Hindu-Muslim problem, the settlement of the problem of the untouchables was necessary if the Indian political goal was to be achieved. In his reply on 6 August, 1944, Gandhi regretted his inability on the plea that to him the question of the depressed classes was of a religious and social reform.[49]

A good number of modern social reforms have condemned the institution of caste in the strongest terms. The most vocal amongst them was Har Dayal. He observes, "caste is the curse of India. Caste, in all its forms, has made us a nation of slaves. Priesteraft and caste have slain us, India can never establish and maintain a free state so long as caste rules in our society".[50] Strangely enough, Gandhi, who had set *'Purna Swaraj'* as his goal not only believed in caste system but even went to the extent of justifying it. In an article in the *Navajivan* in 1921, he said that he was opposed to all those who were out to destroy the caste system, and summarised his views as follows:

1. "I believe that if Hindu society has been able to stand, it is because it is founded on the caste system.
2. I believe that inter-dining or inter-marriage are not necessary for promoting national unity … . Taking food is as dirty an act as answering the call of nature … . Just as we perform the act of answering the call of nature in seclusion so also the act of taking food must also be done in seclusion.
3. To destroy caste system and adopt Western European social systems means that Hindus must give up the principle of hereditary occupation which is the soul of the caste system. Hereditary principle is an eternal principle. To change it, is to create disorder … . It will be a chaos if every day a Brahmin is to be changed into a Shudra and a Shudra is to be changed into a Brahmin."[51]

Ambedkar, on the contrary, believed that,

(1) caste has ruined the Hindus;
(2) the reorganisation of the Hindu society on the basis of *chaturvarna* is impossible because the *varna vyavastha* is like a leaky pot or like a man with a runny nose. It is incapable of sustaining itself by its own virtue and has an inherent tendency to degenerate into a caste system unless there is a legal sanction behind it which can be enforced against everyone transgressing his *varna*.
(3) the Hindu society must be reorganised on a religious basis which would recognise the principles of liberty, equality and fraternity; and
(4) in order to achieve this object the sense of religious sanctity behind caste and *varna* must be destroyed.

Ambedkar's verdict that the caste has ruined the Hindu society does not seem to be difficult to sustain in view of the very grave and fundamental drawbacks pointed out by him. In brief, his indictment of the caste system runs as follows:

1. "Practically speaking in a class structure, there is on the one hand, tyranny, vanity, pride, arrogance, greed, selfishness and on the other, insecurity, poverty, degradation, loss of the liberty, self-reliance, independence, dignity and self-respect.
2. These caste are anti-national because they bring about separation in social life. They are anti-national also because they generate jealousy and antipathy between caste and caste.
3. A society which rests upon the supremacy of one group over another irrespective of its national or proportionate claims inevitably leads to conflict.
4. The group set-up prevents an individual from acquiring consistency of mind which is possible only when society has common deals, common models. His thoughts are led astray and this creates a mind whose seeing unity is forced and distorted.

5. The group set-up leads to stratification of classes. Those who are masters remain masters and those who are born in slavery remain slaves. Owners remain owners and workers remain workers. The privileged remain privileged and serfs remain serfs.
6. The caste system is a system which is infested with the spirit of isolation and in fact it makes isolation of one caste from another a matter of virtue".[52]

Although many other nations are characterised by social inequality, perhaps nowhere else in the world has inequality been so elaborately constructed as in the institution of caste in India. In independent India, despite constitutional mandate, caste system prevails in all its forms and manifestations. It is more predominant in the countryside than in urban areas and more in the realms of kinship and marriage than in personal interactions. The *dalits* are deprived of education, right to possess assets and right to posses weapons to protect themselves. The practice of untouchability was abolished by law in 1950, yet the *dalits* experience the agony of untouchability in all walks of life. One cannot understand the pain of being a *dalit* unless he or she experiences it.[53]

Many status differences in Indian society are expressed in terms of ritual purity and pollution. Notions of purity and pollution are extremely complex and vary greatly among different castes, religious groups, and regions. However, broadly speaking, high status is associated with purity and low status with pollution. Some kinds of purity are inherent, or inborn, for example, gold is purer than copper by its very nature, and similarly, a member of a high ranking Brahmin caste is born with more inherent purity than a member of low ranking sweeper caste. Unless the Brahmin defiles himself in some extra-ordinary way, he will always be purer than a sweeper. Other kinds of purity are more transitory, a Brahmin who has just taken a bath is more ritually pure than a Brahmin who has not bathed for a day. This situation could easily reverse itself temporarily, depending on both schedules, participation in polluting activities, or contact with temporarily polluting substance. Purity is associated with ritual cleanliness – daily bathing in flowing water, dressing in properly laundered clothes of approved materials, refraining from physical contact with people of lower rank, and avoiding involvement with ritually impure substances.

No one practices untouchability when it comes to sex. Rape is a common phenomenon in rural areas. Women are raped as part of caste custom or village tradition. According to *dalit* activists, *dalit* girls have been forced to have sex with the village landlord. In rural areas, "women are induced into prostitution (Devadasi system) which is forced on them in the name of religion". The prevalence of rape in village contributes to the greater incidence of child marriages in those areas. Early marriage between the age of ten years and sixteen years persists in large parts because of *dalit* girls' vulnerability to sexual assault by upper caste men; once a girl is raped, she becomes unmarriageable. *Dalit* women are also raped as a form of retaliation. *Dalit* women face the triple burden of caste, class and gender. *Dalit* girls have been forced to become prostitutes for upper caste patrons and village priests. Sexual abuse and other forms of violence against women are not uncommon and the police is a silent spectator.

Because of the insurmountable problems they faced in remaining within the Hindu fold, the *dalits* always try to switch over to other religions in search of equality and dignity. Buddhism was one of their first alternatives as it rejected caste system and the authority of the *Vedas*. The arrival of the Christian missionaries to India, especially after the 16th century, provided an occasion for many *dalits* to embrace Christianity. The Portuguese Padroado, the English Christian merchants, the French and the Irish missionaries and others converted thousands of *dalits* to their faith. It must be noted that economic benefits also played a major role in these conversions. For the *dalits* who lived in extreme poverty, the economic benefits as a result of conversions provided the much-needed relief. Many of them were labelled as "wheat

Christians" or "milk powder Christians" but in truth hundreds of *dalits* escaped starvation solely due to the humanitarian efforts of these missionaries. But it is also true that many of the missionaries were instrumental in maintaining the caste system in the Indian Church. Just a casual look at the history of the Indian church reveals how the missionaries tolerated and accepted the caste system in a subtle way. The missionaries had to make compromises in order to escape the wrath of the upper caste converts. The equality and the human dignity promised by Christianity has remained only a dream in the case of the millions of *dalit* Christians.[54]

The plight of *dalits* even in the post-independence era remained by and large unchanged. This is evident from the following:

(i) The Constitution (Scheduled Castes) Order, 1950.

(ii) Report of the First Commissioner for Scheduled Caste and Scheduled Tribes for the period ending 31st December, 1951.

(iii) Report of the Backward Classes Commission, (popularly known as Mandal Commission), 1980.

The Constitution (Scheduled Castes) Order, 1950

The Constitution of India under Article 341(1) provides that the President of India, "... by public notification, to specify the castes, races or tribes or parts or of groups within castes, races or tribes which shall, for the purpose of this Constitution be deemed to be Scheduled Castes ..." Again, the Constitution without defining in Article 366(24), only refers back to the power given to the President of India in Article 341. But once the President has issued such an order, the list prepared on the basis of Article 342(2) or scheduled castes can be changed only through an Act of Parliament. While exercising the powers conferred under Article 341(1), the President of India promulgated an order in 1950, known as the Constitution (Scheduled Castes) Order 1950. The order almost re-enacted the list of the Constitution of India (Scheduled Castes) Order, 1936.

Concerning the Scheduled Castes, the Constitution has followed the basis the British Government laid down in 1936. This applies not only to the list, but also to the criterion, which the British Government used to define "Scheduled Caste", because the same is followed by the Order of 1950. On that basis, the third paragraph of this order reads, "Notwithstanding anything contained in paragraph 2, no person who professes a religion different from Hindu, shall be deemed to be a member of a Scheduled Caste". This paragraph was changed in 1956 by parliament to "Hindu or Sikh" and again in May 1990 it was changed by the Parliament to "Hindu or Sikh" or "Buddhist".

So, the positions of the President and Parliament are the same as that of the British Government in 1932–36, because it has used "religion" as the criterion to define the scheduled castes, but a political party like Bhartiya Janata Party (BJP) has a still more orthodox and biased criterion in regard to the scheduled castes, or the *dalits*. On June 12, 1990, at Thiruvananthapuram, L.K. Advani stated his party's stand that it is opposed to any move by the V.P. Singh government to extend reservation to converts to Islam and Christianity from scheduled castes and scheduled tribes. It had supported the extension of reservation to scheduled castes/scheduled tribes to Buddhism because under the Constitution Buddhists and Sikhs and Jains were classified as Hindus and that reservation to converts to other religions would violate the recommendation of the Constituent Assembly. This is the basic contradiction, which the Constitution of the country and those responsible for its implementation are faced with, because the view expressed above, and decisions based on such views, not only violate the fundamental rights [Article 15(1)] but also raise the question of human rights based on the principle of equality.[55]

Report of the First Commissioner for Scheduled Castes and Scheduled Tribes (for the period ending 31st December, 1951)

The Constitution of India stipulates under Article 338(1) to appoint a Special Officer for the scheduled castes and scheduled tribes and "it shall be the duty of the Special Officer to investigate all matters relating to the safeguards provided for the scheduled castes and scheduled tribes under the Constitution and report to the President on the working of those safeguards at such intervals as the President may direct, and the President shall cause all such reports to be laid before each House of Parliament". Under this provision, the President of India appointed L.M. Shrikant as the first Commissioner (Special Officer) on November 18, 1950. The Report states that caste in Hindu society is still the most powerful factor in determining a man's dignity. Such a rigid caste system is not found anywhere else outside India. All such professions that involve handling of the so-called dirty jobs like tanning and skinning of hides, manufacture of leather goods, sweeping of streets, scavenging, etc., are allotted to those castes, also known as Harijans, who are about 5 crores according to the latest figures available. It further observes, by the force of habit, the Harijan (*dalit*) has lost his self-respect to such an extent that he regards his work to which his caste is condemned not as a curse from which he must protect. He has not much courage to seek another job in field or factory. He has thus become lazy in mind and body and callous to his own condition, and he will not educate his children".[56]

Shrikant, as the first Commissioner, undertook an extensive tour to get first hand information about the *dalits*, on whom he spent much space in his report, while describing what he had observed and has seen personally, he writes, the main reason for this is that Harijans (*dalits*) have no courage to come forward either to draw water from the common wells or to go to shops, public restaurants, hotels, etc., as they are generally economically dependent on non-Harijans in one way or the other. At places where offences committed under these Acts have not been made cognizable, it is very difficult for the scheduled caste people to take any action against culprits because the police are incapable of taking any action if a report is made to them.[57]

Shrikant's view again gets support from the report of the Commissioner for Scheduled Castes and Scheduled Tribes of

April, 1985 to March, 1986. This report, 35 years after the first report of 1951, proves that these atrocities against the *dalits* continue as in 1950–51 or before. These reports show that historically the development of the *dalits* problem is continuing on the same pattern as in the past.[58]

Report of the Backward Classes Commission, 1980 (Mandal Commission)

This Commission was constituted under the chairmanship of B.P. Mandal on January 1, 1979, and the report of the Commission was submitted on December 31, 1980. The Commission's terms of reference included determining the criteria for defining the socially and educationally backward classes, recommending steps for the advancement of the socially and educationally backward classes of citizens so identified, and examining the desirability or otherwise of making provision for the reservation of appointments or posts in favour of such backward classes which are not adequately represented in public services at the Union and state levels.

Marc Galanter, in his work, *Competing Equalities: Law and the Backward Classes in India,* observes, India's system of preferential treatment for historically disadvantaged sections of the population is unprecedented in scope and extent. India embraced equality as a cardinal value against a background of elaborated, valued, and clearly perceived inequalities. Her constitutional policies to offset these proceeded from an awareness of the entrenched and cumulative nature of group inequalities. The result has been an array of programmes in the form of compensatory discrimination.[59]

The above analysis makes it clear that:

1. The *dalits* are the descendants of the earliest settlers of India.
2. The problems of the *dalits* can be traced to 1500 B.C. For more than 3500 years they have suffered and continue to suffer multiple oppressions, which have always been supported by religion, directly or indirectly.

3. Because of the long history of oppression, the *dalits* have even lost their self-identity as human beings, which they have now accepted "as a part of the natural order of things" or "as a privilege".

Notes

1. Cited in Sarajit Kumar Chatterjee, *The Scheduled Castes in India*, Vol. I, Gyan Publication House, New Delhi, 1996, p. 11.
2. Ibid., p. 12.
3. Ibid., p. 15.
4. Ibid., p. 16.
5. C.P. Yadav, *Encyclopaedia of Scheduled Castes and Scheduled Tribes*, Vol. I, Anmol Publications, New Delhi, 2000, p. 1.
6. John C.B. Webster, *Religion and Dalit Liberation: An Examination of Perspectives*, Manohar Publishers, New Delhi, 1999, p. 11.
7. Sarajit Kumar Chatterjee, op. cit., p. 12.
8. Ibid., p. 12.
9. Walter A. Fairservis Jr., 1967: It does suggest that the Indus valley civilisation was an indigenous development that arose out of the evaluation of developed village cultures in a favourable environment. It emphasises the sub-continental roots and the consequent "style" which gives the civilisation its uniqueness; Ernet Mackay, 1935: Who were these people who built Mohenjodaro and Harappa? No definite answer can be given at present to this question, though it is certain that they were a pre-Aryan race, for their cities were flourishing some thousand years before any Aryan-speaking people had entered India, which took place according to modern ruling about 1500 BC; Mortimer Wheeler, 1953: Thus of the twelve seals for which any sort of dating can be postulated, seven may be Sargonid, one pre-Sargonid and four of the Larsa or later period. On current dating the maximum period required to cover these possibilities would be 2500–1500 BC with a strong focus on 2550 BC.

10. N.N. Bhattacharyya, *Ancient Indian History and Civilization: Trends and Perspectives*, Manohar Publishers, New Delhi, 1988, p. 21.
11. James Massey, *Roots of Dalit History, Christianity, Theology and Spirituality*, ISPCK, Delhi, 1996, p. 1.
12. Ibid., p. 18.
13. Ram Sharan Sharma, *Sudras in Ancient India*, Motilal Banarsidas, Delhi, 1990, p. 33.
14. S.M. Michael, *Dalits in Modern India: Vision and Values*, Vistaar Publications, New Delhi, 1999, p. 13.
15. J.H. Hutton, The origin of the position of the exterior castes is partly racial, partly religious and partly a matter of social custom. There can be little doubt but the idea of untouchability originates in taboo.

    J.H. Hutton, *Caste in India: Its Nature, Function and Origins*, Oxford University Press, Bombay, 1969, p. 16.
16. Cited in S.M. Michael, op. cit., p. 14.
17. Rebati Ballav Tripathy, *Dalit: A Sub-Human Society*, Ashish Publishing House, New Delhi, 1994, p. 7.
18. Ibid., p. 8.
19. Ibid., p. 10.
20. H. Kotani, *Caste System, Untouchability and the Depressed*, Manohar Publishers, New Delhi, 1997, p. 4.
21. Ibid., p. 15.
22. Dr B.R. Ambedkar, *The Untouchables*, Amrit Book Co., New Delhi, 1948, p. 30.
23. Stephen Fuchs, *The Aboriginal Tribes of India*, The Macmillan Company of India, Delhi, 1973, p. 42.
24. www.cwo.com/lucumi/caste.html
25. Human Rights Education Movement in India.
26. www.india_resource_tripod_com/social.html
27. www.dalitsolidarity.org/untouchability2.htm
28. Sarajit Kumar Chatterjee, op. cit., p. 68.
29. Ibid., p. 71.
30. J.S. Grewal, *Muslim Rule in India: The Assessments of British Historians*, Oxford University Press, Calcutta, 1970, p. 26.

31. Imtiaz Ahmad, *Caste and Social Stratification among Muslims in India*, Manohar Publishers, New Delhi, 1978, p. 28.
32. James Massey, op. cit., p. 26.
33. Cited in ibid., p. 31.
34. Ibid., p. 33.
35. Cited in Sarajit Kumar Chatterjee, op. cit., p. 147.
36. Ibid., p. 149.
37. Ibid., p. 152.
38. G.S. Ghurye, *Caste and Race in India*, Popular Prakashan, Bombay, 1979, p. 74.
39. Sarajit Kumar Chatterjee, op. cit., p. 154.
40. Cited in H. Kotani, op. cit., p. 76.
41. Ibid., p. 80.
42. *Indian Law Reports*, Calcutta Series, Vol. 51, p. 488.
43. Manickam v. Poongavanammal, 66 *M.L.J.* 543.
44. Sankaralinga Nadan v. Rajeswara Dorai, *Indian Law Reports*, Madras Series, Vol. 31, p. 236.
45. Sarajit Kumar Chatterjee, op. cit., p. 68.
46. Cited in ibid., p. 80.
47. Cited in D.C. Ahir, *Gandhi and Ambedkar: A Comparative Study*, Blumoon Books, New Delhi, 1995, p. 10.
48. Ibid., p. 11.
49. Ibid., p. 12.
50. Cited in ibid., p. 13.
51. Cited in ibid., p. 14.
52. Cited in ibid., p. 15.
53. www.dalitsolidarity/reality.htm
54. www.india_resource_tripod_com/social.htm
55. James Massey, op. cit., p. 37.
56. Ibid., p. 40.
57. Ibid., p. 41.
58. Ibid., p. 39.
59. Marc Galanter, *Competing Equalities: Law and the Backward Classes in India*, Oxford University Press, Delhi, 1984, p. 42.

2

Constituent Assembly Debate *vis-à-vis* Suppressed Humanity

The country became independent on August 15, 1947. On August 29, 1947, the Constituent Assembly announced the names of the Committee for drafting the Constitution of free India. It was headed by Ambedkar as its Chairman and included persons of eminence such as Sir Alladi Krishnaswamy, Sir B.N. Rau, Syed M. Sadullah, Sir N. Gopalaswami Iyengar, K.M. Munshi, Sir B.L. Mitter and D.P. Khaitan. Subsequently, the Drafting Committee was reconstituted when, N. Madhava Rao was appointed to replace Sir B.L. Mitter and T.T. Krishanamachari to fill in the vacancy caused by the death of D.P. Khaitan.

Ambedkar was now fully immersed in the task of drafting the Constitution of India, with his characteristic single-mindedness of purpose inspite of deterioration in his health. A speech delivered by T.T. Krishnamachari on November 5, 1948 in the Constituent Assembly shows that Ambedkar was in fact the chief architect of our democratic Constitution. In his speech, Shri Krishnamachari drew the attention of the Assembly to the fact that out of the seven members nominated by the Constituent Assembly to the Drafting Committee, most of them were not doing the work for one reason or the other and, therefore, ultimately the burden of drafting the Constitution fell upon Ambedkar.

The draft Constitution underwent three readings by the Constituent Assembly on November 25, 1949, Ambedkar, its principal architect, rose to reply to the debate which followed the third reading. He delivered a 40-minute speech in which he made an impassioned appeal to the people of independent India to defend their freedom with the last drop of their blood. He also cautioned against the hero worship and at the end of his speech he made a fervent appeal to all the Indians to be a nation in the true social and psychological sense by totally discarding the caste system. The entire Constituent Assembly, including Prime Minister Nehru, listened to his speech with rapt attention and all the members applauded him when he sat down.[1]

Rajendra Prasad[2], Chairman of the Constituent Assembly, was so impressed that he made the remark: "Sitting in the Chair and watching the proceeding from day to day, I have realised, as nobody else would have, with what zeal and devotion the membership of the Drafting Committee and especially its Chairman, Ambedkar, inspite of his indifferent health, have worked. We would never make a decision which was or could be ever so right as when we put him or the Drafting Committee and made him its Chairman." He has not only justified his selection but has added lustre to the work which he has done. Jawaharlal Nehru made the remark: "Ambedkar had played a most important part in the framing of India's Constitution. No one took greater trouble and care over Constitution making than Ambedkar."[3]

Ambedkar knew well that unless reservation in jobs and legislature was given to the *dalits*, they would never be in a position to be equal partners in the administration of the country and they will remain oppressed and slaves for ever. The conscience of the Constitution found adequate expression on this. In his final address to the Constituent Assembly, Ambedkar gave a caution and premonition and derived home this point not to interpret but to illumine the scheme of the equality code and the casteless society plea. He observed:

> "The third thing we must do is not to be content with mere political democracy, we must make our political democracy a

> social democracy as well. Political democracy cannot last unless there lies at the base of it social democracy. What does social democracy mean? It means a way of life which recognises liberty, equality and fraternity as the principles of life. These principles are not to be treated as separate items in a trinity. They form a union of trinity in the sense that to divorce one from the other is to defeat the very purpose of democracy. Liberty cannot be divorced from equality, equality cannot be divorced from liberty. Nor can liberty and equality be divorced from fraternity. Without fraternity, liberty and equality could not become a natural course of things. It would require a constable to enforce them. We must begin by acknowledging the fact that there is complete absence of two things in the Indian society; one of these is equality. On social plane, we have in India a society based on the principles of graded inequality which means elevation of some and degradation of others. On the economic plane, we have a society in which there are some who have immense wealth as against many who live in abject poverty. On 26th January, 1950, we are going to enter into a life of contradictions. In politics we will have equality and in social and economic life we will have inequality. In politics, we will be recognising the principle of 'one man one vote and one vote one value'. If our social and economic structure continues to deny the principle of one man one value, how long shall we continue to live this life of contradictions? How long shall we continue to deny equality in our social and economic life? If we continue to deny it for long, we will do so only by putting our political democracy in peril. We must remove this contradiction at the earliest possible moment or else those who suffer from inequality will blow up the structure of political democracy which this Assembly has so laboriously build up."[4]

There were eminent persons of different walks of life who participated in the discussions as members of the Constituent Assembly. For example, P. Kakkan of Madras argued that "the poor Harijan candidates hitherto did not get proper appointments in government services. The higher officers selected only their own people but not Harijans. Even in the matter of promotions we did not get justice. The government can expect necessary qualification or personality from the Harijans, but not merit. If you take merit alone into account, the Harijans cannot come forward. I say in this house that the government must take special steps for the reservation of appointment for the Harijans for same years. I expect that the government will take the necessary steps to give more appointments in police and military services also. For example, in Kashmir the poor Harijans are fighting with great vigour. I say in this house that Harijans must be given more jobs in this government and be encouraged by the government."[5]

T.V. Muniswami Pillai of Madras said that "in the great upheaval of making a Constitution for this country, I feel that the communities that have not enjoyed the leaves and fishes of the services should not be left out. It is for this purpose, I gave notice of an amendment and a further amendment signed by more than fifty members which has been presented to this House, but for reasons well known to you. I specially mean the scheduled caste are given a chance, unless there is an assurance that these communities will at all times be taken into account and given enough and more chances in appointments, their uplift will still stand over. I may tell this House that it is not the object of any of the leaders of the Harijan community to perpetuate the communal bogey in this land for ever, but so long as they remain so backward in getting admission into the services it is highly necessary that they must be given some protection."[6]

T. Channaiah of Mysore (an SC member) remarked that "the backward communities suffer from two disabilities, namely, social disabilities and educational disabilities. I want this reservation for 105 years which has been the period during which opportunities have been denied to them. At present, there is reservation in the elections and thereby we get a chance to discuss our problems here. But if there was no such reservation it would not be possible for us to come here as we would not be able to win in the general elections. I therefore submit that there should be reservation in the services and elections."[7]

If we consider the aspect politically, scheduled caste community is not represented anywhere if no reservation of seats is given. If the qualifications for Harijan candidates are not relaxed, our candidates will not be able to compete with the candidates of the Brahmin community or the so-called *suvarna* Hindus.

The question of reservation in services was handled by the Constituent Assembly in the most vacillating manner. In the initial stages of the framing of the constitution the opinion was in favour of continuation of the policy of reservation in services to minority communities. The report of the Advisory Committee on Minorities under the chairmanship of Sardar Vallabhbhai Patel in 1947 had made recommendation, which reflected this opinion. The Committee, while rejecting a Constitutional guarantee of representation in the public services to the minority communities in proportion to their population, recommended that "consistent with the need of efficiency in administration, it is necessary for the state to pay due regard to the claims of minorities in making appointments to public service". The Centre and the provinces, the Committee recommended should appoint 'Special Minority Officers' charged with the duty to enquire into cases in which it alleged that "rights and safeguards have been infringed" and submit a report to the appropriate legislature. Article 296 of the draft Constitution laid down that "the claims of the minority communities shall be taken into consideration, in the making of appointments to services and posts in connection with the affairs of the Union or a State".[8]

The Advisory Committee on Minorities later modified its view in regard to claims of religious minorities in making appointments to public services. "I can assure the house", K.M. Munshi[9] stated in the Constituent Assembly "that at the time when the Advisory Committee met on the last occasion, there was no question of providing safeguards for any religious minority. The negotiations proceeded on the footing that except the backward classes who are economically and socially backward and scheduled castes and tribes who have special claim of their own, no other minority should be recognised in the Constitution". An exception was made in the case of the Anglo-Indian community due to certain special circumstances. The committee noted that "as a result of historical circumstances the whole economy of the community is at present dependent on finding employment in certain types of posts in the Railways, the Posts and Telegraphs and the Customs Department". The Committee added that "in view of this we feel that if the existing safeguards in this regard are not continued in some form for some years to come, the community will be subjected to a sudden economic strain which it may not be able to bear".[10]

As a social scientist, Ambedkar's views almost bordered on the Marxist frame of a class society with class struggle going on intermittently under a caste facade. Ambedkar sought to identify the class interests of the untouchables. He claimed that under the garb of religion the caste-Hindus exploited them. He had recognised, much earlier, this class-caste identity and made it a political issue. It is in consonance with such a principle that he put forth the claims on behalf of the untouchables for constitutional safeguards to enable them to have due share in the political power of the country. He always maintained that as a political problem it has to be resolved through political means.[11]

Initially, thus, the Constituent Assembly was in favour of abolition of separate electorates but was in favour of reservation of seats for minorities for a fixed period. In July, 1947, the minorities sub-committee recommended the system of reservation of seats for recognised minorities for a period of ten years instead of separate electorates. The Drafting Committee accepted this recommendation and the draft Constitution accordingly provided for reservation of seats in the Union Legislature for the minorities. After the partition of the country the issue was subjected to re-examination in the changed political context. In May, 1949, a proposal was moved in the Advisory Committee that the system of reservation of seats for minorities in the legislature should be abolished. While it was welcomed by the Muslim members, the representative of the scheduled castes put forward the plea that as they were backward the system of reservation would help in safeguarding their interests and facilitate their advancement. Accordingly, it passed the resolution which read: "that the system of reservation for minorities other than scheduled castes in the legislature be abolished". Thus, the Constitution provided for the reservation of seats for the scheduled castes and scheduled tribes in the legislature for ten years.[12]

In the Constituent Assembly, the representative of the Sikh community doggedly fought to the end that constitutional safeguards should extend to all minority communities and that the original provisions of the draft Constitution which were based on the recommendations of the Advisory Committee on Minorities made in 1947 should be retained. Some of the Muslim members also passionately pleaded for reservation in services to Muslims. Z.H. Lahari made the plea that, "in the Legislature you have got statutory reservations where they are meaningless, but when you come to the services it is merely said that their claims shall be considered. This is a very pious wish. Take away the reservation from the Legislature and for God's sake give us reservation in the services. Here I speak not only for the Muslim of the United Provinces but also for other minority people". He also argued that the concessions made for Anglo-Indian community were a blatant discrimination. The Constituent Assembly was not in favour of reservation of posts for the minority communities, except the Anglo-Indian community for a short period. Sardar Patel declared that "this Constitution of India of free India, of a secular state will not hereafter be disfigured by any provision on a communal basis".[13]

The Constituent Assembly was unmistakably opposed to the policy of reservation of posts for the minorities with the exception of Anglo-Indian community. However, it was not against the adoption of the policy of reservation in favour of backward classes and scheduled castes and scheduled tribes. A feeble opposition was put up against this policy as being inconsistent with the concept of secular state. Damodar Swarup Seth maintained that "It is not easy to define precisely the term "backward"; nor is it easy to find a suitable criterion for testing the backwardness of a community or class ... it will give rise to casteism and favouritism which should have nothing to do in a secular state". Ambedkar defended the policy of reservation in favour of backward classes as presently embodied in the Constitution and argued that it reconciled three point of views expressed in the Constituent Assembly "The first is that there shall be equality of opportunity for all citizens. It is the desire of many members of this House that every individual who is qualified for a particular post should be free to apply for that post, to sit for examinations and to have his qualifications tested so as to determine, while he is fit for the post or not and that there ought to be no hindrance in the operation of the principle of equality of opportunity". Another view mostly shared by, "a section of this House is that if this principle is to be operative ... there ought to be no reservations of any sort for any class or community at all, that all citizens if they are qualified, should be placed on the same footing of equality so far as the public services are concerned ... then we have quite a massive opinion which insists that there shall be equality of opportunity, there must at the same time be a provision made for the entry of certain communities which have so far been outside the administration". Thus, the Constitution while adopting the general principle of non-discrimination, based on religion, caste, etc., has made an exception in so far as scheduled castes, scheduled tribes and backward classes are concerned.[14]

In the Constituent Assembly there was a demand for a precise definition of the term "Backward". H.N. Kunzru[15] deplored that "the word 'Backward' is not defined anywhere in the Constitution". He pleaded that "whether any class is Backward or not should not be left to the law courts to decide.

It is our duty to define the term". T.T. Krishnamachari considered the term to be very vague and susceptible to varied interpretations. "It does not apply to a backward caste … . It says class. Is it a class which is based on grounds of economic status or on grounds of literacy or on grounds of birth?" Quite a few members pleaded for the substitution of the word "scheduled caste" for "backward classes" in Article 16(4) as the latter term was very vague. K.M. Munshi[16] contended that "It is perfectly clear that the word 'Backward' signifies that class of people – does not matter whether you call them untouchable or touchables, belonging to this community or that a class of people who are so backward that special protection is required in the services". He referred to the practice in Bombay Province where backward classes were defined in a manner as to include "not only scheduled castes and scheduled tribes but also other backward classes who are economically, educationally and socially backward". He added: "we need not, therefore, define or restrict the scope of the word 'backward' to a particular community. Whosoever is backward will be covered by it …". Munshi's reply is important because it makes clear that "any backward class" in Article 16(4) means not only backward classes but also scheduled castes and scheduled tribes. Further, it lays down that backward class is one which is socially, economically and educationally backward.[17]

In the Constituent Assembly, the scope of Article 16(1) and Article 16(4) also received careful examination. The unequivocal opinion was that the principle of equality of opportunity embodied in Article 15(1) must be effective and for this purpose reservation of posts in public services under Article 16(4) must be restricted. Ambedkar was emphatic on this point, "if reservations were made for a community or a collection of communities the total of which came to something like 70 per cent of the total posts under the state and only 30 per cent are retained as the unreserved, could anybody say that the reservation of 30 per cent as open to general competition would be satisfactory from the point of view of giving effect to the first principle, namely, that there shall be equality of opportunity? It cannot be, in my judgment. Therefore, the seats to be reserved, if the reservation is to be consistent with sub clause (i) of Article 10 (now Article 16), must be confined to a minority of seats. It is then only that the first principle could find its place in the constitution and be effective in operation. We have to safeguard two things, namely, the principle of equality of opportunity and at the same time satisfy the demand of communities which have not had so far representation in the state, then, I am sure they will agree that unless you use some such qualifying phrase as 'backward' the exception made in favour of reservation will ultimately eat up the rule altogether. Nothing of the rule will remain". He believed that the judiciary would provide an effective safeguard if the reservation tended to be excessive. If the local government included in this category of reservations such a large number of seats, I think one would very well go to the Federal Court and the Supreme Court and say that the reservation is of such a magnitude that the rule regarding equality of opportunity is destroyed and the court will then come to the conclusion whether the local government or the State Government acted in a reasonable and prudent manner".[18]

Ambedkar's approach was different in respect of its thrust rather than the basic philosophy of safeguards. It was not at all his intention to score some concessions from the government or to be content with a few more seats for his people. On the other hand, he made use of the opportunity of Constitution-making for solving the problem of minorities in India on more enduring grounds. It is also to be noted that he was not for the perpetuation of the minorities but he pleaded for their merger some day into one. He pleaded with the Constituent Assembly that "in this country, both the minorities and the majorities have followed a wrong path. It is wrong for the majority to deny the existence of minorities. It is equally wrong for the minorities to perpetuate themselves. A solution must be found which will serve a double purpose. It must recognise the existence of the minorities to start with. It must also be such that it will enable minorities to emerge some day into one .... The moment the majority loses the habit of discriminating against the minority, the minorities can have no ground to exist. They will vanish".[19]

When Ambedkar entered the Constituent Assembly, he entered it as a 'protestant'. He had never thought that he was destined to be the 'chief architect' of the Indian Constitution. How could he ever imagine that an untouchable Mahar would be enlisted and marked out for this privilege and honour? When it did come Ambedkar himself was more than surprised. It was all the more great when he was elected Chairman of the Drafting Committee. He had entered the Assembly with the only hope of safeguarding the rights of the scheduled castes. He was overwhelmed by the gesture and acknowledged his election gratefully.[20] The Constituent Assembly of India, which was entrusted with the task of Constitution-making, was composed of the representatives elected from the then elected Legislative Assemblies of the British Indian provinces and the representatives of the princely state, joining at a later stage. It was in no way a body that was elected on the basis of a liberal franchise. It was also true that in view of the special situation in the country, the nominees of the Indian National Congress were predominant, though there were representatives of the other parties too. There were Hindus, Muslims, Christians, Sikhs, Parsis, Harijans and others. A galaxy of freedom fighters led by Jawaharlal Nehru, Patel, Rajendra Prasad and others, with the conspicuous absence of Gandhi, took a leading part in the making of the Constitution. Those prominent among the lady members were Sarojini Naidu, Vijayalakshmi Pandit, and Durgabai. By and large, the best part of the country's leaders of men, thought and ideas participated in the deliberations of this important and historic Assembly.[21]

The Constitution has recognised the right of equality for the religious, linguistic and cultural minorities and has stated them fully. In this connection, special mention must be made of

Article 17 of the Constitution which abolishes the practice of 'untouchability' in any form. Article 17 in a simple and brief way has abolished 'untouchability', and age-old anachronism of our society. It was for that day, on which the Constituent Assembly adopted this Article in one voice, that Ambedkar was anxiously striving for all along his life and was looking forward to. Accordingly, the Untouchability Offences Act, 1955, provided for specific punishment for particular offences under Article 17. As one of the members of the Assembly observed, "... this clause does not propose to give special privileges and safeguards to some minority community, but it proposes to same one-sixth of the Indian population from perpetual subjugation and despair, from perpetual humiliation and disgrace ... for the sake of sustaining our goodwill and reputation beyond the boundaries of India, this clause ... must find a place in the Constitution of free and independent India .... Today, the 29th November 1948 is a great and memorable day for us, the untouchables. This day will go down in history as the day of deliverance, as the day of resurrection of the crores of Indian people .... Last of all, I cannot resist the temptation of saying a few words about our great and eminent Law Minister and Chairman of the Drafting Committee, Ambedkar. It is an irony of fate that the man who was driven from one school to another, who was forced to take his lessons outside the classroom, has been entrusted with this great job of framing the Constitution of free and independent India, and it is he who has finally dealt a death blow to this custom of untouchability, of which he was himself a victim in his younger days ...".[22]

It was pointed out that Article 17 did not 'create' any particular right and privilege. Ambedkar was aware of this fact but as he had pointed out earlier, it was the only effective way in which the determination of the majority communities and also the minorities to eradicate this evil root and branch, could be expressed emphatically. Untouchability was one of the greatest disabilities suffered mutely by nearly one-sixth of the country's population. If a 'right' means 'a remedy against a disability', the fundamental right created in Article 17 should be a great charter of a deliverance to those people. Those who had inflicted and perpetuated such a humiliation and disgrace on these unfortunate people, by writing this right into the Constitution could repent of their sins.[23] By providing joint electorate except the reserved seats for a period of ten years, the Constitution sought to establish equality. Sardar Patel observes: "... it is not our intention to commit the minorities to a particular position in a hurry. If they really have come honestly to the conclusion that in the changed conditions of this country, it is in the interest of all to lay down real and genuine foundations of a secular state, then nothing is better for the minorities than to trust the good sense and sense of fairness of the majority, and to place confidence in them ... . But in the long run, it would be in the interest of all to forget that there is anything like majority or minorities in this country and that in India there is only one community."[24] But a section of the members representing the Sikhs and Muslims were not happy over this, and they demanded some provision for themselves by which they could get political safeguards. Some Muslim members suggested the adoption of the system of proportional representation with multi-member constituencies and cumulative system of voting. Though this suggestion was appreciated in principle, it was rejected owing to practical difficulties that beset such a system in a country with such large number of illiterate voters. Further, Ambedkar himself would have preferred a longer period of special protection, to ten years, for the scheduled castes. But the consensus was in favour of ten years, which was accepted.

Despite the best intentions of the Constituent Assembly, the deep-rooted caste system has sustained the practice of untouchability and discrimination. As Radhakrishnan rightly observes, "the cause of a society's destruction happens not so much in other things as to being gripped by jejune policies and the form of blind beliefs ... what the spiritual truth is, may be permanent; all other rules change according to the requirements of an age, and even moral rules or ideals are not sanatan or eternal. They are relative to the social requirements and circumstances. Whether a moral system is good or bad depends upon the fact that how far it does benefit to mankind. The rules or institutions which have lost their vitality, must be eliminated."[25]

The abolition of the caste system seems, however, an ideal which is not likely to be realised except in the dim and distant future; and to those who hope for the weakening of its hold upon the people it is disappointing to find that candidates for election to the legislature of one province solicit the votes of their castemen simply on the strength of caste fellowship without regard to other considerations, that a solid caste vote has determined the result of some elections, and that there has been a tendency in the legislature itself for groups to be formed on caste lines.[26]

A powerful factor which helped to preserve the essentials of the *varna* system and to downgrade the Shudras was the indoctrination of the masses in the theory of *karma* and of the bad consequences following the non-performance of the *varna* or *jati,* ordained by the scriptures. It is argued that since the masses were widely educated and endowed with critical acumen, they could not believe in the natural superiority of the higher *varnas*, but there is no basis for such a wild claim. On the contrary, the minds of the labouring masses were so strongly enchained by the Brahminical ideology that both direct coercion against the Shudras and violent revolts on their parts were made extremely difficult.[27] Even Nehru despite his strong secular credentials could not make a dent in the attitude of the high caste Hindus. Once in Goa, when he was coming out of the Mangesi temple after *darshan*, he was surrounded by Harijans who were standing at the gate and lamented, "Panditji, we have seen you, but not God in this temple". Nehru was reported to have said, "I am sorry, what can I do? If these Brahman priests allow you, I shall ask them."[28]

Notes

1. *Constituent Assembly Debates*, Vol. XI, pp. 972–981.
2. Ibid., Vol. II, p. 146.
3. Ibid., p. 227.
4. Ibid., Vol. XI, p. 979.
5. Ibid., Vol. VII, p. 38.
6. Ibid., p. 87.
7. Ibid., p. 123.
8. Ibid., Vol. VII, p. 69.
9. Ibid., Vol. V, p. 274.
10. B.A.V. Sharma, *Reservation Policy in India*, Light & Life Publishers, New Delhi, 1982, p. 6.
11. R.G. Misra, *Reservation Policy and Personal Selection*, Uppal Publishing House, New Delhi, 1990, p. 21.
12. Ibid., p. 24.
13. *Constituent Assembly Debates*, Vol. VIII, p. 679.
14. Ibid., p. 11.
15. Ibid., Vol. VII, p. 680.
16. Ibid., p. 683.
17. Ibid., Vol. VII, p. 685.
18. Ibid., p. 690.
19. Ibid., p. 695.
20. A.M. Rajasekhariah, *B.R. Ambedkar: The Quest for Social Justice*, Uppal Publishing House, New Delhi, 1989, p. 169.
21. Ibid., p. 181.
22. *Constituent Assembly Debates*, Vol. III, p. 437.
23. A.M. Rajasekhariah, op. cit., p. 220.
24. Ibid., p. 227.
25. Cited in Shakuntala Devi, *Caste System in India*, Pointer Publishers, Jaipur, 1999, p. 231.
26. Ibid., p. 257.
27. Ram Sharan Sharma, *Sudras in Ancient India*, Motilal Banarsidas, Delhi, 1990, p. 324.
28. Shakuntala Devi, op. cit., p. 230.

3

Protective Discrimination and the Constitution of India

Indian society is composed of intersecting and overlapping groups and sub-groups based on religion, sect, vocation, wealth, language, location and political affiliation. However, one of the most distinctive and powerful features of the Indian society is its division into castes, especially of its majority section. Membership in the caste group is confirmed by birth and is unalterable except, when it is lost, if expelled by the group. Members of each caste, residing in specific areas, have common customs and more or less a similar style of life with a characteristic diet, dress and religious observances. There is a variation in kind and number of castes but due to hierarchical stratification the highest and lowest castes are easily identifiable. Brahmins are considered to be the highest while Shudras the lowest. Shudras were considered inferior to the other three castes and were expected to perform only menial jobs, forbidden to study the *Vedas*, and enjoined to be deferential and subservient to the other castes. In recent times, untouchables have been identified as unclean Shudras in some parts of India, elsewhere they are regarded as outside the four castes. Hence, untouchables are referred to as outcastes. But they are from the castes which have the lowest ritualistic standing and often economically the most depressed class.[1]

The Indian National Congress, till the framing of the Constitution, never mustered a firm stand over the issue of the removal of untouchability. If the brief history of the Congress with its controversy over social reform is closely studied, an impression is formed that it had taken favourable decision on the social uplift of the untouchables in its initial phase only. To be specific, the Congress in its annual session at Calcutta in 1917 passed a resolution to that effect. The focus of the resolution was on the bringing of social justice to the depressed classes and removing their disabilities forced by retrograde customs. An apprehension was also entertained of the hardships of the depressed classes. Natesan moved that resolution and Bhulabhai Desai and Rama Iyer supported it. When Annie Besant was the President in 1922, the Congress Movement came under Gandhi's leadership. He gave it a new life by highlighting the plight of the depressed classes.[2] The Bardoli programme of the Congress provides testimony to it. Apart from lip service nothing substantial was done to improve the lot of depressed classes. To add fuel to the fire, the Congress entrusted the task of eradicating untouchability to the Hindu Mahasabha in May 1923. The problems of the untouchables assumed significance from the First Round Table Conference (1930). Two representatives of the untouchables were invited to the Conference, thus recognising the fact that the interests of the untouchables were different from those of the caste-Hindus. The Conference appointed a committee on minorities under the chairmanship of Ransay MacDonald, the then British Prime Minister.[3] In fact it was not for the first time that the problems and difficulties of the depressed classes were put before the British Government. Earlier, the Montague-Chelmsford Report made certain recommendations for safeguarding their special interests. But the recommendations were pedantic and superficial. [4]

With independence, the Congress took seriously the problem of scheduled castes and scheduled tribes more for political reasons than anything else. The Congress considered these depressed as potential vote banks. The Congress, instead of reforming the caste-ridden society, politicised the institution of caste. Caste became the criterion for the distribution of party tickets and assignment of constituencies. This made the upper castes more caste conscious.[5]

The framers of the Indian Constitution, in their wisdom incorporated various provisions (Articles 330 to 342) concerning scheduled castes, scheduled tribes, Anglo-Indian community, backward classes granting them special privileges. For example, Article 341 empowers the president to notify, territorywise, "castes, races or tribes or parts of our groups within castes, races or tribes which shall for the purposes of this Constitution be deemed to be scheduled castes". Likewise, Article 330 provides reservation of seats for scheduled castes in the House of People and Article 332 in the state legislatures. Article 334 lays down the specific period for which the reservations are to be continued. The period went on increasing as the Congress and other political parties developed vested interests in the sustenance of reservations.[6]

The Constitution also provides for reserved seats, both in the Parliament and state legislatures for the scheduled castes. This led to competition among political parties to hobnob with the sharing of political power with others. In India, every political party considers scheduled castes for political gains. Despite the political and electoral importance of the scheduled castes, they could not make much headway. Lack of committed leadership among these castes, also affected adversely their progress. These leaders behave more like caste-Hindus in their own community. So, the community is deprived of the benefits of the leadership of elite amongst themselves.[7]

The policy of reservation pursued by the state to bring about social transformation of the scheduled castes is also known as "protective discrimination". For various socio-cultural reasons, the scheduled castes, popularly called Harijans, could not even think of occupational mobility which could give them a better status in society.[8]

Article 15(1) states that the state shall not discriminate against any citizen on grounds only of religion, race, caste, sex, place of birth or any of them, also provides in clause (4) nothing in this Article or in clause (2) of Article 29 shall prevent the state from making any special provision for the advancement of any socially and educationally backward classes of citizen or for the scheduled castes and tribes. This policy of reservation attracted severe criticism by foreign observers like Ivor Jennings and others for different reasons.[9] To understand the rationale of this provision, it is necessary to make an assessment of the circumstances leading to its inclusion.

The problem of the untouchables is the problem of minorities even though they are a part of the Hindu religion. As Nehru has rightly observed, "the communal problem as it was called, was one of adjusting the claims of the minorities and giving them sufficient protection from majority action. Minorities in India ... are not racial or national minorities as in Europe; they are religious minorities ... . Religion transcends the racial differences, which fade into one another and are often hard to distinguish."[10] With the advent of the British rule, especially during its last phase, things began to change and this change had some of impact on the mobility of the scheduled castes, generally called the depressed classes then. The British Government did undertake certain protective discrimination measures in favour of the depressed classes. The Government of India had realised that the depressed classes were denied opportunities and appointments because of their relatively less education. The government issued instruction that whenever duly qualified candidates belonging to this group are available for jobs, they should not be denied reasonable amount of opportunities to enter government services just because they could not compete with the caste-Hindus and get through in the open competition. This was a landmark in the history of reservations.[11] In 1942, the status of representation of the depressed classes in government services was reviewed. It was observed that there was little improvement in their representation in government services. Therefore, in 1943, the Government of India resolved to provide for reservation of 8.5

per cent of positions for the depressed classes. It was also decided to increase the quota when qualified candidates were available in larger numbers. It was also felt that the percentage of reservation should be related to the population of these people. By way of further concessions to attract more applications, the age limit was relaxed by three years in relation to other candidates belonging to the upper caste. In 1946, the percentage of reservation was increased to 12.5 per cent and in August 1947 it was 16.75 per cent.

The position in Karnataka (princely state of Mysore) was not favourable to the scheduled castes till the early period of this century. They did not have any definite guarantees of jobs in government services. The backward classes also suffered likewise in general. There was Brahmin domination in the state services. This ultimately led to group prejudices as the non-Brahmins were sore over the discrimination. In 1917, some of the Vokkaliga and Lingayat leaders met the Maharaja and presented a memorandum to him. The Maharaja sympathised with them and appointed a committee under the leadership of the British Jurist, Sir Leslie Miller. This is popularly known as Miller Committee, which submitted a report in 1919. It recommended in a span of seven years, half of the jobs of higher status and two-third jobs of lower status should be filled by taking the backward classes which term included all the castes except the Brahmins. The only point of importance for us at this stage is to know whether the depressed classes were benefited. The available literature proves they were not. These people had developed a fear that the Miller Committee Report would not help them in any measure, though for all purposes of social movement they formed a part of the non-Brahmins.[12]

The rationale for safeguards for the scheduled castes and scheduled tribes is to bring them at par with other communities and once they reached that stage, the distinctions will disappear. There are three distinct kinds of minorities recognised for the purpose of providing protection. "They are the religious, the linguistic and the scheduled castes and tribes.

If the problem of religious minorities is one of the political rights; the problem of linguistic minorities is one of conservation of language, and right to education and employment; and the problem of the scheduled castes is one of social and economic rights, while that of the tribes is of conserving their culture, laws and tribal property. The problems of each one of these minority groups are appreciated fully, and accordingly they are given certain safeguards under Articles 14, 15 and 16 of the Constitution."[13]

In view of the changed circumstances and the adoption of universal adult suffrage, the problem of safeguards had to be approached *de novo*. Ambedkar realised this and abandoned the stand he had taken earlier. The Advisory Committee recommended that the system of reservation for minorities other than scheduled castes in legislatures be abolished.[14]

The scheme of political safeguards that emerged from the Advisory Committee and was finally incorporated in Part XVI of the Constitution (Articles 330 to 342) as special provisions heralded a new era in the political and constitutional life of the country. It abolished the separate electorates, reservation of seats in the legislature on the basis of religion and other safeguards, except for the concessions given to scheduled caste and tribes. It achieved the objectives of preserving the secular character of our polity, and also enabled the scheduled castes and tribes, whose claim for such special treatment is incontrovertible, to receive special protection for a specific period of time which was fixed as ten years from the date of the promulgation of the Constitution.

The Constitution of India authorises special preferential treatment not only for scheduled castes and tribes but also for "other socially and educationally backward classes".[15] They are communities other than the untouchables, or the scheduled castes and tribes. Significantly enough, the Constitution speaks of 'classes' and not castes but these backward classes are by and large identified on a caste basis, which has been strongly contested. The Government of India has repeatedly suggested that it was better to apply economic tests than to go by caste. It is possible that the caste criterion would retard 'social cohesion' and 'emotional integration' by fostering divisive tendencies. Caste criterion goes against the secular spirit of the Constitution. Each state is given the freedom to prepare its own list of 'other backward classes' and most states have adopted the communal criterion, except perhaps in the state of Jammu and Kashmir and partially the state of Kerala.[16]

After the commencement of the Constitution, the Constitution (Scheduled Caste) Order, 1950 (in exercise of powers conferred by clauses (15) of respective Articles 341 and 342) on 10th August, 1950, the Constitution (Scheduled Tribes) Order, 1950 on 6th September, 1950, and the Constitution (Scheduled Castes) (Union Territories) Order, 1951, on 20th September 1951 were issued by the President annexing Schedules incorporating castes or as the case might be, tribes or tribal community for respective states and respective Union Territories or parts thereof. The words "Union Territories" were added by the Scheduled Castes and Scheduled Tribes Lists (Modification) Order, 1956.

The Supreme Court in *Bhaiya Lal v. Hari Kishan Singh*[17] made observations that under Article 341 the President might well come to the conclusion that not the whole caste, race or tribe but parts of or groups within should only be specified and thus the same caste has been included in same districts of the same state and excluded in other districts. It is not necessary here to incorporate as to why two schedules, one as scheduled castes and the other as scheduled tribes were made. Again, in *Kishorilal's* case, the Supreme Court, referring to the Tenth Report of the Commissioner for Scheduled Castes and Scheduled Tribes, laid emphasis on socio-economic conditions in classifying a particular caste as scheduled caste or scheduled tribe.

The expression 'backward classes' is not defined anywhere in the Indian Constitution. The scheduled caste and scheduled tribes are no doubt backward classes. The Indian Constitution clearly shows that there are other backward classes besides the scheduled castes and scheduled tribes. The Constitution recognises three categories of backward classes, namely, (i) scheduled castes, (ii) scheduled tribes, and (iii) other backward classes (OBCs). The other backward classes are those which are not as backward as the scheduled castes and scheduled tribes, but who are backward as compared to the other advanced sections of the society. Sub-clauses (24) and (25) of Article 366 define scheduled castes and scheduled tribes, respectively, but there is no clause defining socially and educationally backward classes of citizens. The Constitution used different terminologies for the other backward classes. For example, Articles 15(4) and 340 use the words 'socially and educationally backward classes'; Article 16(4) speaks of just 'backward classes', and Article 46 is concerned with the 'weaker sections of people'. Even now, the term 'backward classes' is differently defined in the reports of the different backward classes commissions and the judgments of various High Courts and the Supreme Court of India.[18]

The Constitution of India made certain provisions for the welfare of deprived social section which is known as affirmative action, reservation policy and protective discrimination. The aims and objectives of the Constitution, the general agreement and the compromises arrived at in the Constituent Assembly are reflected in the various Articles and provisions relating to backward classes, e.g., the Preamble, Articles 38 and 46 of the Directive Principles of the State Policy, Articles 14, 15 and 16 of the Fundamental Rights and Articles 338 and 340 of the Constitution of India. The Preamble of the Constitution express the determination and aspirations of the people of India in following terms.

"... Justice – social, economic and political, liberty of thought, expression, belief, faith and worship:

Equality of status and of opportunity; and to promote fraternity among them all assuring the dignity of the individual and the unity and integrity of the Nation.

The two objectives, viz., justice – social, economic and political; and equality of status and opportunity of the Preamble are specially relevant and related to the advancement of the weaker sections and backward classes. The Constitution of India promises not only political democracy, but also social democracy as explained by Ambedkar in his speech in the Constituent Assembly: "It means a way of life which recognises liberty, equality and fraternity which are not treated as separate items in a trinity. They form a union of trinity in the sense that to divorce one from the other is to defeat the very purpose of democracy. Nor can liberty and equality be divorced from fraternity." The Constitution of India contains a number of provisions which deal with compensatory preference for the backward classes. The most important among them are Articles 15(4) and 16(4), Articles 46, 335, 338, 340, 341, 342, 366(24) and 366(25).[19]

The Preamble to the Constitution of India expresses the solemn resolve to secure to all Indian citizens equality of status and opportunity. The chapter on Fundamental Rights guarantees the citizens many rights which ensure equality of opportunity and status. Here, we are specifically concerned with those provisions of the Constitution which embody the principles of non-discrimination in general and public employment in particular. For example, Article 15(1) of the Constitution states that ... "the state shall not discriminate against any citizen on grounds only of religion, race, caste, sex, place of birth or any of them". Under 'Cultural and Educational Rights', Article 29(2) states that "no citizen shall be denied admission into any educational institution maintained by the state or receiving aid out of the state funds on grounds only of religion, race, caste, language or any of them." However, Article 15(4) gives special powers to the state by stipulating that "nothing in this Article or clause (2) of Article 29 shall prevent the state from making any special provision for the advancement of any socially and educationally backward classes or citizens or the scheduled castes and the scheduled tribes". These general principles are then applied to more specific areas; like public employment, Article 16(1) states that "there shall be equality of opportunity for all citizens in matters relating to employment or appointments to any office under the state". This is a positive guarantee against discrimination in regard to public employment. It has been stated negatively in Article 16(2), no citizen shall, on grounds only of religion, race, caste, sex, descent, place of birth, residence or any of them be ineligible for, or discriminated against, in respect any employment or office under the state.[20]

Article 16(4) also provides an exception to the general principle of non-discrimination in matters relating to employment or appointment to any office under the state embodied in Article 16(2). It states: "nothing in this Article shall prevent the state from making any backward class of citizens which, in the opinion of the state, is not adequately represented in the services under the state." Article 335 of the Constitution is another exception to Article 16(2). It reads: "the claims of the members of the scheduled castes and scheduled tribes shall be taken into consideration, consistently with the maintenance of efficiency of administration, in the making of appointment to services and posts in connection with the affairs of the Union or of a state. The relationship between these provisions remains somewhat obscure." Article 335 is confined to scheduled castes and scheduled tribes, while Article 16(4) extends to all 'backwards classes'. Article 335 seems to include any method of preference while Article 16(4) is confined to reservation. Finally, Article 320(4) provided that nothing in clause (3) shall require a public service commission to be consulted as respects the manner in which any provision referred to in clause (4) of Article 16 may be made or as respect the manner in which effect may be given to the provisions of Article 335.[21]

Article 16(4) is confined specifically to public services, while Article 15(4) applies to the state in all of its dealings. Thus, the area of employment, offices, and appointments under the state is controlled by Article 16 alone and preference within this area must be within the scope of Article 16(4). This includes judicial offices as well as administrative posts, but not elective offices. The legal opinion is that the constitutional provisions for reservations were not applicable in the sense that public sector enterprises were not constitutionally obliged to have a policy of reservation.

Article 16(4) covers not only preferences in initial recruitment into government services, but also preferences in promotions within the service. After some hesitation in case of *Rangachari v. The General Manager Southern Railway*[22] the Supreme Court reluctantly held that the 'post' referred to in Article 16(4) included promotions as well as initial appointments, but indicated that the preference permissible under Article16(4) would not extend to other aspects of employment covered by Articles 16(1) and (2), e.g., salary, increment, pension, retirement age, etc. Such matters are absolutely protected by the doctrine of equality of opportunity and do not form part of the subject matter of Article 16(4). While the dissenting judges argued that the reservation was limited to securing adequacy of quantitative representation of the favoured group, the majority held that reservation could legitimately be used to secure representation in the posts of higher grades. In the appeal of *Rangachari*[23], the apex court had pointed to the language of Article 335, requiring the state to take into account the efficiency of the services in making provisions for scheduled castes and tribes, and declared the necessity of striking a reasonable balance between the claims of these classes and efficiency of the services. In *Balaji*[24], the court emphasised that the public interest in the efficiency of government services set limits to reservation in promotions, putting outside the scope of Article 16(4) any unreasonable, excessive, or extravagant reservation, for that would, by eliminating general competition in a large field and by creating widespread dissatisfaction among the employees, affecting efficiency. Thus, the court gave notice that it would carefully scrutinise the reasonableness of reservations in the area of promotions.[25]

The wording 'any provision' in Article 16(4) and 'any special provision' in Article 15(4) gives the state a decisive way in prescribing the method of operation of schemes for preference.

Governmental agencies have utilised a wide variety of devices for the purpose of conferring advantage on backward groups. Reservations involve not merely reserved seats but also such preferential rules of recruitment as waiving of age requirements, reduction in fees, educational qualifications (prescribing lower minimum of qualifying marks) and special assistance and training in preparation for competitive examinations.

It can be asked whether such practices are covered by the authorisation of Article 16(4) that the state can make "any provision for the reservation" of government posts. It has been argued that fixing a lower minimum level of successful marks in a competitive examination is outside the power of the state, since it is not "reservation in any sense of the term under Article 16(4)". However, such devices would appear to be included within the constitutional authorisation. While Article 16(4) confines the state to the methods of 'reservations', it is clear that Article 16(4) empowers the state to determine the precise method to be adopted in effectuating the reservation.[26]

The framers of the Constitution were conscious of the backwardness of a large section of the population. It was clear that because of their backwardness they are not in a position to compete with the advanced sections who had all the advantages of so-called affluence and better education. The fact that the doors of competition were open to them would have been a poor consolation to the members of the backward classes because the chances of their success in the competition were far too remote on account of the inherent handicaps and disadvantages. The result would have been that, leaving aside some exceptional cases, the members of the backward classes would have hardly got any representation in jobs requiring educational background. It would have, thus, resulted in virtually keeping out those who were already repressed. The framers of the Constitution, being conscious of the above disadvantage from which the backward classes suffered, enjoined upon the state in Article 46 to promote the educational and economic interests of the weaker sections of the people, in particular, of the scheduled castes and scheduled tribes and also protect them from social injustice and all forms of exploitation.[27]

The condition precedent to the exercise of the powers conferred by Article 16(4) is that the state ought to be satisfied that any backward class of citizens is not adequately represented in its services. This precedent condition may refer either to the numerical inadequacy of representation in the services or even to the qualitative inadequacy of the representation.[28]

Directive Principles of State Policy

The Directive Principles of State Policy enshrined in the Articles 38 and 46 of the Indian Constitution enjoin upon the state to strive to promote the welfare of the people in general and weaker sections, including the backward classes, in particular. To begin with, Article 38 of the Constitution declares that:

1. The state shall strive to promote the welfare of the people by securing and protecting as effectively as it may a social order in which justice, social, economic and political, shall inform all the institutions of national life.
2. The state shall, in particular, strive to minimise the inequalities in income, and opportunities, not only amongst individuals but also amongst groups of people residing in different areas or engaged in different vocations.

Thus, the Directive Principles along with the Preamble embody the socio-economic ideals which the nation had set before itself during the freedom movement. It indicates the political mind of the makers of the Constitution who visualised the creation of a new social order in India based on social, economic and political justice, eliminating the evils of the existing socio-economic system. Though the nature of the 'social order' is not defined in the Constitution, it has been interpreted to mean a 'welfare state'. As a part of this objective, the state is directed to remove the existing inequalities in income, status, facilities and opportunities among the individuals and groups in India. Further, Article 46 directs: "the state shall promote with special care the educational development, and in particular, of the scheduled castes and scheduled tribes, and shall protect them from social injustice and all forms of exploitation."[29]

As can be seen, Article 46 makes it obligatory for the state to take action to ameliorate the conditions of the weaker sections including the backward classes. They are two-fold: (i) to promote with special care the educational and economic interests by taking 'positive measures'; and (ii) to prevent social injustice and all forms of exploitation by taking 'preventive measures'. The Constitution mentioned only the reservation policy. It did not fix any particular percentage of seats in professional and technical institutions and posts in government and semi-government jobs. In 1950, the Government of India reserved 12.5 per cent seats and posts for the scheduled castes and 5 per cent for the scheduled tribes in all-India services to be recruited on the basis of open competition. It also extended the age limit in their case by three years. In 1952, it raised the age limit to five years more than the maximum prescribed for others. Now, in the central and state services, seats and posts are reserved in proportion to population. In 1970, the Central Government raised the reservation for the scheduled castes to 15 per cent, and for the scheduled tribes to 7.5 per cent. As for reservation of jobs, the Constitution mentions no fixed period. Naturally, the state is expected to continue such preferential treatment until the scheduled castes, scheduled tribe and other backward classes make substantial progress educationally and economically and reach a level of equality with the rest of the Indian citizens.[30]

It accelerated the process of socio-economic change in India and specially improving the conditions of the weaker sections and backward classes who constitute a majority of the population. The future of national progress and achievement of an egalitarian society depends on the rapid upliftment of these backward sections of the people. The Constitution has set its goal to achieve this social justice and it can be explained in terms of rising percentage of employees in the various categories of Central Government services. These gainful employments not only improved their economic condition but also provided opportunity to get and maintain administrative power and responsibility. The positive impact of these provisions has been the educational progress and rising literacy rate of the schedule castes and schedule tribe in India. At the time of India's independence in 1947, the literacy rate among them was below one per cent and in the last 47 years there has been considerable increase in their literacy rate. It is true that almost half of the world's illiterate population lives in India, but slowly it is moving towards achieving total literacy.[31]

The special provisions in the Constitution led to the progressive realisation of the creation of a new and just social order as visualised by the Constitution. Further, in the context of economic development of the underprivileged sections of the society, the Constitution set goals for the eradication of poverty.

The data reveal that one-third of Indian population lives in the condition of poverty. They are denied the basic needs of life such as sufficient food, clothes, house and medicine. There is no provision of social security for the poor. Now, the process of liberalisation and the new economic policy have created a market-friendly atmosphere. It could lead to wider disparities within the Indian society. The underprivileged sections will not get benefit of the opportunities, and the competitive market system will take away special privileges provided to them. This will widen the gap between the rich and the poor.[32]

Roster System

With a view to give proper effect to the reservation prescribed, every appointing authority is expected to treat vacancies as 'reserved' or 'unreserved' according to model roster. Model roster is made by keeping hundred posts as component unit.

Before 1990, there were only reservations for scheduled castes and scheduled tribes and chapter IV of the Constitution and other miscellaneous provisions concerning the scheduled castes and scheduled tribes issued by Government of India on February 5th, 1978, provided for model rosters each of 40/100 points. Now reservation is made for other backward classes also, keeping in view 100 posts roster is prepared.[33]

Before the roster system was introduced, there was a lot of scope for calculated mischief in practice. The concerned authorities would devise such mechanisms as would defeat the ends of justice. Therefore, the roster system was introduced. Certain broad guidelines were given by the state government to all the institutions involved in reservation policies. But, we find that in actual practice there is variation from institution to institution. The problem is not that acute so far as the Public Service Commission is concerned where a large number of positions are filled and reservations are done cadrewise. But in other organisations which recruit either a limited number of persons or sometimes a large number, the position is generally different. This is particularly so in the case of the autonomous and semi-government organisations. The roster system was introduced with a view to accommodating the traditionally deprived social groups in administration and teaching. The impact of this system on society depends on the knowledge of its very existence.

If any measure of the government has to be effective and successful, the people should be familiar with the measure in actual practice. Similarly, the roster system would be successful only if people are familiar with its contents. A big majority of the respondents were found to have knowledge of the contents of the system (84%). Those who had absolutely no knowledge were a negligible percentage.[34] Among the scheduled classes and backward castes, the number of persons with full knowledge and partial knowledge of the system is more or less identical. But in the case of the caste-Hindu and Christian, a higher percentage of persons have full knowledge and in the case of the Muslims, a higher percentage has limited knowledge. The implication of this analysis is that scheduled caste people should have a thorough knowledge of the contents of the roster system. On further enquiries, it was explained by the respondents that they generally did not bother to understand the comprehensive knowledge of the system. There are three specific sources, i.e., 'self', 'friends' and 'newspapers'. Self happens to be a source of knowledge for nearly 50 per cent of the respondents, while friends constitute the second position, and newspapers and other sources have third and fourth places.[35]

The observations, in various judgments of the Supreme Court which considered earlier the question of reservation of scheduled caste and scheduled tribe and other backward classes, were in favour of the view that the reservation was to be made with reference to the vacancies and not to the posts. This aspect of reservation was considered to be the reasonable and acceptable approach for implementation of the reservation principles both at the recruitment stage and in promotion matters. The Supreme Court in the case of *Rangachari* observed, "... apart from that we may point out that the government resolution does not contemplate reservation of any post in the service cadre but merely provides for reservation of vacancies. Even if the government had provided for the reservation of posts for schedule castes and schedule tribes, a cent per cent reservation of vacancies to be filled in a particular year or reservation of vacancies in excess of 50 per cent would, according to the decision in Balaji case, not be constitutional."[36] This observation was followed in later cases with approval in *T. Devadasan's*[37], *B.A. Tewari v. Union of India*[38] and *A.R. Choudhury v. Union of India*[39].

The Supreme Court in *Prem Prakash v. Union of India*[40] while considering the provision with regard to the brochure observed, "the correct approach is to fix the number of vacancies available for the reserved candidates on the basis of the total number of vacancies which are intended to be filled at any particular point of time. According to para 2.1 of the

Brochure, 15 per cent of the total vacancies are required to be reserved for the scheduled caste candidates and 7.5 per cent for the scheduled tribes candidates".[41] The position was made very clear beyond any doubt in *Chakradhar Paswan v State of Bihar* by the Supreme Court when it held, "... according to the 50 point roster, if in a particular grade a single post falls vacant it should, in the case of first vacancy be considered as unreserved, i.e., general and on the second occasion when a single post again falls vacant, the same must be treated as reserved". The court held further that "in service jurisprudence, the term 'cadre' has a definite legal connotation. In the legal sense, the word 'cadre' is not synonymous with 'service'. Rule 9(4) defines the word 'cadre' to mean the strength of a service or part of a service sanctioned as a separate unit. The conclusion is irresistible that the posts of Director and those of the Deputy Directors constitute different cadres of the service."[42]

The Government of India adopted initially two series of rosters, viz., one of 40 appointments and the other of 100 appointments known as "40-point roster" and "100-point roster" respectively. The former is applicable to appointments on an all-India basis and the latter to appointments on local or regional basis. This system is devised to enable the members of all communities to occupy the vacancies in a cadre by turn. Under this system, if there is only one post in a cadre, it would be occupied by a general candidate at a time despite the first vacancy, according to roster, being a reserved one. The normal working of the 40-point roster would not cause any disadvantage to any community, but on the other hand it ensures a sort of balancing. However, there is a possibility of dislocation by the chance factor or some strange situations arising on account of fortuitous circumstances by which the number of posts could fluctuate.[43]

The full Bench of the Central Administrative Tribunal in the case of *V. Laxmi Narayan v. Union of India and Other*[44] held that, the government's policy envisages that the reservation of posts to schedule castes and schedule tribes should be made and implemented with reference to the number of vacancies and not from the available posts. A thorough study of various orders issued by the government from time to time will reveal that though the words and expressions used in some of the orders, viz., "the existing reservation of 12.5 per cent of vacancies filling up by direct recruitment", "appointment to the services, reservation in recruitment to posts and services", "appointment to posts and services, etc." denote reservation of vacant posts for scheduled castes and scheduled tribes, but in the actual implementation they refer to only the appointment to the vacancies. Hence, according to the government orders, the reservation quota of appointment for schedule castes and schedule tribes should be marked out on the basis of vacancies as available from time to time and not on the basis of posts available in a particular cadre for every year. However, there is a possibility of dislocation by the chance factor or some strange situations arising on account of fortuitous circumstances by which the number of posts in a cadre becomes very much low or even high if in a cadre consisting of three posts on scheduled caste it inducted, it will look as if 33.3 per cent of the vacancies have been filled up by the scheduled caste. If by some chance another scheduled caste is also inducted into the cadre either by way of getting appointment on merit, transfer or promotion, it would look as if 66.66 per cent of the vacancies have been given to the scheduled caste. If the cadre consists of only one post and the post is given to scheduled caste as per the turn on the roster, it would look as if 100 per cent of the posts have been given to the scheduled caste. Similarly, if the post is given to non-scheduled caste and non-scheduled tribe, it would look as if 100 per cent of the cadre strength has gone to non-scheduled castes and non-scheduled tribes on the above principle. This indicates how the chance factor due to posting, promotion, death, transfer, etc., influences the communal composition in the cadre.

Similarly, if in a specific cadre no scheduled caste and scheduled tribe candidates exist at a particular point of time, it would be reasonable to conclude that the government is not providing any opportunity to the scheduled castes and scheduled tribes to enable them to capture posts in that cadre. It may so happen that scheduled castes and scheduled tribes after taking appointment in that cadre may not be suitable. Likewise, if in any specific cadre, scheduled castes and scheduled tribes are represented sufficiently or in excess, it would be a reason to say that the government is giving more representation to the scheduled castes and scheduled tribes in that cadre but it may so happen that non-scheduled caste/scheduled tribe candidates may not have come forward to take up the job in that cadre. So, in computing the total number of scheduled caste and scheduled tribe candidates in a particular cadre for ensuring the reservation with the maximum percentage, care should be taken to see that the scheduled caste and scheduled tribe candidates, who got selected and were appointed to that cadre on merit by competing with the members of non-scheduled caste and non-scheduled tribe candidates, are not reckoned reservation number.[45]

As per the Ministry of Home Affairs order no. 16/2/67–Estt. 601, dated 27th September, 1967 the reservations do not apply to:

(i) Vacancies filled by transfer.
(ii) Exempted vacancies filled by promotion.
(iii) Temporary appointment of less than 45 days duration.
(iv) Purely temporary establishment such as work-charged staff (daily rated) in the construction/organisation.
(v) Posts filled by deputation unless the deputation is a process for filling up the vacancies in the transferee department.
    In such cases, the roster need not be maintained.[46]

Reasons for the Support

There are three major reasons advanced by the respondents in favour of the system. These are:

(i) expectation that the monopoly on jobs of certain groups would end,
(ii) would act as a check against groups working for exploitation, and
(iii) would permit a close vigilance over misuse. However, for these three reasons it is in respect of the first reason that a majority has expressed its opinion (69%).

So far as different social groups are concerned, we find that all, except the higher castes, advanced by a majority the reason that the monopoly would end. However, among the Muslims, just a little more than half of them gave this reason, whereas among the others the percentage is 70 per cent and above. The second reason that the roster system as a check against exploitation finds the support of the majority among the caste-Hindus (44%) and about (25%) among the Muslims and Christians and much less among the scheduled castes and backward castes. The third reason that it permits close vigilance draws a good support of about 22 per cent from the caste-Hindus and 20 per cent from the Muslims. These reasons were further elaborately explained by some of the respondents in group discussion.[47]

There is a strong argument that the roster system is prepared by a set of persons who are generally members of the higher caste, often known to be anti-reservation. These people, it is said, manipulate the roster system in such a manner that its very purpose is defeated. Some people invite reference to the maximum concept of superstructure. Anyway, a few case studies presented here illustrate the point.[48]

Defects

The defects inherent in the roster system are: post-wise reservation, unrealistic qualification, negligence of representation in higher cadres. Each one of these defects is extremely important since much agitation is noticed today. Of the three defects, post-wise reservation occupies the top place (43%). Post-wise reservation means that when advertisement is issued, there may be a number of positions in separate disciplines or departments of varying status. Generally, a post is reserved for scheduled caste candidate and such a candidate is not available for that post. The post is readvertised three times and even if on the third occasion no scheduled caste candidate is available, the vacancy is converted to general merit category or some other category and advertised. Normally, such candidates are available and the post is filled. Thus, the chances of scheduled caste candidates are ruled out. The second defect lies with unrealistic qualifications. A large number of all the groups, and a reduced number of the backward castes have furnished this defect. Unrealistic qualification means either the qualification is of a higher order or not suitable in the case of the scheduled caste candidate. For the post of Accounts Officer, Chartered Accountancy (CA) was prescribed by a university in the state. This high qualification had not been prescribed for the post in the earlier advertisement when the post was open to all. Why then this time higher qualification was prescribed for the post reserved for the scheduled caste. Respondents would conclude that this was another instance of calculated mischief. The third instance of such a social situation is that the post of Professor in Sanskrit was reserved for the scheduled caste candidates and advertised. Again, the question is do we have scheduled caste candidates to occupy this position? A large number of respondents had no hesitation to call this "a hypocrisy of the highest order".

Some of the caste-Hindu respondents presented a different dimension and its relation. The explanation is that it is in the process of application of some principle that roster system is prepared and no intention or motivation to deprive the scheduled caste candidates is seen. Some responsible caste-Hindus said the issue is overblown or exaggerated. We should not take one or two instances and generalise. The answer of some of the scheduled caste respondents is that this is definitely intentional. If the intention was to help the scheduled castes, the roster system would have been suitably prepared.

Carry Forward Rule of Reservation

The Supreme Court in *Devdasan v. Union of India*[49] was called upon to pronounce the constitutionality of the 'carry forward rule' framed by the Central Government to regulate appointment of persons belonging to backward classes in public services. According to this rule, if sufficient number of candidates belonging to the scheduled castes were not available for appointment during a particular year, the unfilled posts will be reserved in the next year in addition to their reserved quota of the next year. The result was to carry forward the unutilised balance, that is, unfilled vacancies in the second and third year at one time. In the above case, the Supreme Court by majority of four to one held the rule ultravires and invalid. It was also held that a proviso or an exception could not be so interpreted as to nullify or to destroy the main provision.

The observation of J. Khanna, in *State of Kerala v. N.M. Thomas,*[50] brings out the rationale for the constitutional provisions in relation to reservation. The court held, "... those sections of the population would not be in a position to compete with advanced sections of the community who had all the advantages of affluence and better education. The fact that the doors of competition were open to them would have been a poor consolation to the members of the backward classes because the chances of their success in the competition were for too remote on account of the inherent handicap and disadvantage from which they suffered. The result would have been that, leaving aside some exceptional cases, the members of backward classes would have hardly got any representation in job requiring educational background. It would have thus resulted in virtually repressing those who were already repressed ..."

Again, in *A.B.S.K. Sangh Railway v. Union of India,*[51] the above period was further raised from two years to three years. This was challenged by the petitioners as unconstitutional. Rejecting the contention the Supreme Court held, "likewise, the carry forward rule being raised from 2 to 3 years also cannot be struck down. It must be realised that law is not an abstraction but an actual prescription in action. So, what we have to be more careful about is to scrutinise whether the carry forward rule by being increased to 3 years is going to confer a monopoly upon the Scheduled Caste and Scheduled Tribe candidates and deprive others of their opportunity for appointment ...". Furthermore, Krishna Iyer J., added that the carry forward rule shall not result, in any given year in the selection of scheduled caste and scheduled tribe candidates considerably in excess of 50 per cent. This rider, like the rest of his judgment, is lacking in precision and will lead to further litigation. For, what does 'considerably' in excess of 50 per cent mean? Since 'considerable' means 'much', the rider means 'not much in excess of 50 per cent? This leaves counsel free to argue, and judges free to decide, that 55, 60 or 65 or even a large percentage, is not "much in excess of 50".[52]

In *A.R. Choudhury v. Union of India*[53] the fact was that in August 1966 a vacancy arose for the post of Headmistress of the Adra School. The Headmistress of the Kharagpur School was to retire in January, 1969. Four names according to seniority were called for interviews on December 18, 1968. On December 25, 1970, the Calcutta High Court allowed the writ petition accepting the contention of the respondent Lila Bhattacharyya. Upon this, on November 6, 1971 the CPO issued a memorandum stating that it was "decided to hold a selection to draw up panel of two approved candidates to fill the post of Headmistress, one post being reserved for the scheduled castes against the existing vacancy and another to cover unforeseen requirement, viz., unreserved". The petitioner then filed a writ petition challenging the memorandum and despite the order of injunction, the railway administration issued a letter on August 19, 1972, asking the respondent to appear before the selection board on August 30 and again the petitioner and the other, also separately filed the writ petition and acting in pursuance of the Home Ministry's memorandum dated December 4, 1963, as modified from time to time, the Railway Board by its letter of

January 16, 1964, prepared a new 'model roster' signifying the turns of reserved and unreserved vacancies. Under this roster, 12.5 per cent of the vacancies were reserved for scheduled castes and 5 per cent of the vacancies reserved for the scheduled tribes.

The roster contained some important explanations: If there are only two vacancies to be filled on a particular occasion, not more than one may be treated as reserved and if there be only one vacancy, it should be treated unreserved. If on this account a reserved point is treated as unreserved, the reservation may be carried forward in the subsequent two recruitment years. This was in terms of Home Ministry's instructions said above.

In order to remove a still surviving grievance of the scheduled castes and scheduled tribes that in spite of the model roster they were denied appointments whenever there was a single vacancy, such vacancies being invariably treated as unreserved irrespective of the point of roster at which they occurred, the Railway Board by their circular of August 23, 1971, directed that if there was one post to be filled, selection should invariably be held for two posts, i.e., one the actual and the other to cover unforeseen circumstances. It was in pursuance of these instructions that on November 6, 1971, the CPO had issued the impugned order.

The virus of rules impugned in Devadasan's case was though the unutilised reserved quota could not be carried forward for more than two years, the carry forward mechanism envisaged by the rules could almost completely swamp recruitment to open, general seats. The court tested the memorandum by illustration by taking a hypothetical example in that if in each of the first two years of recruitment, the total number of seats to be filled in was 100 per cent, 18 vacancies would have to be treated as reserved in each year. If suitable candidates were not available to fill these reserved vacancies, the reservation would have to be carried forward to the third year, but not beyond it. If the total number of seats for recruitment in the third year was 50, the backlog of 36 seats with the addition of nine reserved seats for the current year would cover 45 out of 50 vacancies leaving only five vacancies for open recruitment. This virus was rectified effectively soon after the judgment in Devadasan's case by the issuance of the Memorandum of December 4, 1963, as amended on September 2, 1964. It was specifically directed by these curative prescriptions that "in any recruitment year, the number of normal reserved vacancies and the carried forward reserved vacancies together shall not exceed 45 per cent of the total number of vacancies".

The court held that the rules thus were no longer open to the objection that the reservation was excessive. As regards the model roster, the court observed that in the note appended to the roster, the words "on a particular occasion" were substituted on September 2, 1964, by the words 'year of recruitment' thus if two vacancies occur, say, within an initial span of three years, the first vacancy has to be treated as unreserved vacancy and the second is reserved. The court held that the South-Eastern Railways runs only two secondary schools for girls, one at Adra and the other at Kharagpur. In August, 66 vacancies at Adra were filled in as unreserved and the vacancy at Kharagpur occurred on 1st January, 1968, on retirement so it fell within the two financial years, hence was rightly treated as reserved.

In *R.P. Dutta and Others v. Union of India*[54] the case was that one Shri Harecharan Singh, one of the Assistant Labour Commissioners, who was appointed on the recommendation of U.P.S.C. was due for retirement on 5th August, 1969, and consequently the Delhi administration sent a requisition to U.P.S.C. to advertise the post for scheduled castes and only the scheduled castes candidates were called for interview. The method of recruitment prescribed on 15th February, 1963, was by promotion 50 per cent and 50 per cent by direct recruitment. For eligibility of promotion, labour officer/labour officer-cum-inspector of shops and establishments, with three years' service in the grade were eligible. In 1969 when the dispute arose, R.P.

Dutta, petitioner 201 and B.P. Jain, the petitioner 3, who were officiating as Assistant Labour Commissioner since 1968 and 1969, respectively, pending selection according to rules, challenged the post being reserved for scheduled castes against Articles 14 and 16(1) and rule contained in the Ministry of Home Affairs order dated 2nd September, 1964. The question then arose before the Delhi High Court whether this vacancy should be reserved for scheduled castes or not. The court observed that Home Ministry memorandum dated 2nd September, 1964 and the note appended with the model roster laid down that if there be only one vacancy, it should be treated as unreserved. Relying on the decision in *Arti Ray Choudhury v. Union of India and Others*[55] that if there was only one vacancy on a particular occasion, it is not to be treated as reserved on the basis of the said memorandum, the court held that each year of recruitment was directed to be considered separately and as there was only one vacancy in the year of recruitment, i.e., 1969, it could not be treated as reserved for scheduled caste and B.P. Jain should be considered against direct recruitment for seniority.[56]

In *Harbans Singh v. Union of India*,[57] the Rajasthan High Court speaking on reservation observed, after the coming into force of the Constitution of India, the Government of India vide Resolution dated 14th September, 1950, issued the first policy statement on the issue of better representation of scheduled castes and scheduled tribes in government services. In the said resolution, the government had taken note of the policy of communal representation in the services before the Constitution and the constitutional ban on discrimination by way of reservation on the ground of caste in the case of scheduled castes and scheduled tribes and it was declared that pending the determination of the figures of population at the census of 1951 the government had decided that the existing reservation of 12.5 per cent vacancies filled by direct recruitment in favour of scheduled castes would continue in the case of recruitment of posts and services made on an all-India basis by open competition and whose recruitment was made otherwise than by open competition the reservation for scheduled castes would be 16 ⅔ per cent at that time. As regards the scheduled tribes it was declared that the reservation in their favour would be 5 per cent of the vacancies filled by direct recruitment.

It was found that sufficient number of qualified candidates from among the scheduled castes and scheduled tribes were not available. The Government of India, therefore, issued supplementary instructions on 28th January, 1952, whereby it was directed that if a sufficient number of candidates of the communities for whom the reservations were made were not available, the vacancies that remained unfilled would be treated as unreserved and filled by the best available candidates, but a corresponding number of vacancies would be reserved in the following year for the communities whose vacancies were thus filled up in addition to such number as would ordinarily be reserved for them under the orders contained in the resolution. This provision for carrying forward of vacancies of a particular year to the next succeeding year was further modified by office memorandum dated 7th May, 1985, of the Government of India, whereby the vacancies of a particular year could be carried forward for next two succeeding years. By the circular of 20th April of the Railway Board, the carry forward Rule referred to above was extended and the vacancies could be carried forward to next three succeeding years.

By circular dated 27th April, 1959, of the Railway Board the prescribed quota of reservation was made applicable to selection posts to which promotion was made by a positive act of selection. By circular dated 20th April, 1970, of the Railway Board the reservations prescribed by the resolution dated 13th September, 1950, for scheduled castes and scheduled tribes was modified in light of the population of these communities in the 1961 census and it was decided that the reservation of scheduled castes might be raised from 12.5 per cent to 15 per cent and the reservation for scheduled tribes be raised from 5 per cent to 7.5 per cent. In order to give effect to this circular the roster was also revised by the Railway Board by its letter dated April 29, 1970. Under the revised 40-point roster, posts at points 1, 8, 14, 22, 28 and 36 are reserved for scheduled castes candidates and posts at points 4, 14 and 31 are reserved for scheduled tribes candidates.[58] By its direction dated 11th January, 1973, the Railway Board decided a quota of 15 per cent and 7.5 for scheduled castes and scheduled tribes respectively might also be provided in promotion to the categories and posts in class I, II, III and IV filled on the basis of seniority-cum-suitability provided the element of direct recruitment to these grades, if any, did not exceed 50 per cent.

The validity of the circular dated 27th April, 1959 came for consideration before the Supreme Court in *General Manager, Southern Railway v. Rangachari* upholding the circular by majority of the court, Gajendra Gadkar J. as he then was, observed:

> "the condition precedent for the exercise of the powers conferred by Article 16(4) is that the State ought to be satisfied that any backward class of citizens is not adequately represented in its services. This condition precedent may refer either to the numerical inadequacy of representation in the services or even to the qualitative inadequacy of representation. The advancement of the socially and educationally backward classes requires not only that they should have adequate representation in the lowest rung of services but that they should aspire to secure adequate representation in selection posts in the services as well. In this context, the expression 'adequately represented' imports consideration of 'size' as well as 'values', numbers as well as the nature of appointments held and so it involves not merely the numerical test but also the qualitative one. It is, thus, by the operation of the numerical and a qualitative test that the adequacy or otherwise of the representation of backward classes in any service has to be judged; and if that be so, it would not be reasonable to hold that the inadequacy of representation can and must be cured only by reserving a proportionately higher percentage of selection posts should also be reserved, for reservation of such posts may make the representation of backward

classes in the services adequate, the adequacy of such representation being considered qualitatively. If it is conceded that 'posts' in the context refers to posts in the services and that selection posts may be reserved but should be filled only in the manner suggested by the respondents then we see no reason for holding that the reservation of selection posts cannot be implemented by promoting suitable members of backward class of citizens to such posts as the circulars intend to do."[59]

It would be in the fitness of things if the periodical extension of the privileges is limited to a specified period. These extensions are in reality against these classes and would be in favour to their interest as these classes would not exert on improving their skill. It is, therefore, humbly submitted that these should not go beyond this century.

Notes

1. R.G. Misra, *Reservation Policy and Personal Selection*, Uppal Publishing House, New Delhi, 1990, p. 2.
2. Ibid., p. 3.
3. A.K. Vakil, *Reservation Policy and Scheduled Castes in India*, Ashish Publishing House, New Delhi, 1985, p. 2.
4. Ibid., p. 3.
5. H. Kotani, *Caste System, Untouchability and the Depressed*, Manohar Publishers, New Delhi, 1997, p. 5.
6. Sheo Kumar Lal, *Extent of Untouchability and Pattern of Discrimination*, Mittal Publications, New Delhi, 1990, p. 3.
7. Ibid., p. 5.
8. Mumtaz Ali Khan, *Reservation for Scheduled Castes*, Uppal Publishing House, New Delhi, 1994, p. 7.
9. Ibid., p. 10.
10. Cited in ibid., p. 15.
11. Ibid., p. 16.

12. Ibid., p. 19.
13. B.A.V. Sharma, *Reservation Policy in India*, Light & Life Publishers, New Delhi, 1982, p. 32.
14. Ibid., p. 33.
15. Article 15(4): Nothing in this article or in clause (2) of Article 29 shall prevent the state from making any special provision for the advancement of any socially and educationally backward classes of citizens or for the scheduled castes and the scheduled tribes.
16. Ram Kumar Jha, *Commentary on Reservations for SC, ST, OBC and Others*, Shail & Beeraj Law House, Patna, 2001, p. 3.
17. *AIR* 1965 SC 1557.
18. S.N. Singh, *Reservation Policy for Backward Classes*, Rawat Publications, Jaipur, 1996, p. 76.
19. Ibid., p. 78.
20. Ibid., p. 81.
21. Ibid., p. 83.
22. *AIR* 1961 Madras 356.
23. *AIR* 1962 SC 36.
24. *AIR* 1963 SC 649.
25. R.G. Misra, op. cit., p. 28.
26. Ibid., p. 30.
27. Ibid., p. 33.
28. Ibid., p. 36.
29. S.N. Singh, op. cit., p. 85.
30. Ibid., p. 87.
31. Ibid., p. 90.
32. Ibid., p. 94.
33. Anirudh Prasad, *Reservational Justice to Other Backward Classes (OBCs) Theoretical and Practical Issues*, Deep & Deep Publications, New Delhi, 1997, p. 232.
34. S.N. Singh, op. cit., p. 97.
35. Mumtaz Ali Khan, op. cit., p. 123.
36. *AIR* 1962 SC 36.
37. *AIR* 1965 SC 179.
38. *AIR* 1965 SC 1436.

39. *AIR* 1974 SC 532.
40. *AIR* 1984 SC 1831.
41. The brochure on 'Reservation for Scheduled Castes and Scheduled Tribes in Services' (5th Edition 1978) issued by Government of India.
42. *AIR* 1988 SC 959.
43. Ram Kumar Jha, op. cit., p. 458.
44. Decided on February 27, 1992, reported in (1993) 24 Administrative Tribunal Case (FB) 420.
45. Ibid., p. 461.
46. Ibid., p. 465.
47. Mumtaz Ali Khan, op. cit., p. 128.
48. Ibid., p. 130.
49. *AIR* 1964 SC 179.
50. *AIR* 1965 SC 490.
51. *AIR* 1981 SC 298.
52. S.M. Mehta, *A Commentary on Indian Constitutional Law*, Deep & Deep Publications, New Delhi, 1990, p. 110.
53. *AIR* 1974 SC 532.
54. 1967 5 *LJ* 16.
55. 1974(1) *SCR* 659.
56. S.M. Mehta, op. cit., p. 116.
57. 1985 (2) *SCJ* 423.
58. *AIR* 1962 SC 36.
59. *AIR* 1962 SC 36.

4

Analysis of Findings of Commissions/Committees on Reservation

Kalelkar Commission, Mandal Commission, Sachar Committee and Ranganathan Mishra Committee

Politics in society does not hang in the air. Many forces operate in the shaping of politics and politics in itself is a force, which leaves its impact on the society. This dual character of politics is its essence and the relationship between politics and society reveals multiple complexities and contradictions. A few salient features of politics in India may be identified to grapple with its specificity. First, India was subjected to colonial exploitation and in the process it was structurally linked with the world capitalist system. Second, during its long anti-imperialist struggle, Indians evolved a new level of consciousness and the goals of freedom which, defined in a broad manner, helped in raising the levels of participation and awareness among the Indian masses. Third, the democratic experiment of the last four decades has revolutionalised the levels of consciousness and the aspirations of the Indian masses and it has created competitiveness among all classes, social groups and strata to compete for a share in the state power. Fourth, the model of capitalist development has brought supporters and opponents with serious political conflicts, which are resolved through accommodation or suppression of the movements of the poor.[1]

Since independence, India has operated an open democratic political system based on universal adult franchise. Elections have been held at regular intervals, and political parties have competed and participated openly in electoral politics. The actual operation of the democratic process in India has brought into sharp focus the complexity of the relationship between politics and society. The framework of politics in any democratic society is characterized by the general and specific features of interaction between politics and the social structure. The general feature of politics in all democratic societies is that it intervenes to influence the society and that it also reflects the social reality. This interventionist and reflective character of politics cannot, however, be taken for granted. It has been empirically observed that instead of playing an activist role in society, politics becomes passive and reflective of social forces. The activist and reflective roles of politics in society can also lead to a conflict between politics and society.[2]

Indian politics, by and large, is caste-ridden. The caste factor is dominant in every sphere of life. It has reduced the bulk of society to serfdom. The plight of untouchables has deteriorated with the passage of time. Even during the freedom struggle, they were neglected by the British, the Congress and the Muslim League and none of the political and social movements have touched the problems of the untouchables. It was Ambedkar who raised a banner of protest against the practice of untouchability, questioning the very social order. He did so with a deep sense of duty and devotion, unmindful of the opposition from the orthodox section of the Hindu society. He played a very significant part at a crucial period in the history of this country and offered solutions to the several ticklish problems India was confronted with during the struggle for political reforms. With a passionate zeal and relentless fight he hammered out constitutional provisions for the upliftment of the depressed classes.[3] Ambedkar believed that the constitution of society prescribed by *Purushasukta,* a part of *Veda*s, as a *chaturvarnya*. He was of the view that *chaturvarnya* provided the base for the caste system which has ruined the Hindus. According to him, the portions of *Vedas*, at any rate, particularly the *Purushasukta* were fabrications by Brahmins intended to serve their own purpose.[4]

According to Ambedkar, the *Purushasukta* has elevated real to ideal, and that class composition is natural and, therefore, sacred and divine. And that the *Purushasukta* provides for a fixed and permanent gradation of society with an ascending scale of reverence and descending scale of contempt. Such a classification has compartmentalised the society and converted the *de-facto* state of affairs into a *de-jure* connotation of an ideal society. According to Ambedkar, the attempt of *Parushasukta* to realise the ideal was a kind of political jugglery, the like of which was not to be found in any book of religion. Almost all the Hindu books are replete with the concept of *dharma*. Both Manu and Yajnavalkya, learned Hindu seers, refer to *dharma* as compulsory duties and obligations of the different *varnas*. The concept of *dharma*, as has been included in the *varnashramadharma,* has completely destroyed the concept of social solidarity.[5]

The ideal of *varnashrama* as an embodiment of *dharma* gave more privileges and immunities to the Brahmins than the people from the rest of the *varna*. Dutta, in his book *Beginning and Growth of Caste in India*[6], writes that during the period of *Brahmanas*, as the Brahmin had become the lord of the whole creation. He further writes that the Brahmin is by right the lord of the whole creation. Whatever exists in the world is his rightful property. He has a special claim to be honoured if he goes as a guest to any householder. He has thus various privileges in the society. But that is not all. Even the king must give him preferential treatment. While emphasizing the king's duty to act with justice, he enjoins upon him to be lenient towards Brahmins – it is a privilege of the Brahmin to investigate law suits and the Shudra is explicitly debarred from settling the law. Thus, virtue is assumed to be the possession of Brahmin, while the shudras are looked down on as essentially sinful. It is this attitude that reveals itself in the graded punishment prescribed for four *varnas* for the same offence.[7]

All the Shudras were living in deplorable conditions. Therefore, Ambedkar vehemently criticised the Hindu civilization and called it an infamy. He blamed the intellectual class, that is, the Brahmins for the deplorable conditions of the masses because they could not change the state of degradation in which they were placed. He writes: "Under the old Hindu law the Brahmin enjoyed the benefit of the clergy and could not be hanged even if he was guilty of murder, and the East India Company allowed him the privilege till 1817. His profession has lot of nobility. The Brahmin systematically preyed on society and profiteered in religion. The *Puranas* and *Shastras,* which he manufactured are used to fool, beguile and swindle the poor, illiterate and the superstitious." Ambedkar was critical of Gandhi for his adherence to the caste system in spite of the fact that he himself did not follow his own ancestral profession of *bania*. Gandhi was *bania* by caste but he did not become a businessman. He abandoned trade and business in favour of law and politics, which are meant for Brahmins.

Gandhi considered Ambedkar as a challenge to Hinduism. He praised Ambedkar as the most competent critic of Hinduism and also the most uncompromising and the oldest among such critics. He writes about Ambedkar: "No Hindu who prizes his faith above life itself can afford to underrate the importance of the indictment." In fact, Ambedkar was not only the most uncompromising exponent but also the most irreconcilable among them. Thank God, in the front rank of leaders, he is singularly alone and yet as a representative of a very small minority. But what he says is voiced with more or less vehemence by many leaders belonging to the depressed classes, only the latter, for instance, Rao Bahadur, M.C. Rajah and Dewan Bahadur Srinivasan, not only do not threaten to give up Hinduism but find enough warmth in it to compensate for the shameful persecution to which the vast mass of Harijans are exposed. When Ambedkar was asked by his critics that if he did not want caste, what would be his ideal society. Ambedkar replied that, "My ideal would be based on liberty, equality and fraternity." Ambedkar criticized Gandhi's theory of *chaturvarnya* as impracticable in this age and there was no hope of revival in the future. Further, he said that Gandhi was doing a great disservice to social reform by advocating his imaginary utility of division of *varnas*, for it created hindrances in our way.[8]

Ambedkar disagrees with the western theory that during the Vedic period there was unity of race. Secondly, he refutes the theory that the Aryans were fair and others were dark. Ambedkar quotes *Rigveda* [1.117.8;(I), 117.5; (II).3.9] and writes that these instances show that vedic Aryans had no colour prejudice. How could they have? The Vedic Aryans were not of one colour. Their complexion varied, some were copper in complexion, some white and some black. Ram, the son of Dasharath, has been described as *shyam*, i.e., dark in complexion; so was Krishna, the descendent of *Yadu*, another Aryan clan. The name of *Rishi* Dirghatma, who is the author of many *mantras*, was given to him due to his complexion. Karva was an Aryan *rishi* of great repute who, according to the description given in *Rigveda* (X-32–11), was of dark colour. According to Ambedkar, the dispute between Brahmins and Kshatriya centred round the right to receive gifts, the right to teach the *Vedas* and the right to officiate at the sacrifices, which were considered as monopoly of the Brahmins.[9]

According to Ambedkar, caste problem is the most complex. Practically, it is an institution that protends tremendous consequences. It is a local problem, but capable of much wider mischief, for "as long as caste in India does exist, Hindu will hardly inter-marry or have any social intercourse with outsiders" and if Hindus migrate to other regions on earth, Indian caste would become a world problem. Theoretically, it has been defined by many scholars who have taken upon themselves, as a labour or love, to dig into its origin. The people of India form a homogenous whole. The various races of India occupying definite territories have more or less fused into one another and do possess cultural unity, which is the only criterion of homogenous population. Ambedkar maintained that the caste is a parceling of an already homogenous unit, and the explanation of the genesis of caste is the explanation of this process of parceling.[10]

As regards the position of Brahminism in the Indian polity, it had its dominance in most of the fields – social, political, economic and educational. According to Ambedkar, the legislature, executive and judiciary were completely controlled by Brahminism. According to him, the Indian administration was completely controlled by the caste-Hindus. The position of power and authority was concentrated in hands of the upper strata of society. During the days of the British, the two deliberately manoeuvred to exclude the Shudras and the untouchables from the army and education and from acquiring property. Ambedkar observed that the Brahmins and the *bania* protected their privileges, position of power and authority at the cost of the poor people. Writing about the attitude of the governing classes of India (the Brahmin and the *bania*) in 1945–46 towards the weaker sections of the people regarding reservation policy, he said, "The argument used by governing classes to oppose the demands of service classes (the scheduled castes and scheduled tribes classes), for reservation is based on doctrine of efficiency … . But it cannot be right from the point of view of servile classes? Could the 'best' German be 'best' for the French? Could the 'best' Turk be 'best' for the Greeks? Could the 'best' Pole be regarded 'best' for the Jews?"

There was also another anti-Brahminism movement led by Jotiba Phooley. It flourished during the second and third decades of this century. Shahu Maharaja of Kolhapur was an active supporter of this movement. This movement was based on the ideology of Phooley. The non-Brahmin leaders regarded the Brahmins as enemies of the nation. Javalkar published a pamphlet named "Enemies of the Nation", Ambedkar remarked that it was a good book written in bad taste. A suit was filed against non-Brahmin leaders Jedha, Javalker, and Bagade. Ambedkar defended the accused and they were set free. This movement also fell prey to Brahminism and as a result failed. After analysing the causes, Ambedkar said, "Many of the non-Brahmin party men tried to become second class brahmins, they have not abandoned brahminism. They are holding it as an ideal. He further said, "You people always abuse Brahmins but you never imitate their virtues. Brahmins change their ideas according to the exigencies of the time. They pursue knowledge and money .... Remember! Brahmins have brains within brains. If you want to fight the Brahmins, you must be more intelligent than them. You do not unite, instead you fight among yourselves and chew the poison pills given by the Brahmins that *Mahars* are inferior to Marathas". This was the reason why the untouchables could not become one with the Marathas.[11]

As observed by Aristotle, man is, by nature and necessity, a social animal. Hence, he lives in society. Thus, society is quite natural, essential, eternal and universal. It is instrumental in evolving such an atmosphere, which would be conducive not only for the satisfaction of his primary wants, but also for the development of his personality. However, the structure of society is not common everywhere. Whatever might be its nature, it is primordial in shaping economic and political structure which obviously decides the future of individuals in a given society.

Ambedkar believes that the Indian society is a caste society. The Hindu society, a major component of Indian society, is but "a collection of castes. Each caste is conscious of its existence". And that there is no 'common consciousness' among the castes. "The caste system", he states, "prevents common activity and by preventing common activity it has prevented the Hindu from becoming a society with a unified life and a consciousness of its own being". Even the Hindus in his words "are not merely an assortment of castes but they are so many warring groups each living for itself and for its selfish ideals."[12]

Ambedkar put forward his demand of separate electorate for the depressed classes at first in 1919 while giving evidence before the South Borough Franchise Committee. In his report submitted to the Simon Commission in 1929, he recommended for adult franchise, and joint electorates with reserved seats for almost all the communities except the Europeans. While giving evidence before the Simon Commission in 1928, he replied to a question, "if there is no adult franchise?" saying that, "then we would ask for separate electorate".

In order to decide the nature of future Constitution and settle the communal problem, the British Government convened the Round Table Conference in London consisting of the representatives of India, the British Government and the British political parties on November 12, 1930. It met under the chairmanship of Ramsay MacDonald, the Prime Minister of England. The Conference was adjourned on January 19, 1931. The second Round Table Conference began on September 7, 1931. It was adjourned on December 1, 1931. It is during these conferences that Ambedkar demanded separate electorate for the depressed classes. The British Government, however, conceded that demand of separate electorate under the communal award, but due to antagonistic attitude of Gandhi in that respect, he had to relinquish it and accept joint electorates with reserved seats under the Poona Pact, 1932. The third Round Table Conference was convened on November 17, 1932 to confirm and finalize the minutes of the previous conferences. It was adjourned on December 24, 1932.[13]

What is electorate and separate electorate is a pertinent question. The electorate is the entire body of voters in the state. They exercise their right to vote in favour of any candidate in their respective constituencies. Where separate electorate is in operation in respect of any community, voters list of such community is separately maintained. The voters of such a community vote separately for a candidate of their own community in their respective constituencies. Thus, the voters and candidates belong to the same community and the voting takes place separately.

The obvious purpose of separate electorate is to secure adequate and effective representation to a minority in order to thwart any probable attempt to impose tyranny by communal majority over the communal minority. Due to historical and other reasons there was reasonable apprehension in the minds of the people of minorities that the majority people might impose their communal tyranny over them at their whims. Therefore they thought to enter into power structure in order to protect the interests of their brethren. Ambedkar also thought that separate electorate was the best method of securing true representation of the *dalits*, thereby protecting their interests.

He lost all hopes in the British Government due to their indifferent attitude towards the problem of the *dalits*. He said at the Round Table Conference, "no share of this political power can evidently come to us so long as the British Government remains as it is". It is only in *Swaraj* that they might be able to protect their interests. He, however, thought that political power would be possible to them only through their real representatives, and they would be real only when they are elected by the depressed classes themselves through separate electorate.[14]

Ultimately, Ambedkar demanded *inter alia* separate electorate for the depressed classes through a memorandum submitted to the Round Table Conference jointly by himself and R.B.R. Srinivasan. What was the actual demand and what was its nature is a very curious question. The memorandum submitted to Round Table Conference bears, *inter alia*, the following demand:

> "The depressed classes must be given sufficient political power to influence legislative and executive action for the purpose of securing their welfare. In view of this they demand that the following provisions shall be made in the electoral law so as to give them:
>
> (i) Right to adequate representation in the legislatures of the country, provincial and central.

(ii) Right to elect their own men as their representatives, (a) by adult suffrage, and (b) by separate electorates for the first ten years and thereafter by joint electorates and reserved seats, it being understood that joint electorates shall not be forced upon the Depressed Classes against their will unless such joint electorates are accompanied by adult suffrage."

The main purpose of Ambedkar in demanding separate electorate to the depressed classes was "to destroy monopoly in every shape and form" enjoyed by the so-called high castes. "Our aim is", he stated, "to realise in practice our ideal of one man one value in all walks of life, political, economic and social. It is because representative government is one means to that end that the depressed classes attach to it a great value and it is because of its value to us that I have urged upon you the necessity of making your declaration subject to its fulfillment." Thus, in the words of M.P. Mangudkar, he wanted "to share political power with others mainly to transform the Indian society".[15]

It was, however, a period of political transition. Power was being transferred from British Parliament to Indian legislature. The nationalist forces in India were consistently demanding self-government to India, but at the same time they were not ready to share power with the hitherto underprivileged people. Those who were saying that no foreign country had any right to rule over other country like India, they were also of the view that "no country was good enough to rule another and it was equally true that no class was good enough to rule over another". Thus, he was against the imperialism of one country over another; at the same time, he was also against the monopoly of one class over another class.

What was Gandhi's attitude towards the demand of separate electorate is an important question. It is true that Ambedkar could ably convince Aga Khan (Muslims), R.B. Pannir Selvam (Indian Christians), Sir Henry Gidney (Anglo-Indians) and Sir Hubert Carr (Europeans), the Indian delegates to the conference. Even he could convince the British delegates, including the Prime Minister. However, Gandhi, who participated in the second Round Table Conference as a representative of the Congress, was not convinced of the demand of separate electorate. He opposed this demand tooth and nail. He said very emphatically that, I would not bargain away their rights for the kingdom of the whole world. It will create a division in Hinduism, which I cannot possibly look forward to with any satisfaction whatsoever. "I do not mind untouchables, if they so desire, being converted to Islam or Christianity, I should tolerate that, but I cannot possibly tolerate what is in store for Hinduism if there are two divisions set forth in the villages. I would resist it with my life".[16]

In order to foil the efforts of Ambedkar in demanding separate electorate, Gandhi played some foul tactics. He argued that almost all the delegates to the Round Table Conference were not elected by the parties or groups whom they were to represent; but they were nominated by the government. Hence, they were not properly authorised by their respective parties. On the other hand he argued, "the Congress claims to represent the whole nation". Thus, he vainly tried to demoralise all the delegates and tried to create an impression that only Congress delegates represent the whole nation. Ambedkar, however, ably said that, "I am a nominee or not, I fully represent the claims of my community". Regarding the claim of Congress to be representative of whole nation, he said that, "I can only say that it is one of the false claims which irresponsible people keep on making, although the persons concerned with regard to those claims have been invariably denying them". The British Government did not see any substance in the argument of Gandhi and continued the proceedings of the Round Table Conference uninterrupted.

Gandhi was, in fact, very firm on not conceding the demand of separate electorate. It was his firm conviction that the depressed classes do not need political right at all. He said very categorically before the Round Table Conference that "what these people need more than election to the legislatures is protection from social and religious persecution". In order to win over the Muslim delegates to its side so that they may oppose the demand for a separate electorate for the depressed classes, he tried to convince Agha Khan but in vain. Further he agreed to concede "fourteen points" put forth by the Muslim League, which included that India should be federal with residuary powers vested in the provinces, one-third representation to the minority in the central legislature, full liberty of belief and worship, one-third Muslims in the central or provincial cabinet, etc.

When the British Prime Minister realised that there was no compromise on the minority problem, he asked all the members of the minorities committee to authorise him to settle the problem on his own. Gandhi signed the pledge to agree with the premier. Ambedkar, however, did not sign the pledge as he believed that his demands are just. The Prime Minister then adjourned the conference on December 1, 1931. The British Government finally declared the Communal Award on August 4, 1932, which, *inter alia*, stated separate electorate for the depressed classes. Gandhi who was in jail in those days finally resorted to go on "fast unto death" on September 20, 1932. Although he signed the pledge to be bound by the verdict of the premier on the issue of communal problem, he did not stick up to his own words.

Gandhi began his epic fast unto death in Yerwada Jail, Pune on September 20, 1932 in protest against the separate electorate for the depressed classes provided under the communal award. The political atmosphere in the country became grim and tense. Several letters threatening Ambedkar poured in and demands were made to save the life of Gandhi at any cost. Ambedkar was very much firm on his stand. He said categorically that, "I shall not deter from my pious duty, and betray the just and legitimate interests of my people even if you hang me on the nearest lamp-post in the street". Hence, tension was mounting day-by-day. He was caught in a big dilemma either to save the life of Gandhi or to lose the special safeguards in the form of separate electorate which he achieved after a long fight against many odds.

Eventually, Sir Tej Bahadur Sapru evolved a scheme of primary and secondary elections for the reserved seats in place of separate electorate. Accordingly, the depressed classes – qualified voters in their respective constituencies were to select a panel of not less than three candidates and then out of those three candidates one was to be elected by the joint electorate. Ambedkar, however, expressed his willingness to accept the proposal provided the number of seats was increased. It was acceptable to the Hindu leaders. In the negotiations, the Hindu leaders accepted to allot 148 seats to the depressed classes in the provincial assemblies. In the central legislature, 18 per cent of the seats allotted to the general electorate were to be reserved for them. Gandhiji consented to the agreement. The agreement was signed on September 24, 1932 at Poona, as such it is known as "Poona Pact".[17]

Why did Ambedkar accept the Poona Pact? Was he not fully aware of the disadvantages of the Poona Pact? It is of course true that he was fully aware of the disadvantages, which the scheduled castes were to sustain due to joint electorates. The scheduled caste candidate contesting reserved seat under joint electorate was to win only on the strength of majority caste-Hindu votes. In other words, the majority caste-Hindus who had but malice for the scheduled castes were to decide the representative of the scheduled castes. They, however, elected such candidates from among the scheduled castes who were to serve the interests of the majority caste-Hindus and not of the scheduled castes. Therefore, Ambedkar rightly observed that, "Poona Pact has completely disfranchised the scheduled castes". Gandhi and the Hindu leaders agreed to joint electorate only because it was to serve their interests in a better way. They must have thought that they would be able to impose 'Hindu-cracy' on the scheduled castes, that too with the easy consent of the 'stooges' of their community. Ambedkar was fully aware of this fact, therefore, he tried his best to secure separate electorate for the scheduled castes since 1919 onwards. He was fully aware of the interrelationship between separate electorate, representation, political power and welfare of the scheduled castes. He said very categorically that the Poona Pact was "fraught with mischief". It was accepted because of the coercive fast of Gandhi and because of the assurance given at the time that the Hindus will not interfere in the election of the scheduled castes".[18]

With due respect to all these interpretations of that great event, it could be said that in the given critical situation Ambedkar moved by the principle of "politics is the game of possible", and the spirit of democracy. Later, Ambedkar was elected as chairman of the Drafting Committee of the Constituent Assembly on August 29, 1947. He, however, refrained from raising the issue of separate electorate in the Constituent Assembly, which was dominated by the Congress. On the other hand, it was going to accept universal adult franchise. The whole nation was still alive to the shock of partition, which it has woefully sustained in the recent past. Therefore, Ambedkar who believed in the politics of principle, power and possibility in a given situation kept strategic silence over the matter.[19]

The increasing consciousness of the fact that the British were leaving India prompted Ambedkar to make some compromises with the Congress. The partition of the country made it clear that Congress was the only political organisation which would be able to command confidence and rule the country. He made clear that on the inauguration of the Constitution, India has attained equality in politics but he warned that there was still inequality in social and economic life. He urged for the removal of this contradiction at the earliest moment, "or else those who suffer from inequality will blow up the structure of political democracy which this Assembly has so labouriously built up". The problem before the country was whether people would place the country above their creed or creed above the country. "But if the parties place creed above country, our independence will be put in jeopardy ... and probably be lost forever."[20]

Gandhi tried to close the communal issue by bringing about a settlement among the Hindus, Muslims and the Sikhs. He had been carrying on negotiations privately with them before the Minorities Committee met, but Gandhi failed in his mission. Knowing this as a detrimental move, Ambedkar told the committee that whatever may be the representative character of Gandhi or of the parties with whom he wishes to negotiate, they certainly are not in a position to bind us – certainly not – I want to make that absolutely plain.[21] The Minorities Pact was in no way anti-national or even anti-independence document. It simply provided human rights to all with some special claims, which could be modified in the national interest. Besides, Ambedkar and Rao Bahadur Srinivasan put a supplementary memorandum asking for special representation for the depressed classes in the federal and provincial legislatures in proportion to their population in India. It demanded separate electorates but added that if the system of joint electorates was to exist with reserved seats, it should take place only after a referendum but that also not until after 20 years and until universal adult suffrage has been established. It emphasized that the depressed classes should not only have right to their own separate electorates, but they should also have the right to be represented by their own men. Gandhi's reaction, however, was strong and vehement. He was particularly against the recognition given to the untouchables as a separate political entity. He said, "I would resist it with my life". Thus, Gandhi blocked the inclusion of the necessary safeguards for the depressed classes. At the Round Table Conference, Gandhi's argument was that the Hindus had seriously taken up the cause of the untouchables and, therefore, there was no reason to give them political safeguards. Outside, however, he gave a different version and before he returned to India he said:

(a) The Muslim and the Sikhs were well organised. The untouchables were not. The separate electorates would make their lives miserable. It would throw the apple of discord between the touchable and untouchable Hindus.

(b) The question of separate electorates for untouchables is manufactured by the Government. The only thing needed was to put them on the voting list and provide fundamental rights for them in the Constitution. In case the depressed classes were unjustly treated and their representatives were deliberately excluded, they would have the right to special election tribunal which should provide them protection, and

(c) The separate electorate to the untouchables would ensure their bondage in perpetuity. It would keep them 'untouchables' forever. What was needed was destruction of untouchability and not their separation from the Hindus.[22]

The Poona Pact was accepted by the British Government thereby nullifying the Communal Award, much to the Gandhi's satisfaction. The main points of pact were: increase in the number of seats; voting on the basis of joint electorate; termination of reserved seats after ten years; and adequate representation was to be given to the depressed classes in public services.

The scheduled caste political leadership at the Government of India level has remained the monopoly of an individual from the time of the Constituent Assembly (1947) and even before, when Congress was voted to power at provincial levels during 1937. Gandhi was groomed to fight against Ambedkar and he was anti-Ambedkar. This old Congressman, a veteran freedom fighter, was in fact disapproved of by his party leader for having received a sword in token of his success as a Defence Minister in the liberation of Bangladesh during 1971–72.

That the scheduled caste men have to attach themselves to some upper caste men if they wish to be in politics, is a truism. Since their representation in the Assembly, Parliament and Ministry is almost a constitutional gift, they are seldom tolerated to be original and vocal. They should toe the line of the party bosses both within and outside the party and legislature. Also, the social values which have survived and, to some extent, been directly fortified by the political machinery always try to associate caste status with behaviour pattern and occupation. In this way, scheduled caste political leaders are constantly watched by the party bosses and the public, commented upon and admonished for lapses.

While the generation of freedom fighters is nearly extinct, the lingering few are left away in the Congress organization after the great split of 1969, when the party was divided more as a result of personality clash than of differences in ideologies, as was made out. This entire process can be aptly put in Merton's terms as follows: "The periodic efforts at 'political reform' turning the 'rascals out' and cleaning the 'political house' are typically (though not necessarily) short lived and ineffectual. The reform may for a time bring new figures into political limelight; it may serve the casual social function of reassuring the electorate that moral virtues remain intact and will ultimately triumph; it may actually affect a turnover in the personnel of the political machine, it may even for a time, to curb the activities of the machine, leave unsatisfied too many needs it has previously fulfilled. But inevitably, unless the reform also involves a 'reforming' of the social and political structure, such that the existing needs are satisfied by alternative structures or unless it involves a change which eliminates these needs altogether the political machine will return to its integral place in the social scheme of things".[23]

Gandhi tried to sideline the interests and provisions of political rights of the untouchables and wanted to make a settlement with the Muslim and Sikh communities at the cost of untouchables. "This was nothing but a declaration of war by Gandhi and the Congress against the untouchables. In any case it resulted in a war between the two". At this juncture, the ever vigil saviour of the downtrodden, Ambedkar, rose to be equal to the mischievous situation and thundered his point before the Minorities Committee when it met on 28th September to conclude: "... I have no quarrel with the question whether any particular community will get weightage or not, but I do want to say most emphatically that whoever claims weightage and whoever is willing to give the weightage, he must not give it, he cannot give it – out of my share. I want to make that absolutely clear ... I have made my position absolutely clear."[24]

On this, J. Ramsay MacDonald, the Prime Minister of England, who was the Chairman of the Committee, declared: "Dr Ambedkar's position has been made absolutely clear; in his usual splendid way he has left no doubt at all about it and that will come up when this body resumes its discussion. What I would like to do is to get you all to feel that we are cooperating together for a general settlement, not for a settlement between any two or any three, but a complete settlement."[25]

Ambedkar accused Gandhi of being lost in his double role of Mahatma and politician. As a Mahatma he may be trying to spiritualise politics. Whether he has succeeded in it or not, politics has certainly commercialised him. A politician must know that society cannot bear the whole truth and that he must not speak the whole truth; if he is speaking the whole truth it is bad for politics. The reason why the Mahatma is always supporting caste and *varna* is because he is afraid that if he opposed them he will lose his place in politics. Whatever the source of his confusion the Mahatma must be told that he is deceiving himself and also deceiving the people by preaching caste under the name of *varna*.[26]

Political reservation at higher levels so far has functioned as a family preserve. Only a handful of ambitious persons are fighting to retain the glory. How can this help the cause of scheduled castes in general? Even those who put forth their life mission as service of the downtrodden do not see the contradiction between their lifestyle and that of the scheduled caste masses. Many of them do not know the utterly dependent conditions of scheduled castes in rural areas. For the masses, scheduled caste politicians are as unapproachable as anybody else. The ignorance of the scheduled castes is exploited by the scheduled caste political leaders. Given this, the deliverance of the scheduled castes is no longer in the hands of scheduled caste political leaders. Political reservation has become redundant and it has and will serve another kind of vested interest. The sooner it is replaced by a different system when scheduled caste problems are the direct concern of those getting elected from reserved seats, better it is. Some tangible results could be then expected.[27]

A structurally heterogeneous society reflects its conflicts at multiple levels such as caste versus caste, class versus class and the multiplicity of socio-cultural and socio-political conflicts have been taking place because of the existence of multiple diversities, competitive casteism and peaceful co-existence of the communities has been a great causality. We must not lose sight of the fact that the higher castes have traditionally used force to put down the lower cases and not allowed their "serfs" to raise their voice. Now, the poor lower castes have been activated by militant political leftist groups and they are challenging the feudal structure of rural areas. This has led to the growth of Naxalism and formation of several underground guerrilla units to protect the interests of the lower castes and prevent their exploitation. These units have frequently clashed with the private armies formed by the upper castes/class and threatened to put the democratic and secular identity on the edge of a precipice.[28]

At that time Ambedkar was seriously considering becoming a Sikh. He had discussions with other untouchable leaders. Keer mentions that Ambedkar was advised by some of them to also seek backing of the Hindu Mahasabha. It may have appeared to some of them that the choice of a religion which stood in conflict with Hinduism would only embitter social relationship without serving any spiritual purpose because, whatever their religion, the vast majority of the untouchables would still live in largely Hindu villages.[29]

Another major development in 1936 was the establishment by Ambedkar of the Independent Labour Party. If the decision to given up Hinduism had, at least partly, been the consequence of the failure of the Nasik Satyagraha and the growing disenchantment with the reformist movement under Gandhi, the founding of the Independent Labour Party was a result of the realisation that if the interests of the untouchables had to be protected in the era of electoral politics that was about to begin, the untouchables needed to be organised as a political party. But if a political party were to be created, it would not be effective by being limited to just the untouchables. It had to have broader affiliations, without losing its central focus – the protection and furtherance of the interests of the untouchables. Ambedkar thought that the group with which the untouchables would have some community of interest was that of industrial and agricultural labour. The party was founded in August, 1936, and it was named, significantly, the Independent Labour Party. It sought to establish an identity separate from the communist-led trade unions in the labour field and from the Indian National Congress in the political arena. The party declared itself in favour of working the Government of India Act, 1935, in spite of all its limitations. The Congress took some time deciding whether or not it would fight elections under the new legislation. Ambedkar characterised the Congress as a curious combine of exploiters and the exploited.[30]

As the conversion move towards Buddhism picked up tremendously in almost every state of India, there were reports of mass conversion to Buddhism. *The Asian Age*, 28th September, 1998, reported: "The figures published by the Gujarat government, in its socio-economic review, 1998, reveal that the growth rate of Hinduism in the last one decade in the state was 21.12 per cent, of Christianity 36.96 per cent and Islam 24.05 per cent, compared to these, the growth rate of Buddhism was 53.84 per cent. These figures have been provided by the commissionerate of population studies, Delhi. The trend towards Buddhism is more discernible in the age group of 18 to 30 years and is also reflected in the increase in sale of books on Buddhism and Zen."[31]

The untouchables alone got bewildered and shuddered with their broken backbone after the partition of India. Though they alone could not fight against the casteism and the supremacy of the Brahmins, they did not drop their scheme to conquer back their motherland. As a consequence, gradually, the Republican Party lost its charm and strength. The untouchables gradually overdepended upon the constitutional policy of reservation, political as well as service. As a consequence, they lost their independent political aspiration, in the reserved seats it became impossible to get elected without the support of the governing castes. Ambedkar was the glaring example of this. The democratic movement of the untouchables, the political aspirations of the untouchables and the movement of the annihilation of castes by the untouchables remained dormant for a long time.

In a recent study conducted by the Lal Bahadur Shastri National Academy of Administration, Mussoorie, it has been analysed that till the formation of the RPI in 1958, the *dalit* politics in UP kept swinging between the accommodative policies of the Congress and the revolutionary politics of the Federation. These two tendencies of integration and separatism were to remain within the scheduled caste movement in the post-colonial India. The phase of the RPI lasted merely a decade. The influence of the party was confined to UP and Maharashtra. The party won three parliamentary seats and eight assembly seats in UP in the 1962 general elections. Its performance was marginally better in 1967 when it won 10 assembly seats. After winning only two assembly seats in the 1969 elections, the RPI finally declined to almost a non-entity in the subsequent elections. The decade of the 70s is described by Sudha Pai as a phase of integration and a hiatus between two periods of separatist political activity by the scheduled castes in UP. The Congress was able to co-opt both of them.[32]

The government had launched a political campaign to build his and Janata Dal's support base among scheduled castes and backward classes, which divided the country apart and led to widespread violence. The caste conflicts in the rural areas had not only increased but also become extremely violent. The first anti-reservation stir in Gujarat in 1981 left 40 dead and property to the tune of several crores of rupees burnt, in the course of one hundred furious days. The bloody five months' old anti-reservation movement in Gujarat in 1985 had taken a toll of 335 lives, injury to 904, destruction to 5,323 houses and establishments and property losses of over Rs 40 crore. It left the people frightened, the government shaken and the social fabric in the state totally ruined. Long duration of curfew resulted in business losses of around Rs 2,375 crore. Finally, Madhav Solanki, the then Chief Minister was forced to resign. Panic ruled the mixed localities and when the disturbances spread to hundreds of caste-Hindus living around Harijan localities, they migrated to other areas fearing a backlash. The worse was the anti-reservation stir which turned into communal riots between the Hindus and Muslims. The caste conflicts also engulfed the state of Bihar resulting in violence and loss of public property and the Chief Minister Karpoori Thakur had to resign.

There were divergent opinions whether caste is the basic denominator of backwardness. Time and again, commissions on backward classes have come out with purely caste-based reports that satisfied none. There was no justification for the Congress (I) in granting the *Momins*, a group among the Muslims, the backward status in Bihar, creating castes where there were none. The feeling was why should the son of Jagjivan Ram, one of the richest Harijans, or sons of many other rich Harijans, be given the benefit of reservation. In a bid to woo backward votes, Congress (I) ruled-states propose, through a constitutional amendment, to remove the restrictions imposed by the Supreme Court. The biggest election sop is the move by the centre to amend the Constitution in a bid to circumvent the restrictions placed by the Supreme Court on the reservation policy. Some states have been affected by the judgment because they had for years provided quotas much higher than the quotas fixed by the court. This led to violence throughout the country. The residents of Dalal Chock and Baghaura under Madanpura police station in Bihar are mostly

Thakurs. On the night of 29 May, 1987, an armed mob of over 700 persons descended on the two settlements lying at the foot of the Umga hills, situated 25 km from Aurangabad (Bihar), men, women and children were pulled out of their beds, their hands and feet tied before they were either shot dead or brutally hacked to death. Their houses were set on fire and children hurled into a makeshift pyre. The mob, mostly Yadavs, left the place leaving 55 men, women and children dead. It was a revenge carnage as earlier the Rajputs had killed seven Yadavs in the neighbouring villages.[33] In a massacre on July 11, 1996, in Burki Khargaon and adjoining villages of Bhojpur district in Bihar which left 22 people dead and more than 50 injured, mostly women and children, in the course of a four-hour long violence perpetrated by the pro-upper caste landlord "Ranbir Sena", consisting mostly of Bhumihars and Rajputs suggests the collapse of the law and order administration in the lawless state. The victims of the tragedy are the poor scheduled castes and backward classes.

The situation of the violence-prone districts of South and Central Bihar has been largely out of control over the years, but the government and the political leadership, deeply entrenched in caste politics, have refused to heed the danger signals that have been hoisted. Internecine pulls and pressures resulting from the politics of caste that dominates the Bihar scene have only added to the woes and travails of the police leaving them in no position to restore order anywhere. Caste politics thus became highly criminalised.

In Maharashtra, caste tension had been endemic. *Mahars*, a scheduled caste, had held their resentment against the upper caste since 1972. There was large scale violence during Marathwada agitation in 1977–78. During the agitation, a total of 227 villages comprising scheduled castes were attacked and 153 atrocities against them were reported. Police opened fire to control the situation and registered 153 cases covering six districts. In most cases, some government functionaries joined hands against the scheduled castes.[34]

The history of the party system in India is linked with the struggle for freedom from British colonial rule. During the struggle for freedom, the Indian National Congress emerged as a kind of united front of all regions, religions and linguistic and caste groups: the nationalist leadership mobilized the Indian masses under that umbrella organization. After independence, the Congress became a political party and regularly participated in the democratic electoral process. It now based its strategies on the experience that its leadership had gained during the struggle for national freedom. During all elections held for the Lok Sabha, the Congress party nominated its candidate on the basis of caste arithmetic. After winning the elections, the Congress Chief Ministers and ministers, whether at the centre or the state level, continued to operate on the basis of caste. The caste factor thus linked the party, the government and the elections. One's caste became a ladder through which one reached the heights of power in politics. The Congress is a multi-caste, multi-religious and multi-linguistic party, whereas the Bhartiya Janata Party (BJP), the Lok Dal and the Janata Party are essentially based on narrow social constituencies. The Bhartiya Janata Party is essentially a party of high-caste Hindus, and the "untouchable" castes have not been attracted towards it.

The Janata Party has an important component of the erstwhile socialists whose ideologue was Ram Manohar Lohia. Lohia believed that a socialist transformation could be achieved in India by mobilising the 'backward', 'depressed' castes in the rural areas, and the Janata Party has adopted his strategy of caste mobilisation. The Lok Dal was established by Charan Singh on the basis of 'backward' peasant castes. Charan Singh has posed a formidable challenge to the Congress in northern India by mobilizing the 'backward' peasant castes against the Congress multi-caste coalition. Caste in India has been employed as a factor for achieving political power. One consequence of this has been the growth of competition and confrontation among the various castes. Since politics protects caste interests, the caste factor in politics has been solidified irrespective of its growing confrontational and competitive role.[35]

The policy of reservation in India was quite firmly established during the decades of the British rule but such a policy was designed more to redress communal inequalities in the representation in public services rather than a social engineering device to redress the deep-rooted socio-economic inequalities of the disadvantaged sections of the society. The British Indian government had introduced special provisions and concessions for the educational advancement of backward classes, which were later converted into caste reservations for jobs. The entry of a scheduled caste person into educational institutions in the country was recorded in 1856. It was in June, 1856, that a scheduled caste boy applied for admission to a government school in Dharwal, Bombay Presidency, which created furore in the administration attracting the attention of the rulers. The Board of Directors was then forced to formulate an educational policy where it was stated that as long as the schools are maintained by the government students are to be given admission without any distinction of caste, religion and race. This policy was further strengthened with the enactment of the Caste Disability Act of 1872.[36]

Political representation, as a means to emancipate the backward sections of the Indian society from the age-old disabilities, was not given recognition during the nineteenth century. Thus, the Government of India Act of 1858 and the Indian Council Acts of 1861 and 1892 did not recognise the special claims of the depressed classes. The dawn of the 20th century also did not herald their recognition as a political entity. For the first time the census report of 1910 divided the Hindus into three categories: (a) Hindus, (b) animists and tribals, (c) the depressed classes or untouchables. Thus, the untouchables acquired a new political dimension by virtue of the distinctive importance accorded to them. On the basis of representations received from the depressed communities in 1918, the Maharaja of Mysore appointed in the same year the Miller Committee to recommend steps for adequate representation of non-Brahmins in the services of the state.[37]

The untouchables do not constitute a homogeneous group. They belong to different ethnic and cultural groups. But segregated together on the basis of untouchability, they all are often pushed to live in a distant part of a village or ghettos of a city. It is an accepted phenomenon that the scheduled castes are still lagging behind in almost all fields and undergoing hardships, sufferings and oppressions, but consciousness dawned on them during the freedom movement about their plight. National leadership was already worried about them. Long before the era of struggle for recognition of human existence and socio-political rights (1920–50), attempts were made to emancipate them from the clutches of upper caste exploitation and degradation by various saints and social reformers. But they tried to do so on the basis of philosophical and religious grounds. But they failed as they insisted on the continuation of the *varna* system. Basic challenge to this exploitative and inhuman system came from emergence of Buddhism and Jainism, which more or less did not believe in the philosophical tenets underlying the caste system.[6] The British Raj as usual was not concerned with social reforms or removal or untouchability or the amelioration of the condition of depressed classes. Their policy was to divide the people and rule over them. It was more concerned with preserving their power, maintaining law and order, and collecting taxes.[38]

The government responded in a very cool and slow manner to the reformers, when they introduced progressive bills like the Hind Gains of Learning Bill and the Temple Entry Bill in the Central Legislative Council. This complaint was reiterated by progressive Englishmen like H.N. Brailsford, and by the untouchable leaders like B.R. Ambedkar. Actually, the British often preferred to exercise a restraining function over the untouchables in order to appease the upper castes. It did not like to displease the upper castes by introducing social reforms to improve the conditions of the untouchables.[39]

Kalelkar Commission

For the first time a commission was set up for backward classes on January 29, 1953, under the chairmanship of Kaka Kalelkar. Its terms of reference were as follows:

(a) To determine the criteria to be adopted in considering whether any sections of the people in the territory of India (in addition to the scheduled castes and scheduled tribes specified by notifications issued under the Articles 341 and 342 of the Constitution) should be treated as socially and educationally backward classes; and, in accordance with such criteria, prepare a list of such classes setting out also their approximate number and their territorial distribution;

(b) To investigate the conditions of all such socially and educationally backward classes and the difficulties under which they labour; and make recommendations (i) as to the steps that should be taken by the Union or any state to remove such difficulties or improve their conditions; and (ii) as to the grants that should be provided for the purpose by the Union or any state, and the conditions subject to which such grants should be made;

(c) To investigate such other matters as the President may hereafter refer to them; and

(d) To present to the President a report setting out the facts as found by them and making such recommendations as they think proper.

The Commission worked for about two years and submitted a three volume report to the President of India on 30 March, 1955, making, among others, the following important recommendations:

(i) That caste was the main cause of backwardness of the other backward classes;

(ii) That after taking into consideration the social position which a community occupied in the social hierarchy, the percentage of literacy and its general educational advancement; and its representations in the government service or in the industrial and other economic spheres, 2,399 castes comprising about 32 per cent population stood at a low level in the Indian society as other backward classes;

(iii) That women and backward communities among the Muslims, Christians, etc., be also treated as other backward classes;

(iv) That to bring these people into the national mainstream, reservation of 70 per cent seats in all technical and professional institutions for their qualified sons and daughters be made;

(v) That special economic measures be taken to uplift the other backward classes economically through such programmes as extensive land reforms, reorganisation of village economy, Bhoodan movement, development of livestock, dairy farming, cattle insurance, bee-keeping, piggery, fisheries, development of rural housing, public health and rural water supply, adult literacy programme, etc.; and

(vi) That to enable the other backward classes to come on a par with the high castes in the government/local bodies services, the following reservations be made for them for some time: Class I: 25 per cent, Class II and III: 33⅓ per cent and Class IV: 40 per cent.[40]

The attachment of untouchables to the Congress during the 1930s and 40s was far less than is sometimes assumed. In the years after Independence, untouchable support for the Congress clearly strengthened. From 1952 until 1989, with the exception of the post-Emergency elections of 1977, the untouchables tended to function in both national and state elections as a 'vote bank' for Congress. Their vote for Congress was a vote for the party of government, a party that had committed itself to a programme of action on untouchability and poverty. While the untouchables were a crucial Congress vote bank in India as a whole and in a majority of individual states, even before the recent flux they did not cling to Congress in regions where another party of movement rose to dominance. The major examples of long-term non-Congress dominance are West Bengal, Kerala, Tamil Nadu and Andhra Pradesh. A number of Ezhavas associated themselves with the fledgling Communist Party from the early 1940s, but with increasing prosperity the caste vote has been split along class lines between communists and Congress. But in the state of Kerala, the scheduled castes were more inclined towards the left parties. In West Bengal, the communist movement was slower to gain control of the state: the first United Front government came to power in 1967, a decade after the first such government in Kerala. The untouchables of Kerala and West Bengal behaved according to the logic of their class position within a political culture, more directed to considerations of class than anywhere else in India. But, from another perspective, the untouchables of these two states have been doing little different from their counterparts elsewhere in India. They have simply aligned themselves with the majority party. It is doubtful that most of these untouchables have been affected with any special passion for Marxism.[41]

Within Congress, the importance of the untouchable vote did not translate itself into great influence for individual untouchables. In particular, the building of the compensatory discrimination system arose more from the arithmetic of elections and the goodwill of sections of the elite than from the efforts of *dalit* parliamentarians. Jagjivan Ram was alone as a scheduled caste politician was able to succeed in becoming a genuinely national figure through Congress. A small number of state and national politicians gained a good measure of political recognition but there was no substantial change.[42]

The Congress framework rested a bit too heavily on the personality factor and on 'networking' through the state apparatus, handing out privileges and promises and thus patronising its support base. The politics of co-option was thus central to the Congress party, but the ever-mounting aspirations of emergent social groups, like the intermediate castes, put the 'inclusivist' system under great strain. In the specific case of Uttar Pradesh (UP) even when the Congress for a good two decades managed to use the levers of power to keep the various components of its support base reasonably contented, this success became less and less pronounced in the later years due to a combination of factors. For one, as Kothari and others have pointed out, the Congress kept uprooting influential state-level leaders to induct them at the Centre, thereby creating a vacuum at the top leadership level. Stalwarts like Gobind Ballabh Pant signify that tendency most vividly, because even before he could settle down in his chief ministerial assignment in Lucknow, he was called upon to 'assist' the party and government at the Centre. Sucheta Kriplani, Hemwati Nandan Bhauguna, N.D. Tiwari, Kamlapati Tripathi and so on – they were all shifted from New Delhi to Lucknow and back.[43]

In the general election of 1984, Congress won 83 out of 85 UP seats with 51 per cent of the total vote. But five years later the party won only fifteen seats with 32 per cent of the vote. In 1991, the Congress vote slipped further to 18 per cent, and it won five seats. This was also its tally of seats in 1996. Congress dominance had been built on a strong command of the Brahmin, Muslim and untouchable 'vote banks', together with considerable but variable support form the other upper castes and also the backward castes.

The electoral politics of the Congress was affected by the rise of two other parties – the Janata Dal and its offshoots, including Mulayam Singh's Samajwadi Party, and the Bhartiya Janata Party (BJP). These parties gained prominence partly because of the vacuum caused by the unpopularity of the Congress and partly because of their own efforts to divert the voters. The Janata Dal and the Samajwadi Party drew their major strength from the backward castes, whereas the BJP has traditionally been strongest among the upper castes of the towns. The Janata Dal and Samajwadi Party attracted a large share of the Muslim votes, disenchanted with the Congress after the destruction of the Babri Masjid. And the BJP has picked up considerable backward caste support, partly because it has had a strong backward caste (Lodhi) leader in Kalyan Singh.[44]

The practitioners of populist politics are consciously dividing the Indian society by following an unprincipled policy on reservations for public services and entry to educational institutions. The Biju Patnaik Government in Orissa has sharpened social conflicts by an abrupt announcement to increase the reservation of seats in educational institutions for scheduled caste and scheduled tribe students from the present quota of 22.5 per cent to 38 per cent. The decision sparked off violent agitations by a large section of students.[45]

The National Front, in its election manifesto of 1989, supported substantial reservation in employment, education and public offices to backward classes observing at the same time that the recommendations of the Mandal Commission will be implemented expeditiously. This intention of the V.P. Singh government was also reflected in the President's address to the joint session of both the Houses of Parliament. While delivering his address to the joint session of both the Houses of Parliament on 20th December, 1989, the President of India, R. Venkataraman, said: "The scheduled castes and scheduled tribes continue to be victims of social and economic injustice. The government's primary aim will be to ensure economic and social justice to them so that they can lead their lives with dignity and honour. The reservation for the scheduled caste and scheduled Tribes in the legislature will be extended by a further period of ten years. The government will take appropriate steps to implement the recommendations of the Mandal Commission."[46] But, the timing of its acceptance by the V.P. Singh government came as a complete surprise to all including even the MPs of ruling Janata Dal. On 7 August, 1990, V.P. Singh stunned the entire nation by announcing the government's acceptance of some recommendations of the Mandal Commission's report in parliament.

Mandal Commission

The Mandal Commission was set up by Janata Party government. But, it is worth noting that Indira Gandhi did not outrightly reject the Mandal Report, nor did she take it up for consideration. Discreetly she shelved it and equally discretely the leaders of the opposition let it remain on the shelf. Later, Rajiv Gandhi also did exactly the same thing.[47] The report was taken up by the National Front after a lapse of ten years and V.P. Singh projected himself as the saviour of backward classes by declaring that the Mandal Commission Report will be implemented. This sparked off anti-reservation movement throughout the country. In Delhi, the student community took to the streets and organized bandhs and rallies. Though the lack of co-ordination between the various student groups spear-heading the stir made some of the bandhs somewhat farcical, the agitation clearly put the government in dock. In Bihar, though Laloo Prasad Yadav, the Chief Minister, who stood to gain the most form the implementation of the Mandal Commission Report, yet his state witnessed some of the bloodiest anti-Mandal protests which claimed several lives. The upper caste in Bihar was so angry that an organisation called the Rashtriya Swarna Mukti Morcha was set up in Bhumidhar-dominated Muzaffarpur district to demand a separate *'Swarna Rajya'* comprising areas in Bihar, Uttar Pradesh, Madhya Pradesh, West Bengal and Haryana. The other big beneficiary of the Commission Report Mulayam Singh Yadav had to face less music.[48]

The Mandal Commission Report was politicised for electoral gains by the Janata Dal. The party has decided to launch a countrywide 'Mandal Yatra' from August 25 to November 7, 1992, with a view to mobilise the backward castes on the issue of reservations in jobs. The caste approach of the Janata Dal is quite clear when it wants a "caste census".[49]

The Narasimha Rao government inherited the agenda of the Janata Dal on reservations, and modified it to give some representation to the poor. Every major political party has come to agree on the policy of reservations, but each wants to take the sole credit for it. They are championing the cause of reservation without accepting the responsibility of initiating genuine socio-economic programmes for the real poor. The legitimate role of politics is to provide opportunities for upward mobility of the suppressed sections of society, governments must launch direct attacks against poverty. But Mandal-based reservations are a shortcut adopted by politicians to seek votes.[50]

On August 19, 1993, the *Times of India* reported about a meeting of the *dalits* and indigenous political leaders belonging to the ruling Congress party. The *dalit* movement was recognized as a force to reckon with. The report noted, the leaders of the backward castes (including *dalits*) and tribes in the Congress (ruling party) ... have raised their voice against the neglect of these sections of society and demanded firm measures to redress their grievances. They recently held a one-day meeting ... . It was demanded that the party should project a candidate from this section as the Chief Minister during the campaign for the assembly election. The idea was mooted by Ajit Jogi (a Christian *dalit*), Rajya Sabha member .... Almost all attributed the rise of the Bahujan Samaj Party (a *dalit* political party) in certain regions of the state (Madhya Pradesh) to the discontent in this section ... .[51] The Dalit Panthers were recognised as a new force in the politics of India. Panthers released a manifesto, which indicated Marxist influence. Dhosal was one of the main leaders of the *dalits*. Most of the Panthers owing allegiance to Ambedkar were against communists. The Panthers got split and many of them were involved in criminal cases, because of the violent acts committed by them. The Panthers often criticised the RPI leaders for their intemperate habits, anti-Ambedkarite activities, going around with Congressmen and so on, those involved in criminal cases individually approached Congress leaders for help and managed to get the cases withdrawn.[52]

Sachar Committee

In March, 2005, the UPA government appointed a high level committee under the chairmanship of Justice Mr Rajendra Sachar to study the social, educational political and economical status of the Muslim community with the seven members, namely, Syyid Hamid, Dr T.K. Oaman, Mr M.A. Basin, Dr Akhtar Majeed, Dr Abu Saleh Shariff, Dr Rakesh Basant and Dr Syed Zafar Mahmood. The committee submitted its report on November 17, 2006, which was tabled in the Parliament. The report sent shock waves not only within the Muslim Community but also among saner elements of the Indian society because it revealed that the Muslims are lagging behind every other community in all fields but the finer point is that the Indian citizenry has realised that the Muslims need upliftment and the state should take up its responsibility in this respect.[53]

Sachar Committee has done a lot of analysis about the Indian Muslims with statistical report based on information from government agencies, banks, Indian Minority Commission, different state governments and their agencies. The committee has found that the Muslims have been marginalised in the employment sector, which even sidelined them. On the all-India level, Muslims are nearly 15.4 per cent of total population but their share in government jobs is only 6.4 per cent. The presence of Muslims has been found to be 3 per cent in the IAS, 1.8 per cent in the IFS and 4 per cent in the IPS. The Muslim community has a representation of only 4.5 per cent in Indian Railways while 98.7 per cent of them are positioned at lower levels. Their share in Police Constables is only 6 per cent, in health 4.4 per cent and in transport 6.5 per cent.[54] Representation of Muslims is very low in the universities and banks. In IIMs and IITs, their share is 1.3 per cent and 1.7 per cent respectively. Statistics indicate that the number of poor within the Muslim society soared. Consequently, nearly 40 per cent Muslims fall under poorest monthly per capita expenditure class. Politically also, they are marginalised, their representation in decision-making bodies is negligible and they are counted only at the time of elections. Successive governments have made promises before elections leading to persistent accusations of appeasement but ironically these promises have generally been forgotten after elections.[55]

The report put forward some recommendations to eliminate the situation raised for Indian Muslims. Justice Sachar explained that the upliftment of minorities and implementation of these recommendations would strengthen the secular fabric of Indian society as well as increase patriotism due to their all-inclusive progress. The Sachar Committee has recommended corrective measures in two categories, i.e., General Policy and Specific Policy measures.

Within General Policy it recommends:

1. Creation of a National Data Bank (NDB) where all relevant data for various SRCs are maintained.
2. Enhancement of legal basis for providing equal opportunities.
3. Establishment of an Equal Opportunities Commission (EOC) to look into the grievances of the deprived groups.
4. Enhancement of participation in governance.
5. Establishing a more rational procedure for delimitation of constituencies.

On Specific Policy to be adopted by the government, the committee recommends that:

1. Free and compulsory education upto the age of 14 years is the obligation of the government and is critical for the improvements in the educational conditions of Muslims.
2. School textbooks should reflect social diversity.
3. The pre-entry qualification for admission to it should be reduced to class VIII and Madarsa educated children should be treated as eligible to such courses.
4. The University Grants Commission (UGC) should be encouraged to evolve a system where part of the allocation to colleges and universities is linked to the diversity in the population.

5. Hostel facilities to the students of the minorities should be provided on priority basis.
6. The state should run Urdu medium schools.
7. Linkage of the madarsas with higher secondary school boards and recognition of degrees awarded by them for competitive examinations.
8. Recommendations for promoting and enhancing access to Muslims in priority sector advances.
9. Representation of the community in interview panels and boards.
10. For providing financial support to the occupation in which there is Muslim concentration and has growth potential.
11. Registration of trusts such as wages and mosque committees.
12. Improvement of employment opportunities and conditions.[56]

After Sachar Committee findings, the UPA government has taken some steps in uplifting the Muslim community. The response of the government seems not only a sloganeering and the Muslim community expects concrete measures. Muslims are the second largest religious group inhibiting India's every nook and corner. Without their participation, India cannot be a fully developed country. Its Constitution begins with "We, the people of India" and naturally "We" includes Muslims also. Hence, it is now upon the ruling elite to remove the wrong done to the community.

Ranganathan Mishra Commission

The National Commission for Linguistic and Religious Minorities was set up on March 15, 2005, popularly known as the Ranganathan Mishra Commission. The Commission, led by Justice Ranganathan Mishra, Chief Justice of India, and Dr Tahir Mahmood, submitted its report to the government on 22 May, 2007. According to the report, discriminating the deprived either in the name of religion or in the name of technicalities is contradictory to the basic premise of the Indian Constitution. It was reported that the Mishra Commission was addressing the problems identified by the Sachar Committee fundamentally. The National Commission for Linguistic and Religious Minorities was set up on October 29, 2004, under the chairmanship of Chief Justice of India Ranganathan Mishra, with Tahir Mahmood, Anil Wilson and Mohinder Singh as its members.

The Commission recommended that in deciding the criteria for identifying backward classes there should be absolutely no discrimination whatsoever between the majority community, whatever that criteria may be these must be unreservedly applied also to all the minorities.[57]

As the meaning and scope of Article 30 of the Constitution has become quite uncertain, complicated and diluted due to their varied and sometimes conflicting judicial interpretations, the Commission recommend that a comprehensive law should be enacted without delay to detail all aspects of minorities, educational rights under that provision with a view to reinforcing its original dictates in letter and spirit. As by the force of judicial decisions, the minority intake in minority educational institutions has, in the interest of national integration, been restricted to about 50 per cent, thus virtually earmarking the remaining 50 per cent or so far the majority community, the commission strongly recommend that by the same analogy and for the same purpose at least 15 per cent seats in all non-minority educational institutions should be earmarked by law for the minorities as follows:

(a) The break-up within the recommended 15 per cent earmarked seats in institutions shall be 10 per cent for the Muslims and remaining 5 per cent for the other minorities.
(b) Minor adjustments can be made in the 15 per cent earmarked seats. In case of non-availability of Muslim-candidates to fill 10 per cent earmarked seats, the remaining vacancies may be given to the other minorities if their members are available over and above their share of 5 per cent but in no case shall any seat within the recommended 15 per cent go to the majority community.

(c) As is the case with the scheduled castes and scheduled tribes at present, those minority community candidates who can complete with others and secure admission on their own merit shall not be included in these 15 per cent earmarked seats.[58]

In respect of the Muslims, who are the largest minority at the national level with a country-wide presence and yet educationally the most backward of the religious communities, the Commission recommends certain exclusive measures as follows:

1. Select institutions in the country like Aligarh Muslim University and Jamia Milia Islamia should be legally given a special responsibility to promote education at all levels for Muslim students by taking all possible steps for this purpose.

In the funds to be distributed by Maulana Azad Educational Foundation, a suitable portion should be earmarked for the Muslims proportionate to their share in the total minority population. Out of this portion, funds should be provided not only to the existing Muslim institutions but also for setting up new institutions from nursery to the highest level and for technical and vocational education anywhere in India but especially in Muslim-concentration areas.

Since the minorities, especially the Muslims, are very much underrepresented, and sometimes wholly unrepresented in government employment, the Commission recommends that they should be regarded as backward in this respect within the meaning of that term used in Article 16(4) of the Constitution – notably without qualifying the word 'backward' with the words "socially and educationally" and that 15 per cent of posts in all cadres and grades under the central and state governments should be earmarked for them as follows:

(a) The break-up within the recommended 15 per cent shall be 10 per cent for the Muslims (commensurate with their 73 per cent share of the former in the total minority population at the national level) and the remaining 5 per cent for the other minorities.

(b) Minor adjustment can be made within the 15 per cent earmarked seats. In the case of non-availability, remaining vacancies may be given to other minorities but in no case shall any seat within the recommended 15 per cent go to the majority community.

The Commission recommends that para 3 of the Constitution (Scheduled Castes), Order 1950, which originally restricted the scheduled caste net to the Hindus and later opened it to Sikhs and Buddhists, thus still excluding from its purview the Muslims, Christians, Jains and Parsis, etc., should be wholly deleted by appropriate action so as to completely delink scheduled caste status from religion and make the scheduled caste net fully religion-neutral like that of the scheduled tribes.

The Commission further recommends that all those groups and castes among the Muslims and Christians, etc., whose counterparts among the Hindus, Sikhs or Buddhists are included in the central or state scheduled castes lists should also be covered by the scheduled caste net. If any such group or class among the Muslims and Christians, etc., is somehow included in an OBC list, it should be deleted from there while transferring it to the scheduled castes.[59]

Dalit Panthers Movement

Dalit Panthers provided courage to fight against the ghastly incidents perpetrated on the *dalits* and exploded the myth that the untouchables are mute and passive. They vehemently attacked the unjust caste system. They acted as a check and balance against the power politics and Republican Party leaders. They initiated a debate on Ambedkar's ideology. They compelled the government to fill the backlog. They coined the term 'dalit' and were opposed to terms like Harijans and untouchables. And, they captured the imagination of the younger generation, projected a militant image through a policy of confrontation. However, it had its own limitations.

There is a substantial gap between their goals and the efforts to achieve them due to lack of organisational infrastructure. They also failed to link themselves with other parallel movements. The programme was largely inconsistent. It was marked by absence of cadre building programme. Lack of funds also posed a problem in building an effective organisation. No substantial efforts were made by the Panthers to understand the rural position of the *dalits*. It is punctuated by lack of coordination between the *dalit* intellectuals and Panthers.[60]

The Rise of Bahujan Samaj Party

Kanshi Ram, the founder of the party, who was himself a victim of caste discrimination, launched this new outfit with the lofty objectives of confronting social discrimination and establishment of a just social order. He found an ally in Mayawati whose dynamism and energy was considered an asset to the organisation. Consequently, in North India, several branches were opened and committed persons were given the key positions. Soon, the BSP emerged as a political force. Numerous *dalits* thronged under the banner of Kanshi Ram, who apprised them of their basic and fundamental rights and advised them not to rest until their goal was achieved. They could understand soon that here was a leader who could do much for them.

The results of his efforts were quite favourable. Mayawati became Chief Minister of Uttar Pradesh (UP) twice. In the parliamentary election, Kanshi Ram and BSP could capture a few states which gave them same political clout. They are very hopeful that they would do better in the coming years and would like to act either independently or would have coalition with another party of their choice. The Bahujan Samaj Party (BSP) has generated new spirit in other states with the enthusiasm of Kanshi Ram. Again people were apprised of their basic and fundamental rights, which indeed could elevate their socio-economic status. The main idea is to make the *dalits* realise their social worth and put in efforts to elevate their status.[61]

The Election Commission's data shows that BSP did improve its vote percentage in Madhya Pradesh from 3.5 per cent in 1991 to 8.18 per cent in 1996. Another state where the BSP performed reasonably well is Jammu and Kashmir (Jammu region) where it shared 5.95 per cent of the polled votes. Since the party draws its strength mainly from among the scheduled castes its scheduled caste vote share in these states is considerably high. In UP it shared 59.5 per cent of scheduled caste votes; 22.9 per cent in MP, and 12.2 per cent in Haryana. Due to the underrepresentation of scheduled caste voters in the sample of Punjab, scheduled caste vote percentage cannot be calculated constituencywise. Though the party failed to get any seat in Haryana, on the six seats that it contested, its vote share varied from 5.01 per cent to 20.58 per cent. On Jammu seat, the party got 16.14 per cent of total votes. In MP, the party polled more than 20 per cent of votes in as many as six seats, and between 10 to 20 per cent of votes in seven seats. Obviously, the share of scheduled caste votes in these seats must be very high.[62]

The rise of BSP in the four states seems to be linked with the decline of the Congress. In UP, the Congress has been reduced to a peripheral party and the main players are now BJP, SP and BSP. The BSP is firmly rooted in the Jatavs, the largest caste grouping among the scheduled castes in UP. Around 73.8 per cent of its voters belong to this caste group. Parsis constitute 45.7 per cent and other scheduled castes 60.6 per cent of its electorate. The scheduled castes have almost deserted the Congress and switched over to the BSP. In Haryana and Punjab too the Congress has been reduced to a diminutive force and the scheduled caste voters no longer repose total faith behind it. In MP the BSP could spread its influence only in the areas adjoining UP and in the Chhatisgarh region, which has a long tradition of political mobilisation of marginalised groups. In Jammu also, the Congress has taken a back seat and the BJP has taken over but scheduled caste votes have not gone in favour of the BJP. There seems to be a close association between the decline of the Congress and the emergence of the BSP as the representative of scheduled caste interests in these states.[63]

The figures presented above also dispel the commonly held belief that the BSP has a powerful electoral appeal only among the urban educated middle class of the scheduled castes. The voters background figures of UP reveal that the BSP draws 62.7 per cent of its votes from non-lettered voters though they constitute only 44.8 per cent of the total sample of respondents. The next large share to BSP votes comes from the voters having education up to middle level constituting 27.4 per cent of total BSP voters. Voters having completed graduation or above constitute only 2 per cent of BSP voters though their representation in the sample has been 5.6 per cent. In fact, only 6.3 per cent of the graduates preferred to vote for the BSP whereas this figure is as high as 51.3 per cent for the BJP. Occupationwise BSP's voters mainly belong to the unskilled workers, agricultural and allied workers, and artisans and small and marginal farmers. Persons engaged in business and white collar jobs constitute only 2.6 and 1.6 per cent, respectively, of the BSP voters. The all-India figures also resemble the trends as observed in UP, for example, the all-India figures reveal that 85.3 per cent of BSP votes come from the lower class alone.[64]

The only other party known for representing mostly the scheduled castes is the Republican Party of India (RPI). In 1996 parliamentary elections, the party emerged as obvious choice of the scheduled caste voters wherever it contested elections in Maharashtra. Of the 11 seats it contested in the state, though without a win in five seats, its vote share has been more than 20 per cent and in four constituencies between 10 and 20 per cent of the polled votes. The party could poll more than 2 lakhs of votes in two constituencies.

The study reports also have disclosed the truth that with the emergence of their own political party, the *dalit* Bahujans who were merely used by the Brahminical political parties as their stored votes in their vote banks refused to be used as mere ballot in favour of the Brahminical social order and in detriment to the lower stratum of society.

The most important feature of the recent upsurge in *dalit* politics has been change in their party preference, since independence, the scheduled castes had been considered the "committed" vote bank of the Congress. It was the Congress in the pre-independence period, which first of all provided the political space for the scheduled castes to participate in a political activity in form of the freedom struggle. This participation had a pan-Indian character and it gave them, at least in the political sphere, the opportunity to stand somehow at par with the upper castes. This is not to deny the role of power, hegemony and dominance exercised by the upper caste people who dominated the upper layer of the Congress leadership. No wonder, at times we also find that the scheduled castes waged anti-feudal struggles against the local landlords. At many places, it were the communists who attracted them. Ambedkar too had a following among them. Nonetheless, it was the strength of the Congress that it could hold the majority of the *dalits* within its fold and made them believe that the political system in the independent India would offer a bright future for them. The RPI did try to challenge this dominance in most part of the sixties, but its influence was restricted only to Maharashtra and UP that too only in a few districts. By the end of the sixties, even the RPI lost its attraction. The scheduled caste voters remained loyal to the Congress even in the face of troubled times of 1967 and 1977 (the percentage of scheduled caste votes polled by the Congress was 45.2 per cent in 1967, 47.8 per cent in 1971, 52.8 per cent in 1980. It was only in 1977 that the congress could barely manage 35.7 per cent of the scheduled caste votes with 53.0 per cent of the scheduled caste votes going to the non-Congress parties). Some fluctuations notwithstanding, never in the past the Congress faced any serious threat to this "captive" vote bank except in a few states under the left rule. However, signs of decline in its scheduled caste vote share became the order during the elections held in the late eighties (1989) and the early nineties (1991). The Lok Sabha elections of 1996 finally present a changed electoral landscape. There is a definite trend of desertion of the Congress by the scheduled castes in many states like UP and Bihar. This is also one of the reasons why for the first time the Congress failed to become even the single largest party in the Lok Sabha. Except a few states the Congress no longer remains the choice of the majority of the scheduled castes.[65]

The overall emerging pattern is that wherever scheduled castes could find a viable alternative they preferred it to the Congress. The BSP was their first choice, in its absence the Left Front and the regional parties were preferred in states where they had dominance. However, on account of its all India presence, the Congress could still pull the largest share of the scheduled caste votes (31.4%) though scheduled castes shared only 21.6 per cent of its total polled votes. As compared to this, in 1971 the Congress was able to get 57.8 per cent of the scheduled caste votes. In 1996, the left parties together polled 11.6 per cent of scheduled caste votes. The BSP polled their 12.1 per cent votes. The BSP mostly depends on the scheduled caste votes as 67 per cent of votes polled in its favour came from the scheduled castes. None of the other parties solely relies on scheduled caste votes as the case is with the BSP. The BJP could corner around 13 per cent of the scheduled caste votes as against 45.6 per cent of its votes coming from the upper castes. The Congress, the Left Front and the BSP together accounted for 55 per cent of the scheduled caste votes polled all over the country. These are the parties, which pulled larger percentage of the scheduled caste votes as compared to their overall vote sharing in 1996 elections.[66]

The Shudra and tribal voters have started realising the teachings of their leader, Kanshi Ram, *"Toomlog Jiski Piche Khare Hojate Ho, Ohi Sasak Banta, Islie Pichlagu Banna Chodke Apna Payer Par Khare Ho Jao. Satta Tumarhi Hogi"*. (The political party behind whom you people stand and support, becomes the ruler. Therefore, rely on your own identity and become the governing class of your country). This is not just an emotional statement but also a hard fact of Indian politics. The *dalit*-bahujans have been electing government with their immense majority support by casting valuable franchise. The party which is supported by the lowest stratum of the *dalit*-bahujans, who are of late better know as scheduled castes, is invariably installed on the wheel of the government. The ruling political parties were launched by the brahmins in collaboration with other castes like baniyas, kayasth, etc. They organised, manned and managed the policies of those political parties. The members of the Dalit-Bahujan Samaj neither had any initiative nor contribution to make for those parties. They, therefore, enjoyed no privileges out of those political parties. These parties representing upper castes give false assurances to low caste and untouchable people. The gullible, illiterate and helpless masses depend on them. The parties secure their votes and forget about their assurances.[67]

Blatant caste politics, which catapulted the Mulayam Singh-Kanshi Ram combine to power, proved divisive and dangerous in Uttar Pradesh. But nobody expected the conflict to erupt so soon within the walls of the Assembly on the very first sitting of the newly constituted Assembly in 1993, legislators fought pitched battles. As many as 33 legislators, 6 staff members and a few home guards on duty, were injured. Among them were women legislators. So vicious was the crossfire that of the 221 microphones provided in the House only 16 remained functional by the time the trouble was brought under control. The most visible examples were, of course, the removal of T.S.R. Subramanium as the state's Chief Secretary and that of Surendra Mohan as the Home Secretary, after BSP leader Kanshi Ram publicly rebuked the Government for allowing the "Brahminical order" or upper castes, to dominate the higher tiers of bureaucracy. With the BSP leaders insisting on filling up senior posts with scheduled caste officers, and Mulayam, feeling obliged to cater to his main constituency of other backward classes and Muslims, the state machinery resembled the vote bank of the two parties.[68]

Can our political parties bring harmony in our society by demolishing the caste system at present? Not at all because the main aim of any political party is not to bring political unity but to get political power to serve its own interests. Every political party meticulously avoids the changing of status quo for fear of wrath of its voters. Indian party politics, by and large, is not committed to the philosophy of social change. The base of some political parties is religion, some have casteism and regionalism and still others believe in capitalism. The multi-party system has added to the confusion. Every political party has a vested interest in sustaining the caste system.[69] Democratic participation in governance, a strategy for development, search for social justice, is a far cry. In order to capture votes, the politicians pit caste against caste, religion against religion. The wedges driven by religion, caste and class can be neutralised by redefining secularism. The question of secularism does not apply only in the case of Hindu-Muslim relations, it holds good for caste as well.[70] During the agitation against the implementation of the Mandal Report no political party was prepared to condemn it or support it directly and openly for fear of alienating the vote banks.[71] However, the policy of reservation fractured Indian society besides affecting efficiency. Seen in this context, the observations of Jawaharlal Nehru in his letter to Chief Ministers in June 1961, still holds conviction: "I dislike any kind of reservation, more particularly in service. I regret strongly against anything which leads to inefficiency and second rate standards ... the only real way to hold a backward group is to give opportunities for a good education ... but if we go in for reservations on communal and caste basis, we swamp the bright and able people and remain second rate or third rate .... It has amazed me to learn that even promotions are based sometimes on communal or caste considerations. Let us hold the backward groups by all means, but never at the cost of efficiency."[72]

Notes

1. C.B. Bhambhari, *Politics in India 1947–1987*, Vikas Publishing House, New Delhi, 1988, p. VII.

2. Ibid., p. 177.
3. Prem Prakash, *Ambedkar: Politics and Scheduled Castes*, Ashish Publishing House, New Delhi, 1993, p. 2.
4. Ibid., p. 12.
5. Ibid., p. 16.
6. Ibid., p. 20.
7. Ibid., p. 23.
8. Ibid., p. 31.
9. Ibid., p. 35.
10. Ibid., p. 49.
11. Ibid., p. 55.
12. R.K. Ksahirsagar, *Political Thought of Dr Babasahab Ambedkar*, Intellectual Publishing House, New Delhi, 1992, p. 32.
13. Ibid., p. 73.
14. Ibid., p. 75.
15. Ibid., p. 78.
16. Cited in ibid., p. 80.
17. Ibid., p. 83.
18. Ibid., p. 60.
19. Ibid., p. 85.
20. S.R. Bakshi, *B.R. Ambedkar: His Political and Social Ideology*, Deep & Deep Publication House, New Delhi, 2000, p. 136.
21. Ibid., p. 140.
22. Ibid., p. 143.
23. C. Parvathamma, *Scheduled Castes at the Cross Roads*, Ashish Publishing House, New Delhi, 1989, p. 153.
24. Cited in S.K. Biswas, *Hindu Raj: Today-Yesterday-Tomorrow*, Orion Books, New Delhi, 1996, p. 110
25. Cited in ibid., p. 103.
26. M.S. Gore, *The Social Context of an Ideology: Ambedkar's Political and Social Thought*, Sage Publications, New Delhi, 1993, p. 147.
27. C. Parvathamma, op. cit., p. 167.
28. S.K. Ghosh, *Indian Democracy Derailed: Politics and Politicians*, APH Publishing Corporation, New Delhi, 1997, p. 201.
29. Ibid., p. 155.

30. M.S. Gore, op. cit., p. 150.
31. S.K. Biswas, *Towards a Casteless Society*, Orion Books, Delhi, 1998, p. 70.
32. Ibid., p. 77.
33. S.K. Ghosh, op. cit., p. 221.
34. Ibid., p. 226.
35. C.P. Bhambhari, op. cit., p. 182.
36. Gopal Singh, *Reservation Politics in India: Mandalisation of the Society*, Deep & Deep Publications, New Delhi, 1995, p. 14.
37. Ibid., p. 15.
38. Joseph Benjamin, *Scheduled Castes in Indian Politics and Society*, Ess Ess Publications, New Delhi, 1989, p. 26.
39. Ibid., p. 27.
40. K.C. Yadav, *India's Unequal Citizens: A Study of Other Backward Classes*, Manohar Publishers, Delhi, 1994.
41. Oliver Mendelsohn, *The Untouchables: Subordination, Poverty and the State in Modern India*, Oxford University Press, New Delhi, 2000, p. 207.
42. Pradyot Lal, *Caste vs Caste: Turbulence in Indian Politics*, Ajanta Books International, Delhi, 1998, p. 72.
43. Oliver Mendelsohn, op. cit., p. 218.
44. C.P. Bhambhari, *Politics in India 1992–93*, Shipra Publications, Delhi, 1993, p. 97.
45. Gopal Singh, op. cit., p. 55.
46. Cited in ibid., p. 60.
47. Ibid., p. 67.
48. C.P. Bhambhari, *Politics in India 1992–93*, op. cit., p. 98.
49. Ibid., p. 99.
50. Gopal Singh, op. cit., p. 126.
51. James Massey, *Dalits in India: Religion as a Source of Bondage or Liberation with Special Reference to Christians*, Manohar Publishers, New Delhi, 1995, p. 147.
52. Ibid., p. 152.
53. *The Sachar Committee Report*, p. 30.
54. Ibid., p. 32.

55. Ibid., p. 41.
56. Ibid., p. 224.
57. *The Ranganathan Mishra Commission Report*, p. 81.
58. Ibid., p. 96.
59. Ibid., p. 216.
60. Sanjay Paswan, *Encyclopaedia of Dalits in India*, Vol. 3, Kalpaz Publications, Delhi, 2002, p. 328.
61. Ibid., p. 326.
62. S.K. Biswas, *Towards a Casteless Society*, op. cit., p. 73.
63. Ibid., p. 75.
64. Ibid., p. 76.
65. Ibid., p. 80.
66. Ibid., p. 83.
67. Ibid., p. 86.
68. S.K. Ghosh, op. cit., p. 231.
69. S.R. Bakshi, op. cit., p. 192.
70. S.K. Ghosh, op. cit., p. 234.
71. Gopal Singh, op. cit., p. 126.
72. *Times of India*, New Delhi, November 17, 1990.

5

Judicial Response

India, for centuries, has been the seat of a social system based on inequality, exploitation and injustice. The poor have not only suffered economic exploitation but have undergone and are still being subjected to social indignation of all kinds. After independence, the makers of the Constitution realised the need for social and economic justice. Nehru asserted: "There is a duty cast upon us and to remember always that we are here not to function for one party or one group, but always to think of India as a whole and always to think of the welfare of the four hundred millions that comprise India." Referring to the pervasive and poignant problem of mass poverty, Nehru warned: "If we cannot solve this problem soon, all our paper Constitution will become useless and purposeless."[1]

The Constitution of India is a social document with most of its provisions directly or indirectly aiming at furthering the goals of social justice. The preamble, the chapters on Fundamental Rights and the Directive Principles of State Policy[2] mandate the state to strengthen political, social and economic democracy. Justice, liberty, equality and fraternity are the guiding principles of the new document. The judiciary in India, specially the higher judiciary, has been assigned a vital role in upholding the federal principle, interpretation of laws made by legislatures and testing their constitutional validity, and protecting the fundamental rights of the citizens. The Constitution of India does not recognise the doctrine of separation of powers as it exists in the United

States. Apart from the powers vested in the Supreme Court by the Constitution, the court on its own has expanded its own jurisdiction under the garb of judicial activism to meet the welfare requirements of the Constitution. The prophecy of Sir Alladi Krishnaswami Ayyar[3] that "the future evolution of the Indian Constitution will depend to a large extent upon the Supreme Court and the direction given to it by that Court" has come true.

An important issue that has assumed significance in recent times has been the activist role played by the judiciary, especially the Supreme Court. The expression "judicial activism" has eluded a precise definition as it means different things to different people. Broadly speaking, it implies dynamism, judicial creativity, judicial sensitivity to social and economic problems. This new role is a deviation from its traditional role of administering justice according to law. The new role visualises the urge to meet the hopes and aspirations of the teaming people. Technically, it is the legislature and executive that are responsible for establishing socio-economic justice and when they fail in doing it, the judiciary cannot sit as a silent spectator. During the past four decades, the role of the apex court changed from the "interpreter of laws" to that of "maker of laws". In fact, its activist role began in the fifties when it had to pronounce on the validity of agrarian reforms introduced by the Parliament and the state legislatures.[4] Since then there has been no looking back.

The Constitution of India does not provide for judicial review in explicit terms. It is implicit in Article 13(1) and (2), 32(1) and 226. In *Kishavananda Bharti v. State of Kerala*[5], Justice Khanna observed: "If the provisions of a statue are found to be violative of any Article of the Constitution which is touchstone of the validity of all laws, Supreme Court and High Courts are competent to strike down the said provision."[6]

Scheduled Castes and Scheduled Tribes

The Constitution treats the scheduled castes and scheduled tribes in India with special favour and accords them with certain safeguards. The Constitution, however, does not specify the tribes or the castes which are to be called as the scheduled castes or the scheduled tribes. It leaves the power to list these castes and tribes to the President. The scheduled castes, according to Article 366(24) read with Article 341, are those castes, races or tribes, or parts thereof, as the President may notify. According to Article 341(1), the President may specify castes, races or tribes, or parts of groups within caste, races or tribes, which shall for the purpose of the Constitution be deemed to be scheduled castes in relation to that state. Thus, the classification of scheduled castes may vary with state and union territory. As regards the states, the President issues the notification after consultation with the Governor of the state concerned. The purpose of this provision is to avoid disputes as to whether a particular caste should be specified as a scheduled caste or not. Only those castes can be characterised as scheduled castes which are notified in the Presidential Order under Article 341.[7] Under Article 341(2), however, Parliament may by law include or exclude from the list of scheduled castes occupied in a notification by the President any caste, race or tribe or part of or group within any caste, race or tribe.

The Scheduled Castes Order, 1950, stipulates that "no person who professes a religion different from the Hindu or the Sikh religion shall be deemed to be a member of scheduled castes". This means that if a member of scheduled castes converts to another religion, he would cease to be a scheduled caste. The Supreme Court in *A.B.S.K. Sangh (Rly) v. Union of India*[8] held that Article 341 makes it clear that a 'scheduled caste' need not be a 'caste' in the conventional sense and, therefore, may not be a caste within the meaning of Article 15(4) or 16(4). A scheduled caste becomes caste only if the President specifies any caste, race, tribe or parts or groups within castes, race or tribes for the purpose of the Constitution. So, a group or a section of a group, which need not be a caste and may even be a hotch-potch of many castes or tribes or even races, may still be a scheduled caste under Article 341. It has been held by the Supreme Court in *Triloki Nath v. State of Jammu and Kashmir*[9] that the state has, no doubt, to ascertain whether a particular class of citizens is backward or not, having regard to acceptable criteria, it is not the final word on the question. It is a justiciable issue and may be canvassed if that decision is based on the irrelevant considerations.[10]

The Supreme Court then finally held that in reservation of appointments for backward classes, determination of backward classes could not be on the basis of community, caste, race or religion. The Supreme Court thus held that state policy of distribution of posts community-wise was hit by Articles 16(1) and (4). For the application of clause (4), two conditions must be satisfied:

(i) a class of citizens is socially and educationally backward; and
(ii) the said class is not adequately represented in the service under the state.[11]

Backward Classes

Besides the scheduled castes and the scheduled tribes, the Constitution extended some protection to backward classes, as these classes have been neglected for long. Backward classes are to be found amongst all religious groups – Hindus, Muslims, Christians, etc. Under Article 15(4), the state is empowered to make special provisions for the advancement of any socially and educationally backward class besides the scheduled castes and the scheduled tribes. Under Article 16(4), there can be reservation of posts for backward classes. The backward classes have not been specified in the Constitution for at the time of the Constitution-making not much information was available about them. In Articles 15(4) and 340, the expression used is socially and educationally backward classes. In Article 16(4), the expression used is 'backward' and in Article 46, the term used is 'weaker sections of the people'. To facilitate the task of identifying the backward classes and laying down criteria for the purpose, Article 340(1) empowers the President to appoint a commission consisting of such person as he thinks fit to investigate the condition of socially and educationally backward classes in India and the difficulties which they face. The commission may recommend steps for improving their condition. The commission may also make recommendations as to the grants which should be made for the purpose by the Centre or any state, and the conditions subject to which such grants should be made. The Presidential order is to define the procedure to be followed by the commission. The commission is to investigate the matters referred to it and present its report to the President setting out the facts as found by it and making its recommendations. The report of the commission, together with a memorandum setting out the action taken thereon by the government, is to be laid before each House of Parliament. After the receipt of the commission's report, the President may by order specify the backward classes which shall fall within the jurisdiction of the special officer for the scheduled castes and the scheduled tribes.

The task of devising positive and workable criteria to identify backwardness on an all-India basis is yet to be completed. At present, each state has its own criterion for determining backwardness and often political expediency plays a decisive role. There is, thus, no uniformity in the country in this respect. For purpose of Articles 15(4) and 16(4), it is for the state concerned to list the backward classes. The Centre can also list them for purposes of admission to central educational institutions and central services and also under Article 338(3) for bringing them under the jurisdiction of the Commissioner for Scheduled Castes and Scheduled Tribes. Even in this the Centre has not been able to do much. The task is an extremely difficult one. Many communities desire to be characterised as backward because of the benefits attached to them and it is here that the entire matter gets politicised.[12]

The Government of India appointed the Backward Classes Commission (known as the Mandal Commission) under Article

340 on January 1, 1979. The Commission submitted its report on December 31, 1980. The Commission was *inter alia* "entrusted with the task of determining the criteria for defining the socially and educationally backward classes in the country". The Commission has held that (besides scheduled castes and scheduled tribes that amount to 22.56 per cent of the total population) 52 per cent of the total Indian population can be characterised as backward and, therefore, 52 per cent of all posts could be reserved for them. The Commission, however, refrained from making such a drastic recommendation in view of the Supreme Court's ruling that the total quantum of reservation under Article 16(4) should be below 50 per cent.[13] In view of this legal constraint, the Commission was obliged to recommend reservation of 27 per cent only for backward classes so that the total reservation for scheduled castes, scheduled tribes and backward classes amounts to a little less than 50 per cent. The Commission by and large identified castes with backward classes and more or less entirely ignored the economic tests. The Commission also ignored the fact that even among the so-called higher castes, there may be a number of socially and educationally backward people deserving help. On the whole, the Commission's recommendations have proved to be very controversial.[14] According to Justice Subba Rao, "Casteism has been projected into every walk of life – admissions to educational institutions, appointment to government services, contracts, licences, elections and the formation of Ministry".[15]

The whole controversy regarding government reservation policy revolves around as to who should be the real beneficiaries of the policy and the extent to which the reservations can be stretched. There have been several decisions of the Supreme Court since 1951 which tried to analyse the criteria to be adopted for making reservations for the backward classes. In the case of *State of Madras v. Smt. Champakam Dorairajan and Others*[16] the issue was discussed in detail by the Supreme Court. The State of Madras runs four medical colleges with 330 seats, out of which 17 seats are reserved for students coming from outside the state and 12 seats are reserved for discretionary allotment by the state and the remaining seats are distributed among the four districts in the state. Likewise, the state of Madras maintains four engineering colleges with a capacity of 395 seats. Out of which, 21 seats are reserved for students coming from outside the state, 12 seats are reserved for discretionary allotment by the state and the remaining seats are distributed among the four districts of the state.

For many years before the commencement of the Constitution, the seats in both the medical colleges and the engineering colleges so apportioned among the four distinct groups of districts used to be filled up according to certain proportions set forth in what used to be called the communal government order. Thus, for every 14 seats to be filled by the selection committee, candidates used to be selected strictly on the following basis:

Non-Brahmins (Hindus)	6
Backward Hindus	2
Brahmins	2
Harijans	2
Anglo-Indians and Indian Christians	1
Muslims	1

Champakam Dorairajan prayed for the issue of a *writ of Mandamus* or other suitable prerogative writ restraining the state of Madras and all officers and subordinates thereof from enforcing, observing, maintaining or following or requiring the enforcement, observance, maintenance or following by the authorities concerned the notification or the order generally referred to as the communal government order in and by which admissions to the Madras Medical College were sought or purported to be regulated in such manner as to infringe and involve the violation of her fundamental rights. From the affidavit filed in support of her petition it does not appear that the petitioner had actually applied for admission to the medical college. She states that on inquiry she came to know that she would not be admitted to the college as she belonged to the Brahmin community. No objection, however, was taken to the maintainability of her petition on the ground of absence of any actual application for admission made by her. On the contrary, courts have been told that the state had agreed to reserve a seat for her should her application before the High Court succeed. In the peculiar circumstances, courts do not consider it necessary to pursue this matter any further.[17]

Sri Srinivasan, who had actually applied for admission to the Government Engineering College at Guindy, filed a petition praying for a *writ of Mandamus*, or any other writ restraining the state of Madras and all officers thereof from enforcing, observing, maintaining or following the communal government order by which admission to the engineering college was sought to be regulated in such manner as to infringe and involve the violation of the fundamental right of the petitioner under Article 15(1) and Article 29(2) of the Constitution. In the affidavit filed in support of his petition, the petitioner has stated that he had passed the Intermediate examination held in March 1950 in Group I, passing the said examination in first class and obtaining marks set out in his affidavit. The Advocate General appearing for the state contends that the provisions of this Article have to be read along with other Articles in the Constitution. And that Article 46 charges the state with promoting with special care the educational and economic interests of the weaker sections of the people, and in particular, of the scheduled castes and the scheduled tribes, and with protecting them from social injustice and all forms of exploitation. It is pointed out that although this Article finds a place in part IV of the Constitution which lays down certain Directive Principles of State policy and though the provisions contained in that part are not enforceable by any court of law the principles therein laid down are nevertheless fundamental in the governance of the country and Article 37 makes it obligatory on part of the state to apply those principles while making laws. The argument is that having regard to the provisions of Article 46, the state is entitled to maintain the communal government order fixing proportionate seats for different communities and if, because of that order, which is thus contended to be valid in law and not in violation of the Constitution, the petitioners are unable to get admissions to the educational institutions there is no infringement of their fundamental rights. The chapter on Fundamental Rights is sacrosanct and not liable to be abridged by any legislative or executive act or order, except to the extent provided in the appropriate Article in Part III. The Directive Principles of state policy have to conform to and run as subsidiary to the chapter on Fundamental Rights.[18]

Take the case of the petitioner Srinivasan. It is not disputed that he secured much higher marks than the non-Brahmin candidates and yet the non-Brahmin candidates who secured less number of marks will be admitted into six out of every 14 seats but the petitioner Srinivasan will not be admitted to any of them. It is argued that the petitioners are not denied admission only because they are Brahmins but for a variety of reasons, e.g., (a) they are Brahmins, (b) Brahmins have an allotments of only two seats out of 14, and (c) the two seats have already been filled up by the most meritorious Brahmin candidates. The classification in the communal government order proceeds on the basis of religion, race and caste. In the view of judges, the classification made in the communal government order is opposed to the Constitution and constitutes a clear violation of the Fundamental Rights guaranteed to the citizen under Article 29(2). And there is no need to consider the effect of Article 14 or 15 on the specific Articles discussed above. The communal government order is, therefore, inconsistent with the provisions of Article 29(2) in part III of the Constitution and is void under Article 13. The appeals were dismissed with costs.[19]

This may be true that only two seats are reserved for Brahmins. But when we come to consider the seats reserved for the candidates of other communities, the petitioners are denied admission to any of them based on the sole ground of their being Brahmins and not being members of the community for which those reservations have been made.

It was this positive attitude which convinced the honourable judges to observe that part III is sacrosanct and Directive Principles of State Policy must conform to and run subsidiary to fundamental rights. There is no doubt that fundamental rights, as mentioned in part III of the Constitution, are very important but at the same time one can not neglect the value of Directive Principles of State Policy which enshrine the aspirations of people of the country. As a result, any strict positive interpretation of fundamental rights vis-à-vis directive principles might result in the frustration of the philosophical foundations of both Part III and part IV of the Constitution. Instead if a liberal pragmatic rule of interpretation is applied to these parts that may yield fruitful results which unfortunately the honourable judges failed to adopt in this case.

Although the method of interpretation of various Constitutional provisions in this case is not convincing but the result of the interpretation is quite convincing. Politicisation of reservation is a dangerous sign for a society already fragmented on various grounds. The court took into consideration not only Constitutional provisions touching the issue of reservation but also considered socio-economic factors involved in the case.

M.R. Balaji and Others v. The State of Mysore and Others[20] The state appointed a Committee called the Mysore Backward Classes Committee with Dr R. Nagen Gowda as its chairman to investigate the problem and advise the government as to the criteria which should be adopted in determining the educationally and socially backward classes, and the special provisions which should be made for their advancement. According to the order, which was passed in the light of interim report that 60 per cent of the seats were left open for what may be conveniently described as the "merit pool", available to candidates according to their merits, 40 per cent were reserved for the reservation pool, 22 per cent of which were reserved for the backward classes, 15 per cent for the scheduled castes and 3 per cent for the scheduled tribes.

The Nagan Gowda Committee submitted its report in 1961 and in the light of the said report and the recommendation made therein, the state proceeded to make an order under Article 15(4) on July 10, 1961. This order begins with the observation that the Nagan Gowda Committee has come to the conclusion that in the present circumstances, the only practicable method of classifying the backward classes in the state is on the basis of castes and communities, and it has specified the criteria which should be adopted for determining the educational and social backwardness of the communities.

Out of the 23 petitioners, six had applied for admission to the pre-professional class in medicine in the medical colleges affiliated either to the Mysore University or to the Karnataka University and 17 had applied for admission to the first year of five-year integrated course leading to the degree of B.E. from the University of Mysore. As a result of reservation made by the said order, students who had secured less percentage of marks were admitted, but not the petitioners. The petitioners' case is that the impugned over the order, which has been passed under Article 15(4) is not valid because the basis adopted by the order in specifying and enumerating the socially and educationally backward classes of citizens in the state is unintelligible and irrational and the classification made on the said basis is inconsistent with and outside the provisions of Article 15(4).[21]

In the opinion of learned judges, when the state makes special provision for the advancement of the weaker sections of society specified in Article 15(4) it has to approach its task objectively and in a rational manner. Undoubtedly, it has to take reasonable and even generous steps to help the advancement of weaker elements; the extent of the problem must be weighed, the requirements of the community at large must be borne in mind and a formula must be evolved which would strike a reasonable balance between the several relevant considerations. Therefore, we are satisfied that the reservation of 68 per cent directed by the impugned order is plainly inconsistent with Article 15(4).[22]

The Supreme Court laid down several important points in this judgment. It held that it was not necessary for the government to appoint a commission under Article 340 before passing an order under Article 15(4). This appointment and report of the Backward Classes Commission was only recommendatory. It was not a condition precedent for taking action under Article 15(4). It was further ruled that the executive can pass orders on reservation. It is not necessary for the legislature to make provisions for reservation. The backwardness must be social and educational. Caste is one indicator, but its role cannot be exaggerated, otherwise it would perpetuate caste. Social backwardness is the result of poverty to a large extent. Occupations and place of habitation also determine backwardness.

Classification between backward and more backward classes made by the government was held to be unconstitutional. According to this criterion, nearly 90 per cent of the state population became backward. Reservation of 68 per cent was also inconsistent with Article 15(4) as it was unreasonable. The interests of the weaker sections must be balanced with that of the society in general. It is a difficult task but in the guise of making special provision, practically all seats cannot be reserved. Reservation should be less than 50 per cent. The apex court concluded that the state government's order was a fraud on the constitutional power conferred under Article 15(4). The court said that it was not its task to categorise the valid and invalid percentage. Article 15(4) gives that discretion to the state government.[23]

The judgment of honourable Supreme Court through learned judges like P.B. Gajendragadkar, K.N. Wanchoo, K.C. Das, Gupta, J.C. Shah and the then Chief Justice of India, B.P. Sinha, in the present case, is one of the finest judgments in relation to reservation and related issues.

The most notable observation of the Supreme Court in this case relates to its ruling that the reservation of 68 per cent made by the impugned Mysore government is a fraud on the constitutional provisions relating to reservational provisions as the makers of our Constitution never intended that the special provisions ingrained in Article 15(4), 16(4) should be used in such a manner as to frustrate the most fundamental of all fundamental rights, that is, right to equality. The 68 per cent reservation is nothing but a naked misuse of special provisions to uplift the backward sections of the society. The court further held that there can not be classification within classification so as to confuse the entire concept of backwardness. Again, the backwardness, as given in Articles 15(4) and 16(4), does not mean either socially or educationally; rather it must be both social and educational backwardness so as to claim benefits of Article 15(4). This interpretation given by the honourable apex court is very convincing and acts as a rider against the irrational attitude of politicians vis-à-vis reservations. Moreover, the court's observation that caste is a relevant factor under Article 15(4) but it cannot be the sole test for ascertaining whether a particular class is backward. Other factors like poverty, occupation, place of habitation are equally relevant. The court rightly observed that Article 15(4) does not speak of 'castes' only but speaks of 'classes', and 'caste' and 'class' are not synonyms. Since the impugned government order solely relied on 'caste' without regard to other relevant factors and that is sufficient to render the order invalid. Furthermore, the observations of learned judges with regard to irrational criterion adopted by the state government, which rendered about 90 per cent of the population as backward, are inconsistent with Article 15(4) is highly appreciating. The court noted that Article 15(4) only enables the state to make special and not exclusive provision for the backward classes. The court's observation that national interest would suffer if qualified and competent students were excluded from admission to institutions of higher education, is an excellent analysis of an uncontrolled and irrational reservation policy.

R. Chitralekha and Another v. State of Mysore and Others[24] The Government of Mysore by an order defined backward classes and directed that 30 per cent of the seats in professional and technical colleges and institutions shall be reserved for them and 18 per cent to the scheduled castes and scheduled tribes. It was said that classification of socially and educationally backward classes should be made on the basis of economic condition and occupation. By a letter the government informed the Director of Technical Education that it had been decided that 25 per cent of the maximum marks for the examination in optional subject should be fixed as interview marks. The selection will be decided by a committee composed of heads of technical institutions and in allotting marks for interview factors like general knowledge, personality and extra-curricular activities of the candidates should be taken into consideration. On the basis of this selections were made for admission to engineering and medical colleges. Thereupon some of the candidates whose applications for admission were rejected filed writ petitions before the High Court of Mysore for quashing the orders issued by the government and for directing that they shall be admitted to the college strictly in the order of merit. The High Court rejected the contentions raised on points of law but held that the petitioners be interviewed afresh and admissions be made in accordance with the government order and letter which were declared valid.

It was also contended that the government letter was invalid in as much as it did not comply with the provision of Article 166 of the Constitution. The government had no power to appoint a selection committee for admitting students to colleges on the basis of higher or different qualifications than those prescribed by the university. That selection by viva voce examination was illegal by reason of the fact that it enables the interviewers to act arbitrarily and therefore it contravenes Article 14 of the Constitution. Lastly, it was contended that unless the observation of the High Court that the classification was not perfect since the government has not applied the caste and economic criterion, it will mislead the government.

The government laid down that classification of socially and educationally backward classes should be made on the following basis: (1) economic condition, and (ii) occupation. According to that order a family whose income is Rs 1,200 per annum or less and persons or classes following occupations of agriculture, petty business, inferior services, crafts or other occupations involving manual labour are, in general, socially, economically and educationally backward. The government lists the following occupations as contributing to social backwardness: (1) actual cultivator, (2) artisan (3) petty businessmen, (4) inferior services (i.e., Class IV in government services and corresponding class or service in private employment) including casual labour, and (5) any other occupation involving manual labour. The order does not take into consideration the caste of an applicant as one of the criteria for backwardness. Learned counsel does not attack the validity of the said order.

According to Justice Subba Rao, we do not intend to lay down any inflexible rule for the government to follow. The laying down of criteria for ascertainment of social and educational backwardness of a class is a complex problem depending upon many circumstances which may vary from state to state and even from place to place in a state. But what we intend to emphasise is that under no circumstances a "class" can be equated to a "caste", though the caste of an individual or a group of individuals may be considered along with other relevant factors in putting him in a particular class. We would also like to make it clear that if in a given situation caste is excluded in ascertaining a class within the meaning of Article 15(4) of the Constitution, it does not vitiate the classification if it satisfied other tests.[25]

According to Justice Mudholkar, it would not be in accordance either with clause (1) of Article 15 or clause (2) of

Article 29 to require the consideration of the castes of persons to be borne in mind for determining what are socially and educationally backward classes. It is true that clause (4) of Article 15 contains a non-obstinate clause with the result that power conferred by that clause can be exercised despite the provision of clause (1) of Article 15 and clause (2) of Article 29. But that does not justify the inference that castes have any relevance in determining what are socially and educationally backward communities. That the Constitution has used in clause (4) the expression "classes" and not "castes".

The Supreme Court dismissed the appeal. The judgment asserted that caste was only a relevant circumstance and it could not be a dominant test in ascertaining the backwardness of a class of citizens. Backwardness could be ascertained without reference to caste. If the government does not take caste into consideration, its order will not be bad.[26]

In fact, the judgment of the Honourable Supreme Court on almost all points, in this case, is quite satisfactory. The court's observation that provisions of Article 166 of the Constitution are only directory and not mandatory is very clear from the reading of the said Article. Since the government issued the impugned order to the effect mentioned therein, it does not contravene the requirements of Article 166. Secondly, the mere fact that selection by viva voce could be abused, does not directly violate Article 14. It could be violative of that provision only when it is shown, in a particular case, that the method was actually misused by the authorities. Again, the Court's observation that classification of backwardness on the basis of economic conditions and occupation is not bad and does not offend Article 15(4), is well-founded. The caste of a group may be relevant circumstance in ascertaining backwardness but cannot be the sole criterion.

In *S. Periakaruppan v. State of Tamil Nadu*[27] the petitioners before court appear to have had brilliant academic careers. The petitioner in petition 285 of 1970 came out within first three ranks in the 10th and 11th standards and in the final examination he secured 451 marks out of the total of 700, he stood third in his school. He was an NCC cadet and passed creditably the 'A' certificate examination. After having passed his Anglo-Indian High School examination creditably, he joined Madurai College in the Pre-University Course taking Physics, Chemistry and Biology subjects. In that course he secured first class with Grade 'D' plus in Physics and Chemistry and 'A' plus in Biology. He stood fourth in his college. The Grade 'D' plus implies 85 to 99 per cent marks and 'A' plus 65 to 75 per cent marks.

The petitioners before the court challenged the validity of the selections made on various grounds. They contended that the unitwise selection contravenes Articles 14 and 15 of the Constitution in as much as the same places the applicants of some of the units in a better position than those who applied to other units. It was alleged that the ratio between applicants and number of seats in the Coimbatore unit was 1:13; in Tirunelveli 1:10; in Thanjavur 1:6 and in Madurai 1:7 ½. It was further alleged that several applicants who secured lesser marks than the petitioners were selected merely because their application came to be considered in other units. It was also alleged that this unitwise scheme was merely intended as a device to get over the decision of this court in Rajendran's case.[28] It was next contended on behalf of the petitioners that the interview held was a farce. Each applicant was interviewed hardly for three minutes. During that interview irrelevant questions were asked. The interview marks were manipulated so as to pull up undeserving applicants and downgrade those who had scored excellent marks in their pre-University examination. It was said that a perusal of the marks list would show that the whole selection was a manipulation. The applicants who had failed more than once and ultimately secured bare second class were selected while applicants who had secured first class with high marks were rejected. It was urged on their behalf that even the students who got the minimum marks could be pulled up by the selection committee by plumping 70 or more out of 75 interview marks, whereas the students who had secured 170 marks the highest marks that could have been secured under the admission rules in pre-university examinations could be pulled down by giving them less than 10 marks out of 75. The petitioners' complaint is that after the interview the selection committee carried the marks given by them to Madras and there the government manipulated the marks in such a way as to select their favourites and reject those in whom the government is not interested.

In Rajendran's case[29] it was held that the classification of backward classes on the basis of castes is within the purview of Article 15(4) if those castes are shown to be socially and educationally backward. The court further observed that there is no gainsaying the fact that there are numerous castes in this country, which are socially and educationally backward and to ignore their existence is to ignore the facts of life. Hence, it is not possible to uphold the contention that the impugned reservation is not in accordance with Article 15(4). But all the same the government should not proceed on the basis that once a class is considered as a backward class it should continue to be so for all times. Such an approach would defeat the very purpose of the reservation because once a class reaches a stage of progress, which some modern writers call as take off stage, then competition is necessary for their future progress. The Government should always keep under review the question of reservation of seats and only the classes which are really socially and educationally backward should be allowed to have the benefit of reservation. Reservation of seats should not be allowed to become a vested interest. The fact that candidates of backward classes have secured about 50 per cent of the seats in the general pool does not show that the time has come for a *de novo* comprehensive examination of the question. It must be remembered that the governments' decision in this regard is open to judicial review.[30] The state of Tamil Nadu shall immediately constitute a separate expert committee consisting of eminent medical practitioners (excluding all those who were members of the previous committees) for selection to the 24 unfilled seats. The selection shall be made on state-wise basis. The committee shall interview only those candidates who are on the waiting list, the persons who unsuccessfully moved the High Court of Madras and the two petitioners before this court. They shall allot separate marks under the five heads mentioned in the rule. The committee shall take into consideration only matters laid down in the rule, exclude from consideration all irrelevant matters and thereafter prepare a gradation list to fill up the 24 seats mentioned earlier. It is ordered accordingly. Again, in *Pradeep Jain etc. v. Union of India and Other,*[31] a group of writ petitions, the question that whether consistently with the constitutional values admissions to a medical college or any other institution of higher learning situated in a state can be confined to those who have domiciled within the state or who are resident within the state for a specified number of years or can any reservation in admissions be made for them so as to give them precedence over those who do not possess "domicile" or residential qualification within the state, irrespective of merit. This question has assumed considerable significance in the present-day context, because we find that today the integrity of the nation is threatened by the divisive forces of regionalism, linguism, communalism and regional linguistic.

In the view of the court that so far as admissions to post-graduate courses, such as M.S., M.D. and the like are concerned, it would be eminently desirable not to provide for any reservation based on residence requirement within the state or on institutional preference. But having regard to broader considerations of equality of opportunity and institutional continuity in education, which has its own importance and value, the court directed that though residence requirement within the state shall not be a ground for reservation in admissions to post-graduate courses, a certain percentage of seats may, in the present circumstances, be reserved on the basis of institutional preference in the sense that a student who has passed MBBS course from a medical college or university, may be given preference for admission to the post-graduate course in the same medical college, or university, but such reservation on the basis of institutional preference should not in any event exceed 50 per cent of the total number of open seats available for admission to the post-graduate course.

In *R. Uma Devi v. The Principal, Kurnool Medical College, Kurnool and Others*,[32] where the petitioner who was born in forward community was admitted to MBBS course under the open category, her marriage subsequently with a person belonging to backward community would change her social status and her admission to post-graduate course under reserved quota would not be cancelled on the ground that she belonged to open category specially when there were no allegation that her marriage was a mock marriage. The petitioner, though a Vysya by birth, was admitted to MBBS course under open category when she was not married, but her marriage to a person belonging to Besta (Fisermen) community which is a backward class 'A' category has sought for admission into post-graduate medical course (DGH) mentioning her social status as backward class 'A' category as that of her husband and the same was granted and she had also paid the necessary fee in that regard. The petitioner had secured 153 marks and was assigned 67th rank. She did not conceal facts and has stated that she is a backward class and after admission by the proceeding dated July 7, 1992 she was issued a notice proposing to cancel her selection on the ground that she belonged to open category on the basis of her father's caste and did not belong to backward class 'A' category, even though her husband was from backward class 'A' category. Hindu marriage is not an agreement. It is a '*sanaskara*' and is a sacrament and, therefore, after marriage, the wife passes into the dominion of her husband. She goes and stays with her husband and he becomes her custodian. After her marriage, she no longer a member of her parents' family and becomes part and parcel of her husband's family. Husband's entitlement requiring his wife to live in his house from the moment of the marriage is well recognised under the Hindu

Law. A wife cannot refuse this obligation. This wife, a Binnagotri at the time of marriage, enters into her husband's 'gotra' on her marriage and becomes a 'sagori' of her husband, as she is treated as part of her husband's family. The Supreme Court rejected the stand taken by the respondents herein and accepted the contention of the petitioner that after marriage she comes within the fold of her husband.

In *K. Duraisamy and Another v. State of Tamil Nadu and Others,*[33] an appeal was filed against the decision of the Full Bench of the Madras High Court in *R. Murali v. R. Kamalakkannan*[34] dated 1 October 1999 in writ Appeal No. 929/99. The Health and Family Welfare Department of the Tamil Nadu government, issued an order No. 55 dated 9 February 1999 laying down the procedure for selection of candidates for admission to post-graduate diploma, degree, higher specialty courses for the academic session 1999–2000. The government order envisaged reservation upto 50 per cent in favour of in-service candidates on merit basis and further stipulated that 50 per cent of the seats available in each of the specialty shall be allotted executively to service candidates. According to the applicant, they were not selected due to a particular understanding of the orders of the government and stipulations contained in the prospectus relating to earmarking or allocation of seats for in-service candidates and non-service candidates in a manner by which the claims of in-service candidates based on merit on the basis of marks came to be ignored in respect of 50 per cent of the seats allocated as "open quota" by confining them exclusively to non-service candidates and considering claims of in-service candidates like the appellants only in respect of 50 per cent allocated to and reserved for service candidates.[35]

As the number of candidates seeking admission to colleges far exceeds the number of seats available, the validity of orders passed by government reserving seats for scheduled castes, scheduled tribes and backward classes in engineering, medical and other colleges providing technical education has been considered in a number of cases after clause (4) had been inserted in Article 15. The Supreme Court considered Article 15(4) in *M.R. Balaji v. Mysore,*[36] *Heggade Janardhan Subbarye v. Mysore*[37] and *R. Chitralekha v. Mysore,*[38] which must be read together as the second case "clarified" the first and the third "explained" a part of it. In Balaji's case the order of the Mysore government reserving seats was the fifth order impugned in court. The questions that were raised were of extreme importance, for it involved the interpretation of Article 15(1), Article 29(2) and Article 46. It was not, however, disputed that these Articles justified a reservation of seats for the scheduled castes and scheduled tribes and for backward classes, the dispute was about the extent of such special provision, and the criterion for identifying these classes. The impugned order was based on the report of the Nagan Gowda Committee, and the judgment in Balaji's case considered that report, and other reports, dealing with backward classes and the reservation to be made for them in educational institutions. However, the court first dealt with certain preliminary contentions and rejected them.[39]

Appointments

In *The General Manager, Southern Railway v. Rangachari*[40] a writ petition filed by the respondent K. Rangachari in the Madras High Court under Article 226 of the Constitution a *writ of Madamus* was issued restraining the appellants, the General Manager, Southern Railways, and the Personnel Officer (Reservation), Southern Railway, from giving effect to the directions of the Railway Board ordering reservation of selection posts in Class III of the railway service in favour of the members of the scheduled castes and scheduled tribes and in particular the reservation of selection posts among the Court Inspectors in Class III which is held by the respondent. After the writ was thus issued the appellant applied for and obtained a certificate from the said High Court under Article 132(1) of the Constitution as it involved a substantial question of law, namely, the scope of Article 16(4) of the Constitution.

The respondent was initially recruited to the grade of Rs 200–300 and was confirmed in that grade on November 21, 1956. He was promoted to officiate in the grade of Rs 260–350. He got a chance of another similar promotion to officiate on April 8, 1959. These promotions were purely ad-hoc and temporary. Later, on June 16, 1959, he was interviewed by the selection committee and his promotion to the said higher grade was regularised and an order was passed in that behalf on June 30, 1959. By this order he was allowed to continue to officiate in the said grade. Since then, he has been officiating in that grade. On April 27, 1959, and on June 12, 1959, the impugned circulars were issued by the Railway Board and addressed to the General Managers. As a result of the said circulars the selection committee decided to consider the case of Hiriyanna for promotion to the grade of Rs 260–350.

According to the respondent the two directives issued by the appellants under the two impugned circulars were *ultra vires*, illegal, inoperative and unconstitutional in that they were not justified by Article 16(4). He alleged that a reading of Articles 16, 335, 338 and 339 would show that the Constitution draws a clear distinction between scheduled castes or tribes on the one hand and backward classes on the other and so it was urged by him that the impugned circulars were illegal. The petitioner further urged that the safeguards provided by Article 16(4) applied only to reservation of posts at the stage of appointment and not for reservation of posts for promotion after appointment and so the circulars were outside the provisions of Article 16(4) and as such contravened Article 16(1). The petition expressed the apprehension that if the circulars are implemented the respondent would be reverted and that would cause great loss both financially and in status to him. It is on these grounds that the respondent prayed for the issue of a *writ of Madamus* directing the appellants to forbear from implementing the two impugned circulars.

The first question to be considered is whether Article 16(1) and (2) refer to promotion or whether they are confined to the initial appointment to any post in civil service. The appellants and the respondent both conceded that cases of promotion fell within Articles 16(1) and (2) though they differed as to whether they were included in Article 16(4). It would be immediately noticed that the respondent's petition postulates the inclusion of promotion in Articles 16(1) and (2) for it is on that assumption that he challenges the validity of the impugned circulars.

According to Justice Gajendragadkar it is true that in providing for the reservation under Article 16(4) the state has to take into consideration the claims of the members of the backward classes consistently with the maintenance of the efficiency of administration. It must not be forgotten that the efficiency of administration is of such paramount importance that it would be unwise and impermissible to make any reservation at the cost of efficiency of administration. Reservation of appointments or posts may theoretically and conceivably mean some impairment of efficiency; but the risk involved in sacrificing efficiency of administration must always be borne in mind when any state sets about making a provision for reservation of appointment or posts. It is also true that the reservation which can be made under Article 16(4) is intended merely to give adequate representation to backward communities. It cannot be used for creating monopolies or for unduly or illegitimately disturbing the legitimate interests of other employees. In exercising the powers under Article 16(4) the problem of adequate representation of the backward class of citizens must be fairly and objectively considered and an attempt must always be made to strike a reasonable balance between the claims of backward classes and the claims of other employees as well as the important consideration of the efficiency of administration; but, in the present case, as we have already seen, the challenge to the validity of the impugned circulars is based on the assumption that the said circulars are outside Article 16(4) because the posts referred to in the said Article are posts outside the cadre of services and, in any case, do not include selection posts. Since, in our opinion, this assumption is not well-founded we must hold that the impugned circulars are not unconstitutional. The decision of the High Court under appeal is reversed and the respondent's application for a writ is dismissed.[41]

The High Court of Madras rightly held that the word "backward classes" in Article 16(4) included members of scheduled castes and scheduled tribes but the word "appointments" did not denote promotion and the word "posts" meant posts outside the civil services and thus the impugned circulars of the Railways were not covered by Article 16(4) and were *ultra vires*. It is, indeed, important to note here that the special provisions made in matters of public employment for the "backward classes" in Article 16(4) must be interpreted in the light of Article 16(1) of the Constitution. Any interpretation made in isolation could defeat the very object of this provision.

It is correct that constitutional provisions must not be interpreted in a narrow or pedantic manner (as observed by honourable Justice Gajendragadkar in this case). Yet it is also very important that one must not forget the dangers involved in highly liberal interpretation because that can defeat the very purpose of the Constitution in relation to a specific aspect. Reservation benefits must, therefore, be extended only at the initial stage (at the time of appointment) and thereafter it should be left to the merit of the persons concerned at the stage of promotions. Reservation after reservation would adversely effect the meritorious members and hence could be harmful for the nation as a whole in the long run.

On the basis of above-mentioned points, it is submitted that the observations of Justice Wanchoo and Justice Ayyangar are far more satisfactory than the other judges involved in this case. Moreover, it is the stand of the Honourable High Court and the minority opinion in the Supreme Court which was approved by an eleven-judge bench of the Supreme Court in *Indira Swahany v. Union of India* case around 30 years after this judgment.

In *Triloki Nath Tiku and Another v. State of Jammu and Kashmir and Other*,[42] the injunction to the secretaries to select candidates "keeping in view the policy of adequate representation of such elements as were not adequately represented in the services", is not a provision making reservation of appointments or posts in favour of backward classes. Selections made in pursuance of such order could not be deemed to have been made on the basis of backwardness of the classes to which they belonged. The policy of the state of Jammu and Kashmir whereby 50 per cent of vacancies were reserved for the Muslims of Kashmir for the entire state, 40 per cent were reserved for the Jammu Hindus and 10 per cent were reserved for the Kashmiri Hindus, is a policy not of reservation of some appointments or posts, it is a scheme of distribution of all the posts community-wise. Distribution of appointments, posts or promotions made in implementation of that state policy is contrary to the constitutional guarantee under Articles 16(1) and (2) and is not saved by clause (4) and the promotions granted in accordance with this policy are contrary to the provisions of Articles 16(1) and (4) of the Constitution and therefore void. This will not, however, prevent the state from devising a scheme consistent with the constitutional guarantee for reservation of appointments, posts or promotions in favour of any backward class of citizens which in the opinion of the state is not adequately represented in the services under the state.

The petitioners claimed that they had been discriminated against in the matter of promotion to the gazetted cadre, solely on the grounds of religion and place of residence. The case that junior officers were promoted to the gazetted cadre over officers senior to them on the sole ground that they belonged to the Muslim community or that they were Hindus belonging to the Jammu province of the sate of Jammu and Kashmir. But the prejudicial treatment of senior officers was sought to be supported on the plea that the state had acted in consonance with the principles of clause (4) of Article 16 of the Constitution. It was the case of the state that Muslims as a community in the whole of the state of Jammu and Kashmir formed a backward class of citizens and they were not adequately represented in the services under the state, so are the Hindus from the province of Jammu and on that clause (4) of Article 16 undoubtedly empowers the state to make reservations in favour of any backward class of citizens so as to provide them adequate representation in the services under the state. The provision making such reservation need not be by a statutory enactment, it may be made by an executive order or direction. But there is not even a formal executive order expressly dealing with reservation of posts and appointment in the Education Department. On behalf of the state, it is claimed that as a matter of state policy, in making appointments and promotions, reservations in fact have been made by the state as alleged by the petitioners with some variations as to the percentage reserved for the Hindus from the province of Jammu.

But for the purpose of Article 16(4) in determining whether a section forms a class, a test solely based on caste, community, race, religion, sex, descent, place of birth or residence cannot be adopted, because it would directly offend the Constitution. The promotions granted to respondents are accordingly declared contrary to the provisions of Articles 16(1) and (4) of the Constitution and therefore void. This will not, however, prevent the state from devising a scheme, consistent with the constitutional guarantees, for reservation of appointments, posts or promotions in favour of any backward class of citizens which in the opinion of the state is not adequately represented in the services under the state.[43]

The Supreme Court rejected the argument of the government that under Article 16(4) "backward classes" are those not adequately represented in public services. If that stand was accepted, however advanced a class may be educationally and socially, if it was not represented adequately in the services it was a backward class. This theory would exclude the really backward classes from the benefit of reservation. Therefore, the court asserted two conditions for valid reservation: (1) the class of citizens must be socially and educationally backward, and (2) it should be inadequately represented in the services.[44]

But some important questions left unanswered by the Apex Court in this case are that if a considerable section of a particular community is socially and educationally backward, would reservation for members of such a community or a part of it not be constitutionally required within the meaning of Article16? Would a denial of reservation benefits to the members of such a community on the basis of their religion not frustrate the purpose of Article16? It seems that the court, in this case, has laid a lot of emphasis upon the 'religion' of the backward class and not their backwardness which is the main criterion for deciding whether a group of persons deserves reservation under Article16 or not? However, a noticeable point in this case was that there was no executive order expressly dealing with reservation of posts and appointments in the Education Department. The absence of either a statutory enactment or a formal executive order by the state is a serious omission on the part of state government which provided sufficient space for striking down the order of state government.

In *State of Kerala and Another v. N.M. Thomas and Others*,[45] the respondent alleged in the writ petition that 12 lower division clerks who were members of scheduled castes and scheduled tribes were promoted without test qualification. The further allegation is that by an order dated 15 June, 1972, 19 lower division clerks belonging to scheduled castes and tribes were promoted as upper division clerks, of which five were unqualified scheduled caste and scheduled tribe members and 14 were qualified scheduled castes and scheduled tribes members. By order dated 19 September, 1972, another eight promotions of members of scheduled castes and tribes were ordered of which only two were qualified and the remaining six were unqualified. By another order dater 31 October, 1972, 7 scheduled castes and scheduled tribes members were promoted without qualifying test and one was promoted with the qualifying test. The grievance of the respondent-petitioner before the High Court was that out of 51 vacancies which arose in the category of upper division clerks in the year 1972, 34 were filled up by scheduled caste members who did not possess qualifications and only 17 were given to qualified persons.

The respondent is a lower division clerk working in the registration department. For promotion to upper division in that department on the basis of seniority, the lower division clerks have to pass (1) account test (lower), (2) Kerala registration test, and (3) test in the manual of office procedure. The respondent's grievance is that in view of certain concessions given to members of scheduled castes and scheduled tribes, they were able to obtain promotions earlier than the respondent, though the members of the scheduled caste and scheduled tribe, who were promoted, had not passed the tests. The important question before the apex court was whether it was permissible to give preferential treatment to scheduled castes and scheduled tribes under clause (1) of Article 16, that is, outside the exception clause (4) of Article 16?

The judgment in the light of relevant Kerala Services Rules as well as the analysis of clauses (1) and (4) of Article 16 of the Constitution seems to be extremely convincing. It rightly held that the interpretation of constitutional provisions should not be interpreted in any narrow or pedantic manner as that would defeat the constitutional purpose. That there can be reasonable classification of the employees in matters relating to employment or appointment under Article 16 of the Constitution. Article 16(1) does not prohibit the prescription of reasonable rules for selection to any employment or appointment to any office. The court rightly observed that the purpose enshrined in Article 16(4) cannot be fulfilled if it is not given effect to at the stage of promotions because denying the same would mean bringing a disadvantaged person or section only one step forward and then denying any other step ahead, frustrating the whole purpose of socio-economic upliftment. Again, it stated that the classification of employees belonging to scheduled castes and scheduled tribes for allowing them an extended period of two years for passing the special tests for promotion is a just and reasonable classification having rational nexus to the object of providing equal opportunity for all citizens in matters relating to employment or appointment to public office. Granting temporary exemption from special tests to the personnel belonging to scheduled castes and scheduled tribes by executive does not result in any discrimination in matters of public employment. It is so because the court held that they are only given extended period for qualifying the concerned tests for promotion and not absolute exemption from the same. Once it does not provide an absolute exemption to members of scheduled castes and scheduled tribes, it is no violation of Article 16 (1) of the Constitution rather it intends to serve the purpose of special protection accorded by the Constitution to certain disadvantaged sections of our society.

Moreover, once it is clear from the service rules under consideration that the members of the scheduled caste and scheduled tribe community getting benefit of temporary extension are bound to qualify the necessary tests otherwise they would revert to their original position (prior to promotion), it does not impair the test of efficiency as ingrained in the service rules, etc. So it is differential treatment for the purpose of giving them equality consistent with efficiency.

As far the minority opinion delivered by Justice H.R. Khanna is concerned, it is no less convincing than the majority opinion discussed above. The learned judge in his minority opinion has made a critical analysis of Kerala Service Rules and the constitutional provisions in relation to equality and protective discrimination in favour of scheduled castes, scheduled tribes and other backward classes in the light of Article 16 as a whole. The only point which makes it a bit less convincing than the majority opinion is that it is more positivistic in nature which does not completely fit into the constitutional rules of interpretation.

This court in the *State of Gujarat v. Shri Ambica Mills Ltd., Ahmedabad*[46] decided that the "equal protection of the laws is a pledge of the protection of equal laws. But laws may classify. And the very idea of classification is that of inequality. In tackling this paradox, the court has neither abandoned the demand for equality nor denied the legislative right to classify. It has taken a middle course. It has resolved the contradictory demands of legislative specialization and constitutional generality by a doctrine of reasonable classification. In this case, the respondent contended that apart from Article 16(4) members of scheduled castes and scheduled tribes were not entitled to any favoured treatment in regard to promotion. In *T. Devadasan v. Union of India*[47] reservation was made for backward classes. The number of reserved seats which were not filled were carried forward to the subsequent year. On the basis of "carry forward" principle, it was found that such reserved seats might destroy equality. The "carry forward" principle was not sustained in Devadasan's case. The same view was taken in the case of *M.R. Balaji v. State of Mysore.*[48] It was said that not more than 50 per cent should be reserved for backward classes. This ensures equality. Reservation is not a constitutional compulsion but is discretionary according to the ruling of the court in Rajendran's case[49].

The Constitution makes a classification of scheduled castes and scheduled tribes in numerous provisions and gives a mandate to the state to accord special or favoured treatment to them. Article 46 mandates the state to promote with special care educational and economic interests of the scheduled castes and scheduled tribes and to protect them from any social injustice and exploitation. The court declared that Rule 13–AA[50] of the rules is a valid piece of statutory provision, which is fully justified under Article 16(1) of the Constitution of India and does not fall within the purview of Article 16(4). The court allowed the appeal, set aside the judgment of the Kerala High Court and directed that the *status quo ante* be restored.[51]

In *Dr Chakradhar Paswan v. State of Bihar and Others*,[52] the appeal by special leave against the judgment and order of the Patna High Court dated 16th May, 1980, allowing the writ petition filed by respondent Dr Kameshwar Prasad and quashing the impugned advertisement No. 121, 1978, issued by the Bihar Public Service Commission inviting applications for the post of Deputy Director (Homeopathic) in the Directorate of Indigenous Medicines, Health Department, State of Bihar from scheduled caste candidates, and the consequent order of the state government dated 30th May, 1979, for the appointment of the appellant Dr Chakradhar Paswan to that post.

A few essential facts would elucidate the nature of the controversy. Prior to 1974 the Directorate of Indigenous Systems of Medicines was a part of the Health Department. On 14th March, 1974, the state government appointed Dr Nagesh Dwivedi, Manager, State Ayurvedic and Unani Medical Pharmacy, Bihar, on an ad-hoc basis to the post of Director (indigenous medicines). He assumed charge on the next day and was confirmed in that post on 11th December, 1976. The state government on 6th May, 1978, directed the creation of a separate Directorate of Indigenous Medicines, the Director being from one of the systems of medicines consisting of Ayurvedic, Unani and Homeopathy. At the time of creation of the separate directorate, the government sanctioned the posts of Deputy Directors for the other two systems of medicine. The state government had, in the mean while, on the basis of the decision of this court in *M.R. Balaji v. State of Mysore*[53], by its circular dated 8th November, 1975, prescribed a 50-point roster to implement the policy of reservation to posts and appointment for members of the backward classes under Article 16(4).

Justice Lalit Mohan Sharma, speaking for a Division Bench, held that (1) reservation to the only post of Deputy Director (Homeopathic) for members belonging to the scheduled castes is tantamount to 100 per cent reservation; (2) the two posts of Deputy Director (Homeopathic) and Deputy Director (Ayurvedic) cannot be linked together for purposes of reservation of posts; and (3) the order reserving the post of Deputy Director (Homeopathic) infringes the principles embodied in the 50-point roster according to which if, in a particular cadre, a single post falls vacant, it should, in the case of first vacancy, be considered as general and on the second occasion when a single post again falls vacant, the same must be treated as reserved. The learned judge also said that if it has been laid down that if in a particular cadre there is only one post, then in case when it is being filled up for the second time it will be considered reserved, that is, on the first occasion it must be treated as a general seat. In substance, the High Court was of the view that the posts of Director and three Deputy Directors could not be clubbed together for reservation of posts and appointments. Now, could the posts of Deputy Directors of Homeopathic, Ayurvedic and Unani, which form distinct and separate systems of medicines be grouped for purposes of reservation. And, the court upheld the judgment of the High Court quashing the impugned advertisement issued by the Bihar Public Service Commission as also the appointment of the appellant to the post of Deputy Director (Homeopathic). They directed the Public Service Commission to take steps to re-advertise the post. However, having regard to the fact that the appellant has continued to hold that post since 30th May, 1979, and confirmed against that post, the state government was directed to adjust him in an equivalent post in the Health Department.[54]

The Honourable Supreme Court, consisting of Justice A.P. Sen and Justice B.C. Ray, held that no reservation could be made under Article 16(4) so as to create monopoly. If that sort of policy is allowed, it would render the guarantee of equal opportunity, contained in Articles 16(1) and 16(2), wholly meaningless and illusory. Therefore, the reservation of the post of Deputy Director (Homeopathic) would amount to 100 per cent reservation which was impermissible under Article 16(4) as otherwise it would render the guarantee under Article 16(1) wholly elusive and meaningless. If there is only one post in the cadre, there can be no reservation under Article 16(4) of the Constitution. The whole concept of reservation for application of the 50-point roster is that there are more than one posts, and the reservation, as laid down by this court, can be upto 50 per cent only.

In *Union of India and Other v. Rajiv Yadav and Others,*[55] the central government is the authority under the Indian Administrative Service (Cadre Rules), 1954, to allocate the members of the Indian Administrative Service (IAS) directly recruited to various state cadres/joint cadres under the said rules. The central government has laid down the broad principles of allocation called "the Roster System". The said system was earlier operating from 1966 to 1977. Thereafter till 1984 the allocations were done in accordance with the procedure called "the Limited Zonal Preferences System". Since the 1985 batch onwards, the Central Government has reverted back to the "Roster System" with some modifications. Reservation to the extent of 15 per cent and 7½ per cent for the scheduled castes and scheduled tribes respectively has been provided in direct recruitment to the IAS. The "Roster System" provides that while allocating the scheduled castes and scheduled tribes candidates to their home state (insiders), vacancies shall be reserved for them in various cadres to the extent reservation percentage has been provided in direct recruitment to the IAS.

Rajiv Yadav appeared in the Civil Services Examination held in 1988. He belonged to the Union Territory of Delhi, and had opted for the "Union Territories" cadre. He was selected for appointment to the IAS and in order of merit he was placed at serial number 16. By order dated September 28, 1989, he was allocated to the Manipur and Tripura cadre. His representation for change of cadre from Manipur-Tripura to "Union Territories" having been rejected by the Central Government, he challenged the order allocating him the Manipur-Tripura cadre before the tribunal. The vacancies in every cadre will be earmarked for 'outsiders' and 'insiders' in the ratio of 2:1. In order to avoid problems relating to fractions and to ensure that this ratio is maintained over a period of time, if not during every allocation, the break-up of vacancies in a cadre between 'outsiders' and 'insiders' will be calculated following the cycle of 'outsider', 'insider', 'outsider'.

In the case of candidates belonging to the reserved category, such of those candidates whose position in the merit list is such that they could have been appointed to the service even in the absence of any reservation will be treated at par with general candidates for purposes of allotment though they will be counted against reserved vacancies. In respect of other candidates belonging to the reserved category, a procedure similar to the one adopted for general candidates would be adopted. In other words, a separate chart should be prepared with similar grouping of states and similar operational details should be followed. If there is a shortfall in general 'insiders' quota it could, however, be made up by 'insider' reserved candidates.[56]

The judgment in this case was delivered by a three-judge bench of the Supreme Court consisting of Justice Kuldip Singh, M.M. Punchhi and K. Ramaswamy. It was held by the honourable court that when a person is appointed to an All India Service, having various state cadres, he has no right to claim allocation to a state of his choice or to his home state. The central government is under no legal duty to have options or even preference from the officer concerned. Rule 5 of the cadre rules makes the central government the sole authority to allocate the members of service to various cadres. It is not obligatory for central government to frame rules and regulations or otherwise notify the principles of allocation adopted by the government as a policy.

The court further observed that a selected candidate has a right to be considered for appointment to the IAS but he has no such right to be allocated to a cadre of his choice or his home state. Allotment of cadre is an incidence of service. Moreover, the court refused to accept the contention that the principles adopted in case of allotment of cadre of government letter of

1985 should be tested upon Article 16(4) of the Constitution. It observed that since such rules don't provide reservation of appointments or posts, there is no question of testing such rules on the basis of Article 16 of the Constitution.

The judgment of the Honourable Supreme Court in this case is very satisfactory because although apparently facts of the case do indicate that unnecessary advantage is given to scheduled castes and scheduled tribes candidates in allocation of cadre by the central government. But an in-depth analysis of things in the light of "Roster System", as followed by the government for allotting cadres to different candidates as well as the clauses of 1985 government letter show that no discrimination results against other candidates by adopting the said criteria. In fact, the distribution of reserved vacancies in each cadre between 'outsiders', and 'insiders' was done in the ratio 2:1. This ratio was operationalised by following a cycle 'outsider', 'insider', 'outsider', as is done in the case of general candidates. Hence, the method does not result in unrequired discrimination.

In *Jatinder Pal Singh and Others v. State of Punjab*,[57] the appeals were filed by Gurbachan Kaur and six others (Head Mistresses), all belonging to the reserved category, praying for writ of certiorari to quash the promotion order dated 3 July 1997 and for a mandamus seeking promotion of the said writ petitioners as principals, and Charan Singh and nine others (Head Masters) all belonging to the reserved category for similar relief and also for promoting the writ petitioners in the place of the opposite party. The array of the parties shows that the writ petitioners (Head Masters/Head Mistresses) (reserved category) were all working as Head Masters in 1997 while the non-official respondents (general candidates) were working as Senior Lecturer/Principal or as Deputy District Education Officers.

So far as this department is concerned the relevant rules are as follows. Under Rule 10 of the Class II Rules, the posts of Principal, Deputy District Education Officers, Senior Lecturers, etc., are to be filled up by promotion in respect of 75 per cent and 25 per cent by direct recruitment under Class II Rules, 1976 sub-clause (3) of Rule 10 states that all appointments to the posts shall be made on the basis of seniority-cum-merit and no members of the service shall have any right for promotion merely on the basis of seniority.

We are acceding to this request made on behalf of the Railways as a special case but subject to a reservation, which was accepted by learned senior counsel. We agree that there is no need to revert those reserved category officers, if they were promoted even beyond 1 March 1996 but before 1 April 1994. But their promotions shall have to be deemed ad-hoc as they were otherwise irregular and further their seniority in the promoted category shall, however, have to be determined by following *Virpal*[58] and *Ajit Singh*[59] as if they were not promoted. To give an example: in the case of roster points at two levels, i.e., from level 1 to level 2 and level 2 to level 3, if the reserved candidate was promoted before 1 April 1997 to level 4, such reserved candidate need not be reverted. If by the date of promotion of the reserved candidate from level 3 to level 4 before 1 April 1997, the senior general candidate at level 2 had reached level 3, he has to be considered as senior at level 3 to the reserved candidate because the latter was still at level 3 on that date. But if such a general candidate's seniority was ignored and the reserved candidate was treated as senior at level 3 and promoted to level 4, this has to be rectified after 1 March 1996 by following Virpal's, Ajit Singh's No. I as explained in Ajit Singh No. II.[60] In other words, if a reserved candidate was promoted to level 4 before 1 April 1997, without considering the case of the senior general candidate who had reached level 3 before such promotion then the reserved candidate need not be reverted, but the said promotion to level 4 is to be reviewed and seniority at level 3 has to be refixed and on that basis promotion/seniority at level 4 (as and when the general candidate is promoted to level 4) is again to be refixed. The seniority of the reserved candidate at level 4 will be refixed on the basis of when his turn would have come for promotion to level 4, if the date of the senior general candidate was considered at level 3 in due time.[61]

The Supreme Court, while considering the Punjab Education Service (School and Inspection Cadre) (Class II) Rules, 1976, in general and Rule 10(3) in particular, held that appointment by seniority-cum-merit rule is interlinked with the promotional rule based on equal opportunity and can't be delinked otherwise that could result in violation of Article 16 of the Constitution. The court observed that candidates from the reserved category who got promoted to feeder post of head master on the basis of roaster points cannot be promoted as Principal in place of general category candidates. This is, indeed, a timely judgment because it puts reasonable limits on undue advantage taken by candidates of reserved category at the promotional level, causing hardship to candidates belonging to general category. It is high time that the highest court of the land should place necessary limitations on the reservation issue so that its politicisation may be controlled.

In *P.A. Haridasan v. State of Kerala,*[62] the economic criterion is not the guiding principle to deny a person the benefit of scheduled caste if he actually belongs to that caste. The question of caste depends upon the caste in which the person is born. Unless there is evidence to show that a person has given up the membership of a caste and has joined the other caste, he should be deemed to be in the caste in which he is born. The crucial point is to ascertain the caste at the time of birth. Thus, the case of the petitioner was that he belonged to Thandan community, i.e., a scheduled caste community in Travancore-Cochin area but evidence showed that his family was an affluent family and the documents produced by the petitioner adored that his ancestors were Thandans and the scrutiny committee ignored documents which proved the petitioner's ancestors and petitioner as belonging to Thandan community on irrelevant grounds and it was made on the ground that petitioner's family had social status that the entries in the documents were not taken into account and there was no case for the committee that these documents were not genuine, denial of benefit of caste to petitioner in service would be improper.

P.A. Haridasan is member of the Subordinate Judicial Service of the Kerala state. He entered into the judicial service as judicial magistrate of second class and now he is working as first class judicial magistrate. The controversy in this case is regarding the caste to which the petitioner belongs. While the petitioner claims that he belongs to the Thandan community, respondents 1 and 2 have the view that he belongs to Thiyya community. The Thandan community was declared to be a scheduled caste so far as the Travancore-Cochin area is concerned from 1950 onwards. The entire controversy arose because petitioner's caste in the High School certificate was originally described as Thiyya but after the coming into force of the Act 108 of 1976, the petitioner got it corrected and changed it to Thandan. It was after this that the petitioner applied for the post of magistrate under the general recruitment as well as the special recruitment for scheduled castes and scheduled tribes. He was appointed in the quota reserved for scheduled castes. Even when he was selected for appointment, there was a controversy as to whether he belonged to scheduled caste or not. At the instance of the Public Service Commission, the government referred the matter to District Collector, Palakkad, and the District Collector called for a report from the Assistant Collector regarding the caste status of the petitioner and the Assistant Collector by his report dated 8 February 1982 came to the conclusion that the petitioner belonged to the community Thandan rather than Ezhava or Thiyya. He also relied on the fact that father and grandfather of the petitioner belonged to Thandan community and that it can be seen from the endorsement made on certain documents which came into existence even prior to the birth of the petitioner. Not satisfied with this report, another report was called for and the Assistant Collector made further enquiries and gave a report dated 6 March 1982. According to this report, the Assistant Collector was fully satisfied that P.A. Haridarsan, the petitioner herein, belongs to Thandan community. The original petition is allowed.[63]

This case was heard and decided by a bench consisting of two judges – Justice A.R. Lakshmanan and S. Sankarasubban. It was held that the question of caste of a person depended upon the caste in which the person is born. Unless there is evidence to show that a person has given up the membership of a caste and has joined any other caste, he should be deemed to be in the caste in which he was born. The crucial point is to ascertain the caste at the time of birth. Thus, where the case of the petitioner was that he belonged to Thandan community, i.e., a scheduled caste community in Travancore-Cochin area, but evidence showed that his family was affluent and the documents produced by the petitioner showed that his ancestors were Thandans and the Scrutiny Committee ignored documents which proved that petitioner's ancestors and petitioner belonged to Thandan community on irrelevant grounds and it was solely on the ground that petitioner's family and social status that the entries in the document were not taken into account and there was no case for the committee that the documents were not genuine.

The apex court observed that denial of benefit of caste to the petitioner in service on the above stated grounds would be improper. Moreover, the economic criteria is not the guiding principle to deny a person the benefit of scheduled caste if he actually belongs to that caste. Consequently, the order stating that community certificates obtained by the petitioner from Tahsildar was false and was set aside, the community certificates were restored. It was further declared that the petitioner was entitled to all the rights, benefits, exemptions or concessions admissible for scheduled castes. It is pertinent to note that the court's observations in the light of the facts of the case are quite convincing because economic criteria is not at all taken into account when the question of reservation for scheduled castes and scheduled tribes arises. It is the caste that matters the most. The case is different in relation to other backward classes and hence the judgment in this case has rightly clarified many issues in relation to the benefits of reservation for scheduled castes and scheduled tribes.

In *Kuldeep Kumar Gupta and Others v. Himachal Pradesh State Electricity Board and Others,*[64] the feeder cadre of Junior Engineers, having been filled up from two recruitment sources, one by qualified diploma holders by way of direct recruitment and the other by unqualified matriculate ITI certificate holders by promotion, there can be a separate consideration for them in the matter of promotion to the post of Assistant Engineer and such separate consideration does not violate any constitutional mandate. Once a classification is permissible notwithstanding that the feeder category is one, when the said classification is challenged as being discriminatory then unless and until sufficient materials are produced and it is established that it is unjust on the face of it by the persons assailing the classification, the court would be justified in coming to the conclusion that such plea of unlawful discrimination had no basis.

In the instant case, the regulations on being examined from time to time unequivocally show that right from the inception, quota has been provided for promotion in favour of the unqualified promotee Junior Engineer though the quota has been changed from time to time and while providing such quota, the longer experience as Junior Engineer has been the basis for being eligible for promotion, providing such a quota in the service history, right from inception, is also a germane consideration for the court, while considering the question of alleged discrimination. That apart when the feeder category itself is filled up by direct recruit diploma holders and promotee unqualified matriculates and if no quota is provided for such unqualified matriculates in the promotional cadre of Assistant Engineer then they may stagnate at that stage which will not be in the interest of administration. If the rule making authority, on consideration of such stagnation, provides a quota for such unqualified promoteee Junior Engineer, the same cannot be held to be violative of any constitutional mandate, therefore, there can be a separate consideration for the promotee unqualified matriculate Junior Engineers in the matter of promotion to the post of Assistant Engineer and the impugned regulation providing a quota for them cannot be held to be violative of Article 14.

Providing a quota is not new in the service jurisprudence and whenever the feeder category itself consists of different category of persons and when they are considered for any promotion the employer fixes a quota for each category so that the promotional cadre would be equibalanced and at the same time each category of persons in feeder category would get the opportunity of being considered for promotion. This is also, in a sense, in the larger interest of the administration when it is the employer who is best suited to decide the percentage of posts in the promotional cadre, which can be earmarked for different category of persons. In other words, this provision actually effectuates the constitutional mandate engrafted in Article 16(1) as it would after equality of opportunity in the matters relating to employment and it would not be the monopoly of a specified category of persons in the feeder category to get promotions. Therefore there is no infraction of the constitutional provision engrafted in Article 16(4) while providing a quota in promotional cadre, as it does not tantamount to reservation.[65]

In *Indira Sawhney etc. v. Union of India*[66], forty-three years after the founding of the Indian Republic, the Supreme Court was asked to settle the law and reservation for backward classes. The occasion arose when the short-lived V.P. Singh government at the centre decided to implement the Mandal Commission Report. It was followed by riots in most parts of northern India.

Through the Constitution guarantees equality of opportunity in matters of public employment, it also provides for reservation of posts in favour of any backward classes. A commission called the Kaka Kalelkar Commission was set up in 1953 to study the conditions of the socially and educationally backward classes. Its report did not find favour with the then government and it was not discussed in Parliament. The second commission called the Mandal Commission was set up in 1979. The report was submitted in 1980. However, no action was taken by the governments at the Centre till 1991 when V.P. Singh decided to implement the recommendations. It was seen as a political play to defeat his opponents in Parliament. There were howls of protests from the upper castes, and many youths in the northern cities immolated themselves against the government decision. Southern states, where the reservation was a fact of life even before the Constitution, remained comparatively claim. Ultimately, the issue was taken to the Supreme Court through nearly four score petitions. They were decided by a nine-judge bench. The majority view was delivered by Justice Jeevan Riddy.[67]

On August 13, 1990, the Government of India, headed by Prime Minister, V.P. Singh, basing itself on the recommendation of the Mandal Commission, issued an office memorandum purporting to extend reservation for socially and educationally backward classes in its services.

The said memorandum reserved 27 per cent of the seats for Other Backward Classes (OBCs) in addition to those already reserved for scheduled castes and scheduled tribes. Reservation was to apply to direct recruitment. OBCs recruited on merit in open competition were not to be counted in the 27 per cent quota. OBCs were to comprise castes and communities common to the state-wise lists in the Mandal Commission Report and state government lists. Reservation was to extend to public sector undertakings and financial institutions including public sector banks.

The issuance of this memorandum led to widespread protest, self-immolations and damage to private and public property, especially by the youth. Writ petitions were filed in the Supreme Court questioning the said memorandum. A three-judge bench of the Supreme Court comprising Chief Justice Ranganathan Misra, Justice K.N. Singh and Justice M.H.

Kania, reviewing its order of September 11, 1990, refused to interfere on the ground that the matter was a political one. The situation not having improved, a petition on behalf of the Supreme Court Bar Association was moved and a five-judge bench of the Supreme Court stayed by its order of October 1, 1990, the operation of the memorandum of August 13, 1990, till final adjudication. The process of identification of castes for locating the other backward classes was to continue.[68]

The constitutionality of this memorandum was also challenged and a nine-judge bench was constituted to hear the matter arising out of the challenge to memorandum of August 13, 1990, tagged to the new writ petitions. The economic criterion having not been fixed, the bench by its order of December 12, 1991, declined to vacate the earlier stay for implementation of the memorandum. The constitution of the special bench of nine judges became necessary to finally settle the legal position relating to reservations in view of the several earlier judgments to the Supreme Court not having spoken in the same voice. The questions before the nine-judge bench as broadly indicated and discussed in the leading judgment of Justice Jeevan Reddy, alongwith the miscellaneous questions discussed therein, were:

1. (a) Whether clause (4) of Article 16 is an exception to clause (1) of Article 16?
   (b) Whether clause (4) of Article 16 is exhaustive of the special provisions that can be made in favour of 'backward class of citizens'? Whether it is exhaustive of the special provisions that can be made in favour of all sections, classes or groups?
   (c) Whether reservations can be made under clause (1) of Article 16 or whether it permits only extending of preferences/concessions?
2. (a) What does the expression 'backward class of citizens' in Article 16 (4) mean?
   (b) Whether the backwardness in Article 16(4) should be both social and educational?

(c) Whether the 'means-test' can be applied in the course of identification of backward classes? And if the answer is yes, whether providing such a test is obligatory?

3. Whether the backward classes can be identified only exclusively with references to economic criterion?
4. Whether the backward classes can be further categorized into 'backward' and 'more backward' categories?
5. To what extent can the reservation be made?
   (a) Whether the 50 per cent rule enunciated in Balaji case is a binding rule or only a rule of caution or rule of prudence?
   (b) Whether Devadasan (1964 4 SCR 680) was correctly decided?
6. Whether Article 16 permits reservations being provided in the matter of promotions?
7. Whether reservations are anti-meritarian?

   To what extent are Articles 335, 38(2) and 46 of the Constitution relevant in the matter of construing Article 16?
8. The concept of positive action and positive discrimination.

The learned judges summarized the answers to the various questions as follows:

1. (a) Clause (4) of Article 16 is not an exception to clause (1). It is an instance and an illustration of the classification inherent in clause (1).
   (b) Article 16(4) is exhaustive of the subject of reservation in favour of backward class of citizens, as explained in this judgment.
   (c) Reservations can also be provided under clause (1) of Article 16. It is not confined to extending of preferences, concessions of exemptions alone. These reservations, if any, made under clause (1) have to be so adjusted and implemented as not to exceed the level of representation prescribed for 'backward class of citizens' as explained in this judgment.

2. (a) A caste can be and quite often is a social class in India. If it is backward socially, it would be a backward class for the purposes of Article 16(4). Among non-Hindus, there are several occupational groups, sects and denominations which, for historical reasons, are socially backward. They too represent backward social collectivities for the purposes of Article 16(4).
   (b) It is not correct to say that the backward class of citizens contemplated in Article 16(4) is the same as the socially and educationally backward classes referred to in Article 15(4). It is much wider. The accent in Article 16(4) is on social backwardness. Of course, social, educational and economic backwardness are closely intertwined in the Indian context.
   (c) 'Creamy layer' can be, and must be, excluded.
3. A backward class of citizens cannot be identified only and exclusively with reference to economic criterion.
4. There is no constitutional bar to classify the backward classes of citizens into backward and more backward categories.
5. (a) and (b) The reservations contemplated in clause (4) of Article 16 should not exceed 50 per cent. While 50 per cent shall be the rule, it is necessary not to put out of consideration certain extraordinary situations inherent in the great diversity of this country and the people. It might happen that in far-flung and remote areas the population inhabiting those areas might, on account of their being out of the mainstream of national life and in view of the conditions peculiar to and characteristic of them need to be treated in a different way, some relaxation in this strict rule may become imperative. In doing so, extreme caution is to be exercised and a special case made out.
   (c) Devadasan's case was wrongly decided and is accordingly overruled to the extent it is inconsistent with this judgment.

6. Article 16(4) does not permit provision for reservations in the matter of promotion. This rule shall, however, have only prospective operation and shall not affect the promotions already made, whether made on regular basis or on any other basis. We direct that our decision on this question shall operate only prospectively and shall not affect promotions already made, whether on temporary, officiating or regular/permanent basis. It is further directed that wherever reservations are already provided in the matter of promotion, be it central services or state services, or for that mater services under any corporation, authority or body falling under the definition of state in Article 12, such reservation may continue in operation for a period of five years from this day. Within this period, it would be open to the appropriate authorities to revise, modify or reissue the relevant rules to ensure the achievement of the objective or Article 16(4). If any authority thinks that for ensuring adequate representation of backward class of citizens in any service, class or category, it is necessary to provide for direct recruitment therein, it shall be open to it do so. (Justice Ahmadi expresses no opinion on this question upholding the preliminary objection of Union of India). It would not be impermissible for the state to extend concessions and relaxations to members of reserved categories in the matter of promotion without compromising the efficiency of the administration.
7. While the rule of reservation cannot be called anti-meritarian, there are certain services and posts to which it may not be advisable to apply the rule of reservation.
8. The Government of India and the state governments have the power to create a permanent mechanism in the nature of a commission, for examining requests of inclusion and complaints of over-inclusion or non-inclusion in the lists of other backward classes and to advise the government, which advice shall ordinarily be binding upon the

government. Where, however, the government does not accept the advice, it must record its reasons therefore.[69]

The following directions are given to the Government of India, the state governments and the union territories:

(a) The Government of India, each of the state governments and the union territories shall, within four months from today, constitute a permanent body for entertaining, examining and recommending upon requests for inclusion and complaints of over-inclusion and under-inclusion in the lists of other backward classes of citizens. The advice tendered by such a body shall ordinarily be binding upon the government.

(b) Within four months from today the Government of India shall specify the bases, applying the relevant and requisite socio-economic criterion to exclude socially advanced persons/sections (creamy layer) from OBCs. The implementation of the impugned memorandum of August 13, 1990, shall be subject to exclusion of such socially advanced persons (creamy layer).

This direction shall not, however, apply to states where the reservations in favour of backward classes are already in operation. They can continue to operate them. Such states shall, however, evolve the said criteria within six months from today and apply the same to exclude the socially advanced persons/sections from the designated OBCs.

By this judgment, the other backward classes of India achieved their long-cherished dream of reserved posts in the central government services. In March, 1993, R.N. Prasad committee determined the creamy layer or advanced sections of other backward classes and in September, 1993, reservation of 27 per cent posts in central services became operative. Now, it can be said that the judiciary not only created hurdles for their caste-based preferential treatment but also gave directions to the government for its proper implementation. Although most politicians did not accepted the judgments in letter and spirit. It is also evident from the 85th Constitutional

Amendment for permitting Tamil Nadu for continuing its reservation quota of 69 per cent. Similarly, in the case of Karnataka, the President of India hurriedly gave his assent to the Karnataka Reservation Bill which reserved 73 per cent posts and seats for the different backward class groups, and its stayed by the Supreme Court as found against the Mandal case verdict. These political considerations made a mockery of the judgment of the Supreme Court that not more than 50 per cent of the available seats should be reserved. Now, the Reservation Acts of Tamil Nadu and Karnataka are under the litigation in the Supreme Court although they go blanket over of Article 31(B) and have been immunized from attack on the ground of contravention of the fundamental and other rights. The integrated and comprehensive scheme of reservation policy, as evolved by the supreme court, is politicised by the politicians for its political gain.

In the judgment of the Indra Sawhney case, the Supreme Court rightly excluded creamy layer from the list of other backward classes. It also vehemently negated the policy of reservation regarding promotions. But it has not taken note of exclusion of advance backward castes from the beneficiaries of the policy of protective discrimination. It was pointed out in *Periakarappan v. State of Tamil Nadu*[70] (1972) case that a case or class found to be backward should not be regarded as backward for all time. As soon as the group shows progress, for example, by the way of taking good numbers of seats in the merit pool, the classification must be reviewed and the progressive groups be deleted from the backward list. Similarly, there should be a time limit for the reservation policy so that it may not tend to serve vested interests and it should be reviewed after every ten years or so, to enable the central and state governments to rectify any distortion arising out of it. It is said that reservation will continue till the members of the deprived classes attain a state of enlightenment and become equal partners of a new just social order in our national life. Only time will tell how long the doctrine of protective discrimination will continue in India, and what will be the results?[71]

A survey of the above judicial pronouncements makes it clear that reservations should be justifiable, rational and reasonable. Thus, in some special circumstances even 100 per cent reservation may be permitted if it is no danger to the interest of the society in general. For example, in a nursery school, 100 per cent seats may be reserved for female teachers. Similarly, for filling the vacancies to the posts of waterman or gateman in railway or some other department, hundred per cent reservations may be permissible. Even in the posts of lower office the higher percentage of reservation may be justified. Perhaps this was the view of Justice Krishna Iyyer, when in *State of Kerala v. N.M. Thomas*[72] he said of clerks in irrigation department. "After all, he is a pen pushing clerk, not a magistrate accounts officer, forest officer, sub-registrar, space-scientist or top administrator or one on whose initiative the wheels of a department speed up or slow down".[73]

On the other hand, there may be some services or educational institutions where some restraint is necessary in reservations. And it may be possible under the scheme of the Constitution and proper appreciation of the value-preference enshrined in Articles 15(4) and 16(4) and indicated in the *Balaji-Devadasan* approach. This spirit of accommodation and value preference is clear from the judgment of Justice A.P. Sen, in *K.C. Vasanth Kumar v. State of Karnataka*[74]. The learned judge said: "The doctrine of protective discrimination embodied in Articles 15(4) and 16(4) and the mandate of Article 29(2) cannot be stretched beyond particular limit. This state exists to serve its people. There are some services where expertise and skill are of the essence. For example, a hospital run by the state serves the ailing members of the public who need medical aid, medical services directly affect and deal with the health and life of the public. Professional expertise, born of knowledge and experience, of high degree of technical knowledge and operational skills is required of pilots and aviation engineers. The lives of citizens depend on such persons. There are other similar fields of governmental activity where professional, technological, scientific or the special skill is called for."[75] The learned Judge wished: "In such services or posts under the Union or states, there can be no room for reservation of posts; merit alone must be the sole and decisive consideration for appointments."[76]

In *P.V. Indiresan & Others v. Union of India*,[77] appeal raises an important question relating to the implementation of the 27 per cent reservation for other backward classes in central educational institutions under the Central Educational Institutions (Reservation in Admission) Act, 2006. The question relates to the meaning of the words "cut-off marks" used in the clarificatory order of 14 October 2008 in *P.V. Indiresan & Others v. Union of India*, in regard to the decision of the Constitution Bench in *Ashoka Kumar Thakur v. Union of India*.[78]

The petitioner made an application in *A.K. Thakur* alleging that some central educational institutions were interpreting the decision contrary to the law laid down therein and sought the directions/clarifications that: (a) the limit of cut-off marks for admission of students in the OBC quota in central educational institutions be a maximum 10 marks below the cut-off for the general category; and (b) that all vacant seats in the reserved quota after the seats have been filled in accordance with the above shall automatically revert to the general category.

The Jawaharlal Nehru University (JNU), the second respondent herein, interpreted the said order of this court to mean that the minimum marks for admission to be secured by an OBC candidate should not be less than the marks secured by the last student admitted under general category. The admissions for 2008–09 and 2009–10 were done on that basis. As a result, a considerable number of OBC seats got reverted to general category because of non-availability of eligible OBC students with the required marks. Therefore, the standing committee on admissions of JNU, at its meeting held on 10 June 2010, considered the ways and means to fulfil 27 per cent quota for OBC students for 2010–11.

A legal notice was issued to the JNU on 27 June 2010 on behalf of a students' association contending that the change in the procedure for admissions to the seats reserved for OBCs proposed by the JNU was contrary to the clarificatory order of this court issued on 14 October 2008, and threatening initiation of contempt proceedings, if the said decision of 17 June 2010 of the Deans Committee was implemented. As a consequence, JNU sought legal opinion. It was advised that while the procedure sought to be adopted by JNU for 2010–11, vide its resolution dated 17 June 2010, may not be contempt of court, it may not stand judicial scrutiny and could be viewed as an attempt to circumvent the law declared in A.K. *Thakur* and, therefore, it should continue the policy and procedure adopted during the previous two years. As a consequence, on 12 July 2010, the Deans Committee reviewed the earlier decision of 17 June 2010 and decided to restore/continue the procedure that was followed during the previous year (2009–10), that is to admit only OBC candidates who secure marks within 10 per cent band below the marks secured by the last candidate admitted in the general category and transfer all the unfilled OBC seats to general category.

On the other hand, the learned counsel for the third and fourth respondents (the OBC category candidates who were the writ petitioner before the High Court) contended that the CEI Act does not stipulate or provide any minimum "cut-off marks" for OBC category candidates who are entitled to the benefit of 27 per cent reservation. It is also submitted that there is no mandatory direction either in *A.K. Thakur* or *Indiresan* to fix the cut-off marks for the general category or for OBC category candidates.

The appellant (and other interveners who claim to be concerned about excellence in education) contend that 'cut-off marks' are different from 'eligibility marks' or 'qualifying marks'. There is no dispute that 'eligibility marks' refers to the minimum marks a candidate is required to have in the last qualifying examination. Similarly, there is no dispute that 'qualifying marks' refers to the minimum marks required to be secured in the special entrance examination, which may be held to determine the inter se merit of candidates from different universities/sources and to ensure that candidates to be admitted possess the minimum academic standards required or expected for a special course of study; and it is only those securing the qualifying marks in the entrance examination, where it is a part of the admission process, who will be included in the merit list for admission, or will become eligible for being called for viva voce.

It was held by the Supreme Court that the maximum cut-off marks for OBCs be 10 per cent below the cut-off marks of general category candidates. If in any central educational institution, the OBC reservation seats remain vacant the institution shall fill the said seats with OBC students. Only if OBC candidates possessing the minimum eligibility/qualifying marks are not available in the OBC merit list, the OBC seats shall be converted into general category seats.

Though OBCs are socially and economically not forward, they do not suffer the same social handicaps inflicted upon Scheduled Castes (SCs) and Scheduled Tribes (STs). The object of reservation for the SCs and STs is to bring them into the mainstream of national life, while the object in respect of the backward classes is to remove their social and educational handicaps. The founding fathers of the Constitution, having been aware to the dissimilarities of the socio-economic and educational conditions of the SCs and STs and other segments of the society, have given them separate treatment in the Constitution.

The study has shown the government's attempts to identify the backward classes with no fruitful result of dilution the caste consciousness. It has accentuated caste consciousness and pressure politics for reservational benefits. The courts cannot be proper substitute of legislative-executive combinations which are the formulators of protective discrimination policy. Judicial remedies are sought in cases of abuse of protective discrimination policy. Since rights involved in protective discrimination are only permissive rights and not substantive rights, therefore, generally the beneficiaries of such arrangements do not go to the courts. The persons whose rights are adversely affected by reverse discrimination go to the courts against the governmental action. And disputes arise between the sponsors of protective discrimination and the victims of reverse discrimination. Anyway, the courts have to perform their onerous constitutional duty to allow or disallow the preferential treatment in accordance with the constitutional norms, both as to the issue of identification of the recipients of protective discrimination and as to the issue of the extent of protective discrimination the court has to intervene only if the government or legislature has failed to discharge its primary obligation properly. In doing so, the judiciary has honoured the constitutional mandate of classless or casteless society. The court is expected to act more effectively than the political wings of the government, which are vulnerable to political pressures. And, this vulnerability has been responsible for policies in derogation framers commitment to establish a society free from discrimination on the grounds of religion, race, caste, sex or place of birth. The judiciary has to take care of this commitment and to evolve rational, scientific and secular criterion to identify the backward classes, a label that every community wishes to bear upon itself on one pretext or the other.[79]

Notes

1. M.G. Chitkara, *Law and the Poor: A Socio-Legal Study*, Ashish Publishing House, New Delhi, 1991, p. 2.
2. Dr G.B. Reddy, *Judicial Activism in India*, Gogia Law Publication, Hyderabad, 2001, p. 5.
3. Ibid., p. 32.
4. Ibid., p. 25.
5. *AIR* 1973 SC 1899.

6. Article 13, which appears in part III of the Constitution, dealing with the fundamental rights, provides in clauses (1) and (2) as follows:

(1) All laws in force in the territory of India immediately before the commencement of this Constitution in so far as they are inconsistent with the provision of this part, shall, to the extent of such inconsistency, be void.

(2) The state shall not make law which takes away or abridges the rights conferred by this part and any law made in contravention of this clause, shall to the extent of the contravention, be void.

Article 32, clause (1) provides:

The right to move the Supreme Court by appropriate proceeding for the enforcement of the rights conferred by this part is guaranteed.

Article 226, clause (1) confers on the different high courts the power to enforce any of the rights conferred by part III and for any other purpose.

7. M.P. Jain, *Indian Constitutional Law*, Wadhwa and Company, Nagpur, 2002, p. 753.
8. *AIR* 1981 SC 298.
9. *AIR* 1956 SC 1557.
10. S.M. Mehta, *A Commentary on Indian Constitutional Law*, Deep & Deep Publications, New Delhi, 1990, p. 94.
11. *AIR* 1969 SC 1.
12. S.M. Mehta, op. cit., p. 101.
13. *AIR* 1963 SC 649.
14. S.M. Mehta, op. cit., p. 760.
15. M.P. Jain, op. cit., p. 753.
16. *AIR* 1951 SC 226.
17. Ibid.
18. Ibid.
19. M.P. Jain, op. cit., p. 718.
20. *AIR* 1963 SC 649.
21. Ibid.
22. Ibid.

23. M.J. Antony, *Dalit Rights: Landmark Judgements on SC/ST/Backward Classes*, Indian Social Institute, New Delhi, 1998, p. 3.
24. 1964 (6) SCR 368.
25. 6 SCR 368 (1964), p. 389.
26. M.J. Antony, op. cit., p. 5.
27. *AIR* 1971 SC 2303.
28. *AIR* 1968 SC 1012.
29. Ibid.
30. *AIR* 1971 SC 2303.
31. *AIR* 1984 SC 1420.
32. *AIR* 1993 Andhra Pradesh 38.
33. *AIR* 2001 SC 717.
34. *AIR* 2000 Madras 174.
35. *AIR* 1955 SC 334.
36. *AIR* 1963 SC 649.
37. 1963 Supp. ISCR 475.
38. 1964 6 SCR 368.
39. *AIR* 2001 SC 717.
40. 2 SCR 586 (1962).
41. Ibid.
42. *AIR* 1967 SC 1283.
43. *AIR* 1969 SC 1283.
44. M.J. Antony, op. cit., p. 10.
45. *AIR* 1976 SC 490.
46. *AIR* 1974 SC 1300.
47. *AIR* 1964 SC 179.
48. *AIR* 1963 SC 649.
49. *AIR* 1968 SC 507.
50. (a) The President, Kerala, *Harijan Samskarika Kshema Samithy, Trivandrum*, has brought to the notice of Government that a large number of Harijan employees are facing immediate reservation from their posts for want of test qualifications and has, therefore, requested that all scheduled castes and scheduled tribes employees may be granted temporary exemption from passing the obligatory departmental tests for a period of two years with immediate effect.

(b) Government has examined the matter in consultation with the Kerala Public Service Commission and is pleased to grant temporary exemption to members already in service belonging to any of the scheduled castes and scheduled tribes from passing all tests (unified and special or departmental tests) for a period of two years.

(c) The benefit of the above exemption will be available to those employees belonging to scheduled castes and scheduled tribes who are already enjoying the benefits of temporary exemption from passing newly prescribed tests under General Rule 13–A. In their case, the temporary exemption will expire only on the date of expiry of the temporary exemption mentioned in para (2) above or on the date of expiry of the existing temporary exemption, whichever is later.

(d) This order will take effect from the date of the order.

51. *AIR* 1976 SC 490.
52. *AIR* 1988 SC 959.
53. *AIR* 1963 SC 649.
54. *AIR* 1988 SC 959.
55. *AIR* 1995 SC 14.
56. Ibid.
57. *AIR* 2000 SC 609.
58. *AIR* 1966 SC 448.
59. *AIR* 1966 SC 1189.
60. *AIR* 1999 SC 3471.
61. *AIR* 2000 SC 609.
62. *AIR* 2000 Kerala 313.
63. Ibid.
64. *AIR* 2001 SC 308.
65. Ibid.
66. *AIR* 1993 SC 477.
67. M.J. Antony, op. cit., p. 116.
68. S.N. Singh, *Reservation Policy for Backward Classes*, Rawat Publications, Jaipur, 1996, p. 59.
69. *AIR* 2001 SC 308.
70. *AIR* 1971 SC 2303.

71. S.N. Singh, op. cit., p. 72.
72. *AIR* 1976 SC 2490.
73. Anirudh Prasad, *Reservation Policy and Practice in India: A Means to an End*, Deep & Deep Publications, New Delhi, 1991, p. 164.
74. *AIR* 1985 SC 1495.
75. Ibid.
76. *AIR* 1968 SC 507.
77. (2009) 7 SCC 300.
78. (2008) 6 SCC1.
79. Anirudh Prasad, op. cit., p. 164.

6

Conclusion and Suggestions

Like various other social aggregations in the world, Indian society is also composed of intersecting and overlapping groups and sub-groups based on religion, sect, vocation, wealth, language, location and political affiliation. However, one of the most distinctive and powerful features of the Indian society is its division into castes, especially of its majority section. Membership in the caste group is conferred by birth and is unalterable, except when it is lost, unless expelled by the group. Members of each caste, residing in specific areas, have common customs and more or less a similar style of life with a characteristic diet, dress and religious observances. There is a variation in kind and number of castes but due to hierarchical stratification the highest and lowest castes are easily identifiable.[1]

Relative positions in the local caste hierarchy are related to the division of the Hindu society into four classes or *varnas*. According to this theory, this hierarchical order of these four classes is, first, the Brahmins: priestly and scholarly class, second, the Kshatriyas: rulers and soldiers, third, the Vaishyas: merchants and agriculturists, and fourth, the Shudras: the menial and the service class supposed to serve the other three *varnas*. Mythology says that the Brahmins were born from the mouth, the Kshatriyas from the hands, the Vaishyas from the stomach and the Shudras from the feet of Brahma. As time passed, the *varnas* were replaced by castes and birth rather than occupation became the determiner of one's class. Shudras were considered clearly inferior to the other three castes and were forbidden to perform only menial jobs, forbidden to study the *Vedas*, exceptions apart, and enjoined to be differential and subservient to the other castes.[2]

To build up a just society has been a dream of mankind since the very dawn of civilisation. A society based on inequality can never be just. It is equally true that the process of stratification is inevitable whatever be the form of social or political organisation. So long as the stratification reflects the socio-ethical convictions of the contemporary society no tension arises. But with the passage of time, perceptions change and what had earlier been part of established order is projected as inequality, giving rise to conflicts. A mature and modern society is able to resolve the conflicts by democratic process otherwise the conflicts become violent resulting into disruption.[3]

The history of world is replete with instances of conflicts arising when perceptions regarding equality change due to ideological innovations. The classes excluded from culture, education and jobs have raised the slogan of equality against those whom they saw as the dominators. The post-modernism has thereafter meant that the hitherto 'excluded' should be included. In the western societies these conflicts have been essentially drawn on economic lines. The Third World countries, however, are witnessing conflicts on the basis of primordial divisions like religion, race and caste. This is only natural because these have been the bases of stratification in traditional societies. In India, the 19th century Renaissance and social reform movements created a new awareness, which found expression, amongst other things, in protest against caste inequalities. The movement of certain castes for greater share in government services started in the southern India well before independence but remained confined to local limits because it was overshadowed by the nationalist movement. The entire energy of the nation was directed during the pre-independence period at resolving the political problem, the social problem did not receive the attention it deserved. Consequently, the social problem of caste inequality came to the fore soon after independence. Due to electoral considerations, the entire problem of inequality in the Indian society is projected only in terms of caste. The sole emphasis on caste in the context of inequalities tends to deflect the attention from other kinds of inequalities.[4]

The origin of untouchability and the racial, ethnic composition of the scheduled caste population is shrouded in mystery. They have been the weakest constituent of the Indian social structure except the *adivasis*. They are designated with a variety of nomenclatures such as untouchables, Harijans, depressed classes, *dalits*, servile classes, weaker sections, *panchamas*, *antisudras, avarnas* and scheduled castes. The term 'depressed classes' refers to those castes which belong to the lowest rung of the Hindu caste hierarchy and whose touch or proximity is considered polluting by the caste Hindus.[5]

As we have discussed in the earlier chapter that the origin of untouchables in a complicated theme. We trace their origin to the Vedic period, i.e., the coming of Aryans to India during 2500 B.C. to 2000 B.C., and from the writings of *Rigveda*, which was written during 1200 B.C. to 1000 B.C. So in the early Vedic time, it is said that, all men were equals and there was no trace of untouchability as we see it today. According to *Rigveda*, in those days, perfect brotherhood was prevalent. In course of time, when the Aryans, having grown in overwhelming numbers, scattered and colonised throughout the whole of Aryavarta, they divided themselves into four divisions according to their different qualities and actions in order to organise their society. This four-fold division has been a pre-dominant feature of Hindu social fabric.[6]

Gradually, as the Hindu *varna* system grew fashionable, strong strict measures were adopted to enforce it. Social intercourse and intermarriage were prohibited. Society became strictly endogamous and was divided into water-tight compartments. Those who violated the law of endogamy were ex-communicated and were forced to live outside the community.

During the Muslim rule, amongst the Hindus, caste system was so rigid that both inter-marriage and inter-dining were taboos. Because of much rigidity, the untouchables became prey to the process of conversion started by the Muslims. Many of these untouchables and low caste people embraced Islam and joined the invaders partly to avoid prosecution and partly in search of freedom. After the Mughals, during the rule of Marathas and Peshwas, it is also recorded that the Mahars and Manqsd were not allowed inside the gates of Poona after 3 p.m. and before 9 a.m. It was because before 9 a.m. and after 3 p.m. their bodies cast too long a shadow which falling on a number of the higher castes especially Brahmins – defiled them. Thus, untouchability was institutionalised.[7]

Socially, scheduled castes have been denied status in the traditional Hindu caste system, for they are ritually far below the pollution line. They fall beyond the *varna* system. But surprisingly they are accommodated in the local *jati* system in the villages. The Hindu caste system, despite severe inequalities, is marked by an organic unity among castes made possible through internalisation of the inegalitarian values, embodied in the swine concept of *'karma'* and *'dharma'* observed both by upper and lower castes.[8]

The British role in this was a characteristic mixture of pragmatic, equivocal, calculated and philanthropic, with the proportions varying with time. The British rule initiated the process of westernization of the Indian society which cut down the social prejudices and taboos. The socio-religious reform movements in the 19th century, an outcome of the western impact, awakened the enlightened Indians to the moral responsibility of improving the lot of the untouchables. In terms of uplift in socio-economic status, the untouchables reaped the least benefits from the British rule, compared to the caste Hindus and other communities such as the Christians and Muslims.[9]

But the general thrust of colonial policy and their presence undermined the traditional restrictions on low castes and untouchables. It opened some avenues of mobility unintentionally which, in fact, had not existed before. It was very important to the untouchables that the British themselves did not practice untouchability. As a consequence when new employment and educational opportunities became available in India due to the presence of the British in the field of western education, industrialisation, new trades and professions, some of the untouchables in their own capacity were able to take advantage of this situation. It enabled some of them to seek employment outside their traditional caste occupation. A large number of tribals and untouchables were enlisted in the British army.[10]

When the Indian National Congress was founded at Bombay in 1885, it was felt by the leaders of the movement that the national movement should not be exclusively political, but the consideration of political questions, questions affecting Indian social economy should also be put forth for vitalising Hindu society by removing the social evils and social wrongs. Annie Beasant in the opening session declared, "what can be done for them by those who feel the barbarity of the treatment meted to them, by those who feel that Indians who demand freedom should show respect to others and give to others a share of the consideration they claim for themselves?"[11]

For the Congress party and the Hindu leaders, the British decision came as a rude shock. Gandhi, who represented the Congress during the second Round Table Conference, had vehemently opposed the idea of separate electorates for the depressed classes, he had argued that it would "create a division of Hinduism", and had threatened that "if I was the only person to resist this thing, I would resist it with my life".[12]

Gandhi meant to carry out his threat. In a letter written to the Prime Minister, Ramsay MacDonald, from the Yervada Jail on August 18, 1932, Gandhi announced his fast unto death.[13] Gandhi commenced his epic fast on September 20, 1932. Everyone, including Ambedkar, became worried about Gandhi's health. The government refused to budge from its decision unless some agreement was reached between the Hindu leaders and the depressed classes representatives. Hurried meetings and hectic activities followed. Pandit Madan Mohan Malviya was the leading figure for the caste Hindu, and Ambedkar represented the depressed classes. After several days of discussion and repeated visits to the Yervada Jail to meet Gandhi, an agreement was reached on the basis of which Gandhi agreed to end his fast. This agreement, known as the Poona Pact, gave the depressed classes more reserved seats under the joint electorates. On political implication of the Poona Pact, Ambedkar later commented that Poona Pact, while giving the untouchables a few more seats that had been given to them by the Communal Award, took away from them a priceless privilege and a powerful political weapon. He estimated that the voting strength of the untouchables in each constituency was one to ten. The double voting in his opinion would have made the caste Hindu candidates more dependent on the votes of the "untouchables" and no caste Hindu candidate would have dared to neglect them.[14]

The Chairman of the Drafting Committee, Ambedkar submitted a memorandum to the Advisory Committee and pleaded forcefully for affording the scheduled castes political and social safeguards in the Indian Constitution. He considered scheduled castes as a "minority" community. As a safeguard to minorities (which included depressed classes), he had suggested the establishment of non-parliamentary irremovable executive both in the union and in the units. He proposed the scheduled castes should have a minimum representation according to their population ratio in the legislatures, ministries and municipalities and had to be elected through separate communal electorates. But after assuming chairmanship of the Drafting Committee, his position and outlook changed. However, Ambedkar's suggestions on safeguards were incorporated in the Constitution. His proposal for an independent officer to be appointed by the President to report on the working of the safeguards for the scheduled castes was accepted by the Assembly as Article 338 of the Constitution. He proposed that the safeguards for the scheduled castes should continue at least for a period of 25 years. The advisory committee decided that the reservations for scheduled castes and scheduled tribes should cease to have effect on the expiration of a period of 10 years. Some members in the debate suggested that it should be for longer period. After a long discussion on the concession for the scheduled castes and scheduled tribes, it was agreed to have that reservation should continue for 10 years. Article 334 provided that reservation of seats and special representation shall cease after 10 years.[15]

The setting up of India's Constituent Assembly in 1946 on the eve of Independence, came as a culmination of almost half a century's efforts at preparing a variety of government patterns. All the efforts during this period were mainly the outcome of an alien government's half-hearted response, relaxing their hold over the country as a result of the pressures mounted by the movement for 'self-rule' in the first instance and complete independence subsequently. The Government of India Act, 1935 included in its purview the princely states and spelt out a plan for much more responsible government in the provinces and a diarchy of the old provincial pattern at the centre. The provincial governments envisaged therein were installed after elections but the federal set-up never came into being due to the hesitation on the part of the princely states and the Second World War.[16]

The Advisory Committee received few memoranda from the organisations of scheduled castes and scheduled tribes. A special mention may be made of the Republican Party and All India Adi Hindu depressed classes Association. If these memoranda are to be taken as an index of political, social and economic aspiration of these classes, it would be noted that the provisions of the draft Constitution were below their expectations. The Depressed Classes Association formulated a long list of measures for the uplift of the scheduled castes. In particular it claimed reservation of seats in the various legislatures in proportion to their population and asked that either elections to these reserved seats should be through separate electorates, or, if the principle of joint electorates was adopted, every candidate should, before he was declared elected, secure at least 40 per cent of the votes cast by members of the scheduled castes. Ambedkar's suggestion for the amelioration of the conditions of the scheduled castes included generous provision of funds in the budget of the government for higher education, secondary and college education, and for education abroad of members of this community; the settlement of scheduled castes in separates village; and the setting up of settlement commission for this purpose. Finally, to watch over these measures, he wanted an office of the Superintendent of Minority Affairs to be created, with the same status as the Auditor General, whose duty would be to prepare an annual report on the treatment of minorities by the public as well as by the government; and on any transgressions of safeguards or miscarriage of justice arising out of communal bias by the governments and their officers. These reports were to be placed before the Union and the State Legislatures and discussed by them.[17]

Gandhi and the Indian National Congress seemed to stand for a kind of gradualist, reconciliatory and co-operative political mobilisation of Harijans whereas Ambedkar advocated for rapid political participation of Harijans. In their own ways, Gandhi and Ambedkar have been more successful mobilisers of Harijans presumably because of their peculiar mixes of traditional and modern idioms, symbolism and styles of appeal. The common objectives of Harijan uplift and welfare were sought to be pursued differently by two leaders, while Gandhi emphasized a more universalistic, reformist approach linking the cause of Harijan uplift with that of other similarly deprived groups, Ambedkar stressed a more radical but ethically particularistic approach isolating the struggles for justice from those of the other oppressed groups. One can argue that Ambedkar was too harsh to Gandhi but Ambedkar failed to appreciate that Gandhi was moving both ahead of his time and along with it. It was felt that Gandhi was apprehensive of the wrath of the higher castes who were dominating the socio-political and economic scene of the country. Touchables liked the idea given by Gandhi, because this slogan of upliftment was in no way opposed to the social hierarchy. Gandhi, a proponent of the best in Hinduism, was never communal. He was the embodiment of secularism. He was far-sighted and broad-minded. He stood before the nation as a seer, as his acumen of wisdom, compassion and a composite cultural aspiration in handling the problems of untouchables. Ambedkar with his affability, his gentle disposition, kindness and affection, no less then by his wisdom stood out as a beacon light of courage and fortitude, instilling in the masses of the untouchables self-confidence and self-respect. The pages of the history of untouchables would ever be embossed in golden letters concerning Ambedkar's unique contribution to the cause of untouchability.[18]

The Constituent Assembly of Independent India passed a provision legally abolishing untouchability on November 29, 1948, nine months after the death of Gandhi, which had no use for legalism whereas Ambedkar had. The synthesis came in the form of certain written provisions in the Constitution, which was inaugurated in 1950.[19]

Politics is a competitive enterprise. Its purpose is the acquisition of power for the realization of certain goals. Politicians seek to identify and manipulate the various existing and emerging allegiances for mobilization. The caste system provides an institutional basis for tolerance. A caste-based society is a pluralistic cultural universe, with each caste having its own occupation, customs, rituals, traditions, etc. The involvement of caste in politics is a process of mobilization of different sections of society for political purposes.[20] All political parties reinforce the caste sentiment. In each constituency, during election, they put up candidates belonging to the dominant caste in that constituency. They use caste associations and persuade caste leaders to appeal to their caste fellows to vote for them.

The social basis of a political party can be built on the basis of its ideology and organization. Political parties in India, except the communist parties, are not clear as to their ideologies. The Janata Dal, Bhartiya Janata party and Congress have, from time to time, laid down short-term goals, policies and tactics to win elections. When they are not able to win their voters at local level through ideological and problem-oriented politics, they adopt caste politics. Although castes have been playing an important role in the Indian political system, they have not demanded separate political identification. As part of a larger society, they are symbolically related to one another and are participants in Hindu culture. This relationship is integrated and legitimized when they come to mobilize themselves politically. Political participation in India earlier was only limited to a few upper castes. The British introduced western education, established speedier means of communication, and extended franchise to cover ever increasing number of people in India. The leadership provided by lower castes during the national movement was proof of the increasing participation, which increased manifold after independence. After independence, the intermediate castes started competing for political power. This increased the number of participants. Earlier, power politics was limited to a few upper castes; now the intermediate castes are also in the picture. The caste system is today responding to the processes of representational politics. The caste structures have grown stronger under the impact of adult franchise.[21]

In the caste politics, the Mandal Commission played a very important role. The Mandal Commission, which generated a bitter controversy over the question of reservations for backward classes. Mandal Report could not appeal to the entire nation. Besides, the timing and manner of its implementation raised doubts in the minds of many about the intentions of the politicians in power. The Commission adopted the premise that ritual ranking of castes has enabled the higher castes to hold the lower castes in bondage for ages. The Commission, therefore, rejected a mechanical view of equality and opined that unequals cannot be treated as equals otherwise of eleven social, economic and educational indicators evolved by it and by giving more weightage to social indicators, the Commission made castes and communities as the basis for identification of backward classes in the Hindu society. No doubt, occupation, underrepresentation in government services, beggary, untouchability, etc., were also taken into account. But the Commission insisted that identification has to be on a collective basis, for example, on the basis of caste or hereditary occupation; the basis cannot be individual. Further, poverty in the view of the Commission could not be a basis of identification as poverty of a person may be a transient phase.[22]

The Mandal Report became controversial and was found unacceptable by bulk of non-beneficiaries mainly because of: (1) inadequate data and unsatisfactory survey relics, (2) dominant importance given to caste, (3) an inclusive approach in preparing the list of backward classes, (4) complete neglect of even the very poor amongst the upper castes, (5) extension of the benefit of reservation even to the affluent amongst backward castes, and (6) application of the reservation policy not only at the stage of initial appointment but also at the stage of promotion in service. In view of these factors, no action was taken on this Report for about a decade. It was unfortunate that this Report was implemented without adequately preparing the public opinion and that too in a confrontationist atmosphere. Many observers thought that the report was implemented to score a point in the intra-party rivalry within the ruling party and with electoral considerations in view. The doubts about the motive of the Government also reflected on the legitimacy of the scheme implemented on the basis of the Mandal Report.[23]

Social reformers down the ages had tried to break the barriers, which divided the Hindu society into the upper and the lower castes, the touchable and the untouchables, but with little success. This resulted in conversion to Christianity and

Islam, as and when the latter two entered the scene. Gandhi also, in his own way, tried to change the heart of the higher castes so as to make them accept that Harijans had as much right to worship in a temple, to draw water from a well and to participate in social and religious functions, as any other Hindu. The various legal and constitutional remedies were tried to counteract the discrimination against the depressed classes so as to improve their social and economic status with the result that in independent India the governments at the centre and the states become the main protagonists of the uplift of these unfortunate sections of the Hindu society. Punitive legislations were enacted to prevent discrimination against these sections and positive administrative measures were taken to compensate for the disadvantages and discriminations to which they had been subjected for centuries. After almost forty years of its implementation in independent India, the reservation policy has reached a stage where both its supporters and critics are unhappy about it. The former are unhappy because it has not created a noticeable impact on the social and economic conditions of the scheduled castes and scheduled tribes, majority of whom still continue to be socially isolated, illiterate and poor. Its critics complain that the matters of employment promotion and admissions reservations have been stretched too far at the cost of merit and equity giving rise to frustration and alienation among the unreserved categories. It is high time now what we take a fresh look at this policy in the light of the experiences gained since independence.[24]

Once a concession is granted it takes the form of a right as time passes and the beneficiary individual or group resists with all its might any attempt to withdraw it. Moreover, the non-beneficiaries do not get organised into an opposing counter force strong enough to break this resistance. The scheduled caste and scheduled tribes constitute almost 25 per cent of the population and no party in power at the centre or in the states can take the risk of abolishing the reservation granted to them and lose the support of this solid vote bank in subsequent elections. Parties out of power also cannot displease these categories for almost the same reasons. They put pressure on the ruling party in another way by instigating other backward sections of the society to demand similar benefits. In such a situation, the ruling party cannot afford to remain far behind and in its apparent zeal to help the poor and the downtrodden sometimes overreact. It projects itself as the sole guardian of the weaker sections by granting them all sorts of benefits irrespective of their long-range implications for the nation. The roster system, carry forward rule, creating watch-dog machineries to safeguard the interests of the beneficiaries, special programmes of financial aid, special scholarships, special training programmes, relaxed standards in admissions and recruitment, etc., are illustrations of various steps taken to keep these groups content and happy. Whether these concessions are reaching to the poorest of the poor among them is hardly anybody's concern. During the last forty years, a section of the scheduled castes and scheduled tribes has become economically as well off as any other average middle class man in any other caste or community. Some of its members have even acquired great wealth. They enjoy all the modern amenities of life. Their wards receive education in the most expensive schools and are fully exposed to rich society. Therefore, they have a distinct advantage over the weaker sections of their own caste, so the poorer co-caste candidates fail to get the advantage even when the competition is limited to the reserved categories only. This group has also developed a strong political lobby to ensure that their interests do not get jeopardized in any way.[25]

There is no doubt that no social institution containing so large an element of inequality and discrimination towards the majority of people can survive for a long period in a purely social context. So this reservation policy was the method contemplated by the Indian political leaders to compensate with the centuries long disadvantageous position that the depressed classes had to face due to the stigma of untouchability.[26]

Another aspect of reservation is that it has strengthened an elitist orientation. As a result of which, though the actual percentage of literacy among these classes is still rising, the rate of progress in literacy has been falling and the gap between the educated and the uneducated among the untouchables is increasing. It has delivered much more benefits to upper echelons than to the entry level ones.[27] There is no doubt that the social gap has got to be bridged, but the vast span of time consumed in the process should make us wiser that it cannot be done through reservations. Although the shackles of mental slavery of the downtrodden cannot be forsaken through one generation, but it is difficult to ignore the reality that the stigma and the slur of quota appointments is far worse than unemployment, more so as they help reveal the identity of the man concerned and segregate him from the mainstream. Since the caste quota has come out to be solemn affirmation of the lower level of caste of the so-called beneficiaries, it is high time the national leadership realises that even the subordinates of the quota appointees point towards them an accusing finger, though, behind their backs. There is no doubt that better economy is the main medium for social upliftment, but that can be achieved even without one per cent reservations, to better the lot of the weaker sections of society, without their bifurcation by caste, colour or creed.[28]

The history of reservations is replete with examples that the real benefits have never trickled down to the intended beneficiaries because the latter had never had the opportunity to achieve the educational level required for the earmarked claim, as the persons for whose benefit the provisions were made in the Constitution suffered throughout from the lack of educational upliftment. The unintended outcome of the intended purpose behind reservations went on multiplying, meanwhile which leads one to the crucial point at stake, whether the son of a Deputy Inspector General of Police or that of a Commissioner of Revenue from the scheduled castes or scheduled tribes or other backward classes is entitled to the benefit of reservations? In the same context comes forth the question: whether the son or daughter of an illiterate peasant or labourer from the scheduled castes and scheduled tribes or other backward classes would ever be entitled to claim, much less than get, the benefit of reservations?

There are some problems attributed to the reservation policy:

1. Instead of bridging the gap between the scheduled castes and scheduled tribes on the one hand, and the rest of the Indian society on the other, this policy has indirectly widened the divide between the two. The beneficiaries of this policy have become objects of jealousy for those whose privileges they are imagined to have cut because of reservation. This jealousy gets reflected in various forms in workplaces, towns and villages. This is not a very happy trend for national integration.
2. As a result of the reservation policy it was expected that in course of time the affected groups will throw up local leaders who, like Ambedkar, shall fight for the welfare of these classes and see to it that more and more of them ascend the economic ladder.
3. It is unfortunate that blanket reservation and ad-hoc quotas have been fixed at all levels, from primary education to professional colleges and skilled government jobs, when it is a well known fact that the percentage of literacy among the reserved categories is abysmally low. A number of nationalised banks and other public undertakings have not been able to fill officer cadre reserved vacancies.
4. This policy and its extension to backward classes has given rise to problems of law and order for those who are already facing a serious challenge from various separatist elements in Punjab and the North-East. The most serious agitation against reservations was witnessed in Gujarat where political maneuvers led to the degeneration of this movement into communal riots which, so often, get sparked off in that state on one issue or the other.[29]

Gandhi always considered Harijans as an integral part of the Hindu society. He taught and won the battle against separate electorate for the Harijans because, according to him, it would have created a permanent schism between the two caste groups. Nehru was also against undertaking any steps which would lead to separatism and create a psychology of dependence in this section of the Indian society. He had said, in so many words, that external props like reservation should be used only as a transitory measure to help the reserved categories to overcome the socio-economic handicap. Like Gandhi, he also favoured programmes to help them develop inner strength to compete in a healthy manner with other sections of the Indian nation on an equal footing. So long as they continued to rely heavily on the external props of reservation they would not learn to stand on their own and the moment these external props are withdrawn they would find themselves in a helpless situation from where it may not be possible to pull them out easily.[30]

The foregoing discussion amply demonstrates that all is not well with the reservation policy, as applied to employment and it is high time that a dispassionate thinking is focused upon it. The following suggestions are mooted in order to make the reservation policy judicious and reasonable. The benefits should be extended to the wider sections of the society so as to make the policy of reservation serve its real purpose.

1. Instead of identifying backwardness through caste the state may lay down objective criteria of socio-economic backwardness.
2. As few indicators of backwardness may be used as possible. The possibility of employing annual family income as the sole criterion may be considered.
3. Vacancies may be reserved against the income criterion, their percentage may be worked out on the basis of the prevailing distribution of income. These percentage may be revised, if necessary, after every ten years.
4. Income certificate issued by the block level officer or an equivalent functionary in urban areas may be considered

adequate to allow the benefit of reservation in so far as selection for appointment is concerned.

5. The roster system and the carry forward rule may be gradually phased out.
6. Reservation may be made at all the levels of direct recruitment.
7. Promotions may be made strictly on seniority-cum-merit basis.
8. Greater attention may be paid to develop mental programmes than has been possible so far. Children from poor families may be given adequate financial support in their education and social development. Possibility of reserving a percentage of seats in high fee schools for promising children from poor families may be considered. The entire cost of their education in such schools may be borne by the state.
9. Only one generation should be permitted the benefit of reservation and the exceptional provisions and schemes, even if envisaged by the Constitution should not be made a general and permanent feature.
10. Its gain should not at all be allowed to be concerned by a few who are already better off. Periodic review is necessary. Once a person has been benefited, he should not be further provided with this protective umbrella. The umbrella should be shifted to others who need its protection and this process should continue for one generation only. The benefits of reservation should be given only once, that is, either at the stage of admission, or recruitment or promotion and not at every stage of one's career.
11. Classifications of backward classes should be dictated by different factors at different stages. A class which is declared as backward may turn out to be the most advanced in a particular region or state. One who is economically poor shall be considered as backward because other norms of advancement are dependent upon this very factor.

12. There must be some independent committee to review of the decision made by any government declaring the list of backward classes. In most cases this is political expediency.
13. If an ultimate goal of having a casteless and classless society is to be attained, the lists of scheduled castes and scheduled tribes would have to be reduced from year to year and replaced in due course by a list based on criterion of income-cum-merit. The unfortunate trend of expanding the lists, obviously under communal pressure, is not a healthy sign. A bold step is arresting this trend in the need of time such is the mandate of the Constitution and imperative for building an egalitarian society.
14. The creamy layer among the backward classes must be excluded with a progressive reduction in the percentage of reservation.
15. Creating conditions for the advancement of the backward classes through literacy and poverty eradication, educational and economic improvement programmes rather than substituting such programmes by mere reservations from which in any case only a selected few are to be benefited and not the bulk of backward classes.
16. Persons getting benefits of reservations through corrupt practices must be dealt with severely. Acquisition of false caste certificates is made a cognizable offence punishable with imprisonment upto two years and fine.
17. Reservations contained in Articles 15(4) and 16(4) of the Constitution of India being exceptions should not be permanent and should be restricted to only one generation. This will ensure the benefits of reservations to those who are genuinely needy.
18. Caste cannot be the sole criterion for ascertaining or identifying the backward classes for the purpose of Article 15(4) and 16(4). Article 16(4) speaks of class and not caste and the two are different. If the goal be a casteless society delineation on the basis of castes as such is bound to prove counter-productive.

19. As and when a group which has enjoyed the fruits of reservations and has become fairly advanced compared to other advanced sections of the society, it has to be ousted from the bracket of the backward classes. It will not only be in the interest of the general public but also in the interest of that particular group itself.
20. Instead of providing 'quota system', it would be ideal if the preparatory preferences were awarded to backward classes of the people. In this respect, both the government and judiciary should draw inspiration from case instead of providing 'quota system' emphasis, protective discrimination and preferential treatment.
21. The next important thing is to "pay back to the society". Ambedkar expected the *dalits* to contribute at least five per cent of their earnings for the development of the society. Unless the whole society is reformed, they will never be respected in the society, howsoever wealthy or educated one may be. Educated *dalits* should make it a habit to contribute at least one per cent of their earning for the welfare of the backward sections.
22. The doctrine of protective discrimination embodied in Articles 15(4) and 16(4) and the mandate of Article 29(2) cannot be stretched beyond a particular limit. The state exists to serve its people. There are some services where expertise and skill are of essence. In such services or posts under the Union or States there can be no room for reservation of post, merit alone must be the sole and decisive consideration for appointment.

The above suggestions have been offered, keeping in view the interests of the entire disadvantaged sections of Indian society. The phenomenon of poverty cuts across all the castes, communities and religions in the country. It is unfair to think that only certain castes deserve special attention for the upliftment of their economic condition through the reservation policy. At the same time, it is illogical to think that the biases, prejudices and negative attitudes deeply ingrained in the minds of the so-called non-scheduled caste would gradually be removed as the members of scheduled castes start working shoulder to shoulder with them. It has not happened so far, and is not likely to happen in future also, simply because an effort is being made to treat a psychological malady through economic measures. The present study of reservations in services instead of bridging the gap between the scheduled and non-scheduled castes has further widened it and led to the hardening to the attitudes on either side. In addition, the so-called backward castes among non-scheduled castes have also started demanding reservations in services to overcome their economic handicap.

The policy of reservations needs reconsideration and the criterion for identifying the intended beneficiaries has to be reviewed, so as to determine the question of backwardness of various castes. The reservations must have a time span and should be reviewed after every five years.

Notes

1. R.G. Misra, *Reservation Policy and Personal Selection*, Uppal Publishing House, New Delhi, 1990, p. 1.
2. Ibid., p. 2.
3. Jitendra Mishra, *Equality versus Justice: The Problem of Reservations for Backward Classes*, Deep & Deep Publications, New Delhi, 1996, p. 1.
4. Ibid., p. 2.
5. Rebati Ballav Tripathy, *Dalits: A Sub-Human Society*, Ashish Publishing House, New Delhi, 1994, p. 2.
6. Ibid., p. 3.
7. Ibid., p. 11.
8. Ibid., p. 13.
9. Ibid., p. 22.
10. Joseph Benjamin, *Scheduled Castes in Indian Politics and Society*, Ess Ess Publications, New Delhi, 1989, p. 28.

11. Cited in Rebati Ballav Tripathi, op. cit., p. 22.
12. Cited in Joseph Benjamin, op. cit., p. 33.
13. "I have read the British Government's decision on minorities and have slept over it. In pursuance of my letter to Sir Samud Hoare and my declaration at the meeting of the Round Table Conference on 13th November 1931, at St. James Palace, I have to resist your decision with my life. The only way I can do so is by declaring a perpetual fast unto death ...", Joseph Benjamin, op. cit., p. 34.
14. Joseph Benjamin, op. cit., p. 34.
15. Ibid., p. 35.
16. H.S. Saksena, *Safeguards for Scheduled Castes and Tribes: Founding Father's View*, Uppal Publishing House, New Delhi, 1981, p. XV.
17. Ibid., p. XXII.
18. Rabati Ballav Tripathy, op. cit., p. 34.
19. Ibid., p. 36.
20. S.N. Singh, *Reservation Policy for Backward Classes*, Rawat Publications, Jaipur, 1996, p. 7.
21. Ibid., p. 11.
22. Jitendra Mishra, op. cit., p. 153.
23. Ibid., p. 154.
24. R.G. Misra, op. cit., p. 145.
25. Ibid.
26. K.S. Padhy, *Reservation Policy in India*, Ashish Publishing House, New Delhi, 1988, p. 106.
27. Ibid., p. 108.
28. S.P. Sharma, *Reservation: Bane or Boon*, Northern Book Centre, New Delhi, 1991, p. 26.
29. R.G. Misra, op. cit., p. 150.
30. Ibid., p. 152.

Bibliography

Primary Sources

Debates and Reports

1. Constituent Assembly Debates.
2. Parliamentary Debates, 1951.
3. Reports of the Commission for the Scheduled Castes and Scheduled Tribes.
4. Reports of the Commission for the Backward Classes.
5. All India Reports.
6. Supreme Court Cases.
7. Supreme Court Reports.

Cases – Law

A. Periakaruppan *v*. State of Tamil Nadu, *AIR* 1971, SC 2303.

A.B.S.K. Sangh (Rly) *v*. Union of India, *AIR* 1981, SC 298.

A.P. State Backward Class Welfare Association (Registered), etc. *v*. The State of Andhra Pradesh Backward Classes Welfare Department, *AIR* 1995, Andhra Pradesh 248.

All Saints High School *v*. State of Andhra Pradesh, *AIR* 1980, SC 1042.

Anil Kumar Gupta *v*. State of Uttar Pradesh (1995) 5 SCC 173.

Arti Roy Choudhary *v*. Union of India *AIR* 1974, SC 532.

Arti *v*. State of Jammu and Kashmir, *AIR* 1981, SC 1009.

Auditor General of India, Gyan Prakash *v*. K.S. Jaganathan (1986) 2 SCC 246.

Banmali Das *v*. Pakhu Bhandari, *AIR* 1951, Calcutta, 167.

C.A. Rajendran *v*. Union of India and Others, *AIR*, 1968, SC 507.

Citralekha *v*. State of Mysore, *AIR* 1964, SC 1823.

Comptroller & Auditor General of India and Others *v*. Mohan Lal Mehrotra and Others, (1992) 1 SCC 20.

D.A.V. College Bhatinda *v*. State of Punjab, *AIR* 1971, SC 1731.

D.N. Chanchala etc. *v*. The State of Mysore and Others, *AIR* 1971, SC 1762.

Deepak Sibal *v*. Punjab University, *AIR* 1989, SC 903.

Devadasan *v*. Union of India, *AIR* 1964, SC 179.

Dileep Domodran *v*. Secretary to Government, Education Department, Hyderabad, *AIR* 1991, Andhra Pradesh, 195.

Dr A.N. Thomas, etc. *v*. Union of India and Others, *AIR* 2000, Kerala, 325.

Dr Chakradhar Paswan *v*. State of Bihar, *AIR* 1988, SC 959.

Dr R. Uma Devi *v*. The Principal Kurnool Medical College, Kurnool and Others, *AIR* 1993, Andhra Pradesh, 38.

General Manager Southern Railway *v*. Rangachari, *AIR* 1962, SC 36.

Hindi Hitrak Shak Samiti *v*. Union of India and Others, *AIR* 1990, SC 851.

Indira Sawhney *v*. Union of India (The Mandal Case) *AIR* 1993, SC 477.

Jagdev Singh *v*. Pratap Singh, *AIR* 1965, SC 183.

Jagwant Kaur Kasar Singh Dany and Others *v*. State of Bombay, *AIR* 1952, Bombay, 461.

Jai Singh *v*. Union of India, *AIR* 1993, Rajasthan, 177.

Janaki Prasad *v*. State of Jammu and Kashmir, *AIR* 1973, SC 930.

Jatinder Pal Singh and Others *v*. State of Punjab, *AIR* 2000, SC 609.

K.C. Vasanth Kumar and Another *v*. State of Karnataka, *AIR* 1985, SC 1495.

K.C. Vasanth Kumar *v*. Karnataka, *AIR* 1985, SC 1495.

Kala Ram *v*. State of Punjab and Others, *AIR* 1995, Punjab and Haryana, 98.

State of Kerala *v*. Rey Mother Provincial, *AIR* 1970, SC 2079.

Kesavananda Bharti Sripadagalvaru and Others *v*. State of Kerala, *AIR* 1973, SC 1461.

Kuldeep Kumar Gupta and Others *v*. Himachal Pradesh.

Electricity Board and Others, *AIR* 2001, SC 308.

Kumari K.S. Jayasree and Others *v*. The State of Kerala, *AIR* 1976, SC 2381.

M.R. Balaji *v*. State of Mysore, *AIR* 1963, SC 649.

State of Madras *v*. Champakam Dorairajan, *AIR* 1951, SC 226.

Managing Board M.T.M.V. *v*. State of Bihar, *AIR* 1984, SC 1757.

Minerva Mills *v*. Union of India, *AIR* 1980, SC 1789.

Minor P. Rajendran *v*. State of Madras and Others, 1968(2) SCR 786.

Miss Nishi Maghu, etc. *v*. State of Jammu and Kashmir and Others, *AIR* 1980, SC 1975.

Narsimha Rao *v*. State of Andra Pradesh, *AIR* 1970, SC 422.

P & T Scheduled Caste/Tribe Employees' Welfare Association (Regd.) and Others *v*. Union of India and Others, *AIR* 1989, SC 139.

People's Union for Democratic Rights *v*. Union of India, *AIR* SC 1473 also called as Asiad Project Worker's Case.

S.B.I. SC/ST Employers Welfare Association *v*. State Bank of India (1996) 4 SCC 403.

Smt. Chetana Dilip Motghare *v*. Bhide Girls Education Society, Nagpur and Others, *AIR* 1994, SC 1917.

Smt. D. Neelima *v*. The Dean of P.G. Studies, A.P. Agricultural University, Hyderabad and Others, *AIR* 1993, Andhra Pradesh, 229.

State of Andhra Pradesh *v*. U.S.V. Balaram, *AIR* 1972, SC 1375.

State of Andhra Pradesh *v*. P. Sagar, *AIR* 1968, SC 1379.

State of Bihar and Another *v*. Bal Mukund Sah and Others, *AIR* 2000, SC 1296.

State of Bombay *v*. Bombay Education Society, *AIR* 1954, SC 561.

State of Kerala *v*. N.M. Thomas, *AIR* 1976, SC 490.

State of Madras *v*. C.R.I. Srinivasan, *SCR*, 1951.

State of Madras *v*. Champakam Dorairajan, *AIR* 1951, SC 226.

State of Punjab *v*. Hiralal, (1970) 3 SCC 567.

Subhash Chandra *v*. State of Uttar Pradesh, *AIR* 1975, SC 563.

Trilokinath *v*. State of Jammu and Kashmir, *AIR* 1969, SC 1.

Union of India and Others *v*. Rajiv Yadav IAS and Others, *AIR* 199, SC 14.

Union of India *v*. Brijlal Thakur, *AIR* 1997, SC 2101.

V.V.Giri *v*. D.S. Dora, *AIR* 1959, SC 1318.

Secondary Sources

Books

A Handbook of National Commission for Scheduled Castes and Scheduled Tribes, 1997.

Ahir, D.C., *Dhamma as Told by Dr Ambedkar*, Dalit Sahitya Prakashan, New Delhi, 1990.

——, *Dr Ambedkar on the British Raj*, Blumoon Books, New Delhi, 1997.

——, *Gandhi and Ambedkar: A Comparative Study*, Blumoon Books, New Delhi, 1995.

Ahmad, Imtiaz, *Caste and Social Stratification among Muslims in India*, Manohar Publishers, New Delhi, 1978.

Ambedkar, B.R., *The Untouchables*, Amrit Book Co., New Delhi, 1948.

Anand, Mulk Raj, *Untouchable*, Arnold Associates, New Delhi, 1981.

Antony, M.J., *Dalit Rights: Landmark Judgements on SC/ST/Backward Classes*, Indian Social Institute, New Delhi, 1998.

Bains, Ravinder Singh, *Reservation Policy and Anti Reservationists*, BR Publishing Corporation, New Delhi, 1994.

Bakshi, S.R., *B.R. Ambedkar: His Political and Social Ideology*, Deep & Deep Publications, New Delhi, 2000.

Basu, Durga Das, *Shorter Constitution of India*, Wadhwa Publishers, Nagpur, 2002.

Benjamin, Joseph, *Scheduled Castes in Indian Politics and Society*, Ess Ess Publication, New Delhi, 1989.

Bhambhari, C.P., *Politics in India 1947–1987*, Vikas Publishing House, New Delhi, 1988.

——, *Politics in India 1992–93*, Shipra Publications, Delhi, 1993.

Bhatia, K.L., *Judicial Activism and Social Change*, Deep & Deep Publications, New Delhi, 1990.

Bhatt, Anil, *Development and Social Justice: Micro Action by Weaker Sections*, Sage Publications, New Delhi, 1989.

Bhattacharyya, N.N., *Ancient Indian History and Civilization: Trends and Perspectives*, Manohar Publishers, New Delhi, 1988.

Biswas, Oneil, *Reservations: Legal Perspectives*, Blumoon Books, New Delhi, 1998.

——, *From Justice to Welfare*, Intellectual Publishing House, New Delhi, 1985.

Biswas, S.K., *Towards a Casteless Society*, Orion Books, New Delhi, 1998.

——, *Father of the Constitution of India*, Orion Books, New Delhi, 1997.

——, *Hinduraj: Today-Yesterday-Tomorrow*, Orion Books, New Delhi, 1996.

Briggs, G.W., *The Chamars*, Low Price Publications, Delhi, 1997.

Chanchreek, K.L., *Dr B.R. Ambedkar: Social Justice and Political Safeguards for Depressed Classes*, Shri Publication, New Delhi, 1995.

Chander, Shailja, *Justice V.R. Krishna Iyer on Fundamental Rights and Directive Principles*, Deep & Deep Publications, New Delhi, 1998.

Chandna, R.C., *Spatial Dimensions of Scheduled Castes in India*, Intellectual Publishing House, New Delhi, 1989.

Charsley, Simon R., *Challenging Untouchability: Dalit Initiative and Experience from Karnataka*, Sage Publications, New Delhi, 1998.

Chatterjee, Sarajit Kumar, *The Scheduled Castes in India*, Gyan Publishing House, New Delhi, 1996.

Chaudhary, S.N., *Changing Status of Depressed Castes in Contemporary India*, Daya Publishing House, Delhi, 1988.

Chaurasia, B.P., *Scheduled Castes and Scheduled Tribes in India*, Chugh Publications, Allahabad, 1990.

Chentharassery, T.H.P., *History of the Indigenous Indians*, APH Publishing Corporation, New Delhi, 1998.

Chitkara, M.G., *Hindutva*, APH Publishing Corporation, New Delhi, 1997.

——, *Law and the Poor: A Socio-Legal Study*, Ashish Publishing House, New Delhi, 1991.

Dahiwale, S.D.M., *Emerging Entrepreneurship among Scheduled Castes of Contemporary India*, Concept Publishing Company, New Delhi, 1989.

Devi, Shakuntala, *Caste System in India*, Pointer Publishers, Jaipur, 1999.

Dicey, A.V., *An Introduction to the Study of the Law of the Constitution*, Universal Law Publishing Co. Pvt. Ltd., New Delhi, 1996.

Fernandes, Lancy, *The Fractured Civilisation: Caste Society in the Theories of Change*, Bharatiya Janwadi Aghadi, Mumbai, 1999.

Fuchs, Stephen, *The Aboriginal Tribes of India*, The Macmillan Company of India, Delhi, 1973.

Fuller, C.J., *Caste Today*, Oxford University Press, Delhi, 1998.

Galanter, Marc, *Competing Equalities: Law and the Backward Classes in India*, Oxford University Press, Delhi, 1984.

Ghatak, B.K., *Dr Ambedkar's Thought*, APH Publishing Corporation, New Delhi, 1997.

Ghosh, Ashish, *Dalits and Peasants: The Emerging Caste-Class Dynamics*, Gyan Sagar Publications, Delhi, 1999.

Ghosh, G.K., *Dalit Women*, APH Publishing Corporation, New Delhi, 1997.

Ghosh, S.K., *Secularism in India: The Concept and Practice*, APH Publishing Corporation, New Delhi, 2001.

——, *Indian Democracy Derailed: Politics and Politicians*, APH Publishing Corporation, New Delhi, 1997.

——, *Protection of Minorities and Scheduled Castes*, Ashish Publishing House, New Delhi, 1980.

Ghurye, G.S., *Caste and Race in India*, Popular Prakashan, Bombay, 1979.

Gore, M.S., *The Social Context of an Ideology: Ambedkar's Political and Social Thought*, Sage Publications, New Delhi, 1993.

Grewal, J.S., *Muslim Rule in India: The Assessments of British Historians*, Oxford University Press, Calcutta, 1970.

Gupta, Shanti Swarup, *Varna, Castes and Scheduled Castes*, Concept Publishing Company, New Delhi, 1991.

Hasbnain, N., *Weaker Sections: The Psycho-Social Perspective*, Gyan Publishing House, New Delhi, 1998.

Hooda, Preet Sagar, *Contesting Reservations*, Rawat Publications, New Delhi, 2001.

Hutton, J.H., *Caste in India: Its Nature, Function and Origins*, Oxford University Press, Bombay, 1969.

Iyer, Justice V.R. Krishna, *Social Justice and the Undone Vast*, BR Publishing Corporation, Delhi, 1991.

——, *Dr Ambedkar and the Dalit Future*, BR Publishing Corporation, Delhi, 1990.

Jain, M.P., *Indian Constitutional Law*, Wadhwa and Company, Nagpur, 2002.

Jain, Nabhi Kumar, *Brochure on Reservation and Concessions*, Nabhi Publication, New Delhi, 2002.

Jain, P.C., *Scheduled Caste Women*, Rawat Publications, New Delhi, 1997.

Jaswal, Paramjit, *Human Rights and the Law*, APH Publishing Corporation, New Delhi, 1996.

Jatava, D.R., *B.R. Ambedkar: A Vision of Man and Morals*, ABD Publishers, Jaipur, 1999.

Jha, Makhan, *Scheduled Castes Today*, MD Publications, New Delhi, 1997.

Jha, Ram Kumar, *Commentary on Reservations for SC, ST, OBC and Others*, Shail & Neeraj Law House, Patna, 2001.

Jiloha, R.C., *The Native Indians: In Search of Identity*, Blumoon Books, New Delhi, 1995.

Jogdand, P.G., *Dalit Women: Issues and Perspectives*, Gyan Publishing House, New Delhi, 1995.

Kamble, N.D., *Deprived Castes and their Struggle for Equality*, Ashish Publishing House, New Delhi, 1983.

Kananaikil, Jose, *Scheduled Caste Converts in Search of Justice*, Indian Social Institute, New Delhi, 1993.

Keer, Dhananjay, *Mahatma Gandhi: Political Saint and Unarmed Prophet*, Popular Prakashan, Bombay, 1973.

Kentkar, S.V., *History of Castes in India*, Low Price Publications, Delhi, 1998.

Khan, Mumtaz Ali, *Human Rights and the Dalits*, Uppal Publishing House, New Delhi, 1995.

——, *Reservation for Scheduled Castes*, Uppal Publishing House, New Delhi, 1994.

——, *Identity Formation and Self Identity among Harijan Elite*, Uppal Publishing House, New Delhi, 1994.

Khan, Nazeer H., *B.R. Ambedkar on Federalism, Ethnicity and Gender Justice*, Deep & Deep Publications, New Delhi, 2001.

Khan, Sheeraz Latif, *Justice Bhagwati on Fundamental Rights and Directive Principles*, Deep & Deep Publications, New Delhi, 1996.

Khan, M.Z., *Scheduled Castes: Their Socio-Economic Background and Development Aspirations*, Inter-India Publications, New Delhi, 1996.

Kirpal Viney, *Equality through Reservations*, Rawat Publications, New Delhi, 1999.

Kotani, H., *Caste System, Untouchability and the Depressed*, Manohar Publishers, New Delhi, 1994.

Kothari, Rajni, *Caste in Indian Politics*, Orient Longman, Hyderabad, 1995.

Kshirsagar, R.K., *Political Thought of Dr Babasahab Ambedkar*, Intellectual Publishing House, New Delhi, 1992.

——, *Untouchability in India: Implementation of the Law and Abolition*, Deep & Deep Publications, New Delhi, 1989.

Kumar, Arun, *Cultural and Educational Rights of the Minorities under Indian Constitution*, Deep & Deep Publications, New Delhi, 1985.

Kumar, Vijay, *Scheduled Caste Panchayat Pradhans in India*, Ajanta Publications, Delhi, 1989.

Lal, Pradyot, *Caste vs. Caste: Turbulence in Indian Politics*, Ajanta Books International, Delhi, 1998.

Lal, Sheo Kumar, *Extent of Untouchability and Pattern of Discrimination*, Mittal Publications, New Delhi, 1990.

Lal, A.K., *Dalit in Action*, Concept Publishing Company, New Delhi, 1997.

Limaye, Madhu, *Manu, Gandhi and Ambedkar and Other Essays*, Gyan Publishing House, New Delhi, 1994.

Madholia, Mata Din, *Supreme Court on Reservation*, Kamlesh Publications, Delhi, 1988.

Majeed, Akhtar, *Nation and Minorities: India's Plural Society and its Constituents*, Kanishka Publishers, New Delhi, 2002.

Massey, James, *Roots of Dalit History, Christianity, Theology and Spirituality*, ISPCK, Delhi, 1996.

——, *Dalits in India: Religion as a Source of Bondage or Liberation with Special Reference to Christians*, Manohar Publishers, New Delhi, 1995.

Mathew, Thomas, *Caste and Class Dynamics*, Tech Publication, New Delhi, 1992.

Mehta, S.M., *A Commentary on Indian Constitutional Law*, Deep & Deep Publications, New Delhi, 1990.

Mendelsohn, Oliver, *The Untouchables: Subordination, Poverty and the State in Modern India*, Oxford University Press, New Delhi, 2000.

Michael, S.M., *Dalits in Modern India: Vision and Values*, Vistaar Publications, New Delhi, 1999.

Mishra, Jitendra, *Equality versus Justice: The Problem of Reservation for Backward Classes*, Deep & Deep Publications, New Delhi, 1996.

Mishra, Narayan, *Scheduled Castes Education: Issues and Aspects*, Kalpar Publications, Delhi, 2001.

Mishra, Upendra, *Caste and Politics in India*, Uppal Publishing House, New Delhi, 1986.

Misra, R.G., *Reservation Policy and Personal Selection*, Uppal Publishing House, New Delhi, 1990.

Muralidharan, V., *Educational Priorities and Dalit Society*, Kanishka Publishers, New Delhi, 1997.

Nikam, Shriram, *Destiny of Untouchables in India*, Deep & Deep Publications, New Delhi, 1998.

Omprakash, S., *Development of the Weaker Sections: Problems, Policies and Issues*, Uppal Publishing House, New Delhi, 1989.

Omvedt, Gail, *Dalit Visions: The Anti-Caste Movement and the Construction of an Indian Identity*, Orient Longman, New Delhi, 1995.

——, *Dalits and the Democratic Revolution*, Sage Publications, New Delhi, 1994.

Pal, R.M., *Human Rights of Dalits: Societal Violation*, Gyan Publishing House, New Delhi, 2001.

Panandiker, V.A. Pai, *The Politics of Backwardness: Reservation Policy in India*, Konark Publishers, New Delhi, 1997.

Pandey, J.N., *Constitutional Law of India*, Central Law Agency, Allahabad, 1997.

Pandey, Jitendra, *Civil Liberty under Indian Constitution*, Deep & Deep Publications, New Delhi, 1995.

Padhy, K.S., *Reservation Policy in India*, Ashish Publishing House, New Delhi, 1988.

Pandy, Rajendra, *Minorities in India: Protection and Welfare*, APH Publishing Corporation, New Delhi, 1997.

Parvathamma, C., *Scheduled Castes at the Cross Roads*, Ashish Publishing House, New Delhi, 1989.

——, *New Horizons and Scheduled Castes*, Ashish Publishing House, New Delhi, 1984.

——, *Scheduled Castes and Tribes: A Socio-Economic Survey*, Ashish Publishing House, New Delhi, 1984.

Paswan, Sanjay, *Encyclopaedia of Dalits in India*, Kalpaz Publications, Delhi, 2002.

Patil, Sharad, *Dasa-Sudra Slavery*, Sugama Prakashan, Pune, 1991.

Pinto, Ambrose, *Dalits: Assertion for Identity*, Indian Social Institute, New Delhi, 1999.

Prakasam, Gana, *Social Separation: Scheduled Castes and the Caste System*, Rawat Publications, New Delhi, 1998.

Prakash, Nirupama, *Scheduled Castes: Socio-Economic Changes*, Chugh Publications, Allahabad, 1989.

Prakash, Om, *Caste Hindu and Scheduled Caste Children in Rural India*, Ess Ess Publications, New Delhi, 1985.

Prakash, Prem, *Ambedkar: Politics and Scheduled Castes*, Ashish Publishing House, New Delhi, 1993.

Prasad, Anirudh, *Social Engineering and Constitutional Protection of Weaker Sections in India*, Deep & Deep Publications, New Delhi, 1980.

——, *Reservational Justice to Other Backward Classes (OBCs)*, Deep & Deep Publications, New Delhi, 1997.

——, *Reservation Policy and Practice in India: A Means to an End*, Deep & Deep Publications, New Delhi, 1991.

Pundir, J.K., *Changing Patterns of Scheduled Castes*, Rawat Publications, New Delhi, 1997.

Purohit, B.D., *Handbook of Reservation for Scheduled Castes and Scheduled Tribes*, Jainsons Publications, New Delhi, 1990.

Rao, Hemlata, *Scheduled Castes and Tribes*, Ashish Publishing House, New Delhi, 1994.

Rajasekhariah, A.M., *B.R. Ambedkar: The Quest for Social Justice*, Uppal Publishing House, New Delhi, 1989.

Rayappa, P. Hanumantha, *Backwardness and Welfare of Scheduled Castes and Scheduled Tribes in India*, Ashish Publishing House, New Delhi, 1986.

Reddy, G.B., *Judicial Activism in India*, Gogia Law Agency, Hyderabad, 2001.

Robb, Peter, *Dalit Movements and the Meaning of Labour in India*, Oxford University Press, Delhi, 1996.

Roy, Ramashray, *Dalits Development and Democracy*, Shipra Publications, Delhi, 1999.

Saksena, H.S., *Safeguards for Scheduled Caste and Tribes: Founding Father's View*, Uppal Publishing House, New Delhi, 1981.

Salvanathan, S., *Status of Scheduled Castes*, Ashish Publishing House, New Delhi, 1989.

Sangwan, Om Prakash, *Dalit Society and the Challenge of Development*, Commonwealth Publishers, New Delhi, 1996.

——, *Social System and the Dalit Identity*, Commonwealth Publishers, New Delhi, 1996.

Seervai, H.M., *Constitutional Law of India*, Universal Book Traders, Delhi, 2002.

Sharma, Anuradha, *Caste in Rural India*, Rajat Publications, Delhi, 1998.

Sharma, R.N., *Fundamental Rights: Liberty and Social Order*, Deep & Deep Publications, New Delhi, 1992.

Sharma, Satish Kumar, *The Chamar Artisans: Industrialisation Skills and Social Mobility*, BR Publishing Corporation, New Delhi, 1986.

Sharma, Sudesh Kumar, *Distributive Justice under Indian Constitution*, Deep & Deep Publications, New Delhi, 1989.

Sharma, B.A.V., *Reservation Policy in India*, Light & Life Publishers, New Delhi, 1982.

Sharma, C.L., *Social Mobility among Scheduled Castes*, MD Publications Pvt. Ltd., New Delhi, 1996.

Sharma, O.P., *Reservation: A Gimmick*, Kar Kripa Publishers, New Delhi, 1994.

Sharma, Ram Sharan, *Sudras in Ancient India*, Motilal Banarsidass, Delhi, 1990.

Sharma, S.P., *Reservations: Bane or Boon*, Northern Book Centre, New Delhi, 1991.

Shukla, Nigamendra, *The Scheduled Castes and The Scheduled Tribes (Prevention of Atrocities) Act 1989*, Modern Law Publications, Allahabad, 2002.

Singh, Gopal, *Reservation Politics in India: Mandalisation of the Society*, Deep & Deep Publications, New Delhi, 1995.

Singh, Mahender, *Dalits in India*, Reference Press, New Delhi, 2003.

Singh, Shyama Nand, *Reservation Problems and Prospects*, Uppal Publishing House, New Delhi, 1991.

Singh, Soran, *Scheduled Castes of India: Dimensions of Social Change*, Gyan Publishing House, Delhi, 1987.

Singh, S.N., *Reservation Policy for Backward Classes*, Rawat Publications, Jaipur, 1996.

Sunderraj, Victor, *Scheduled Castes of Rural India: Problems and Prospects*, APH Publishing Corporation, New Delhi, 2000.

Teltumbde, Anand, *'Ambedkar' in and for the Post-Ambedkar Dalit Movement*, Sugama Prakashan, Pune, 1997.

Thakur, Devendra, *Self-Employment Pattern of Scheduled Castes*, Deep & Deep Publications, New Delhi, 1992.

Tripathy, Rebati Ballav, *Dalits: A Sub-Human Society*, Ashish Publishing House, New Delhi, 1994.

Trivedi, Harshad R., *Scheduled Castes Quest for Land and Social Equality*, Concept Publishing Company, New Delhi, 1996.

Upadhyay, H.C., *Status of Scheduled Tribes in India*, Anmol Publications, New Delhi, 1999.

Vakil, A.K., *Gandhi-Ambedkar Dispute*, Ashish Publishing House, New Delhi, 1991.

——, *Reservation Policy and Scheduled Castes in India*, Ashish Publishing House, New Delhi, 1985.

Venugopal, P., *Social Justice and Reservation*, Emerald Publishers, Chennai, 1998.

Wankhede, G.G., *Social Mobility and Scheduled Castes*, Rawat Publications, New Delhi, 1999.

Webster, John C.B., *Religion and Dalit Liberation: An Examination of Perspectives*, Manohar Publishers, New Delhi, 1999.

Yadav, C.P., *Encyclopaedia of Scheduled Castes and Scheduled Tribes*, Anmol Publications, New Delhi, 2000.

Yadav, K.C., *India's Unequal Citizens: A Study of Other Backward Classes*, Manohar Publishers, Delhi, 1994.

Yadav, S.K., *Education of Scheduled Castes*, Commonwealth Publishers, New Delhi, 1991.

Zelliot Eleanor, *From Untouchables to Dalit: Essays on the Ambedkar Movement*, Manohar Publishers, New Delhi, 1996.

Articles

Abraham, Abu, "Between Manu and Mayawati", *The Hindustan Times*, April 10, 1994.

Anand, C.L., "Reservation versus Indication of Source: Judicial Activism and Preferential Treatment", *Civil and Military Law Journal*, Vol. 24, No. 1, 1988.

Baig, M.A.A., "Reservation in Public Employment and Judicial Process", *SCJ*, Vol. 3, 1989.

Buch, M.N., "Caste Aspersion", *The Sunday Hindustan Times Magazine*, March 24, 1993.

Kothari, R., "Essence of Mandal Report", *Mainstream*, Vol. XXVII, No. 50, October, 1990.

Majahan, R.K., "Dr Ambedkar's Views on Constitutional Vision: Caste System and Parliamentary Democracy", *SCJ*, Vol. 3, 1991.

Mander, Harish, "Where Faith is a Matter of Caste", *The Times of India*, March 23, 1994.

Mehta, P.L. and M.G. Chitkara, "Need to Revamp Reservation Policy", *Civil and Military Law Journal*, Vol. 26, No. 3, 1990.

Menon, P.S.K., "Abolition of Untouchability and Removal of Social Disabilities: An Appraisal", *Yojana*, Vol. 37, No. 23, December 31, 1993.

Mishra, Nishi, "Why Reservations?", *Mainstream*, Vol. XXVIII, No. 26, April, 1990.

Palkiwala, Nani A., "Mandal Perpetuates Casteism", *The Hindustan Times*, November 30, 1992.

Padmanabhan, N. Anata, "Caste based Reservation should be given up", *The Hindu*, May 3, 1994.

Shabbir, Mohammad, "Dr B.R. Ambedkar: Massiah of Depressed Classes", *AMU News and Views*, 1994.

——, N.H. Khan and Z.A. Khan, "Legal Safeguards to Scheduled Castes and Scheduled Tribes: An Appraisal", *SCJ*, Vol. 3, Part 2, 1994.

Sharma, S.S., "Dr Ambedkar: The Savior of Human Rights for Depressed Classes", *Civil and Military Law Journal*, Vol. 28, No. 4, 1992.

Sinha, S.K., "Social Disharmony", *The Hindustan Times*, September 27, 1994.

——, "Reservation Politics", *The Hindustan Times*, September 26–27, 1994.

Theordore, Rajiv, "Reservation Going Backward", *Rashtriya Sahara*, November, 1994.

Tondon, M.P., "Property of Reservation based on Prior Supreme Court Decision", *SCJ*, Vol. 2, 1992.

Journals, Periodical, Magazines and Papers

1. *AMU News and Views*, Aligarh.
2. *Indian Express*, New Delhi.
3. *Journal of the Indian Law Institute*, New Delhi.
4. *Onlooker*, Bombay.
5. *Statesman*, New Delhi.
6. *The Hindu*, New Delhi.
7. *The Hindustan Times*, New Delhi.
8. *The Times of India*, New Delhi.
9. *Indian Express*, New Delhi.
10. *The Sunday Observer*, Weekly, Bombay.
11. *Dalit Voice*, Monthly, Bangalore.
12. *Rastriya Sahara*, New Delhi.

Index